DEVELOPMENTS IN HUMAN SERVICES

Volume II

DEVELOPMENTS IN HUMAN SERVICES

Volume II

General Editors

Herbert C. Schulberg, Ph.D.
Frank Baker, Ph.D.

Behavioral Publications, Inc.
New York

Library of Congress Catalog Number 73–6840
ISSN: 0092–5470
ISBN: 0–87705–168–2
Copyright © 1975 by Behavioral Publications, Inc.

BEHAVIORAL PUBLICATIONS, Inc.
72 Fifth Avenue
New York, New York 10011

Printed in the United States of America
56789   987654321

HV
13
.D47
V.2

Contents

INTRODUCTION: SOCIAL VALUES, ECONOMIC
INFLUENCES AND INTEGRATED HUMAN SERVICES

HERBERT C. SCHULBERG
FRANK BAKER

Part I: DEVELOPING PROGRAM MODELS
FOR THE HUMAN SERVICES

MARK A. LAWRENCE

v

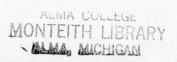

Part II: THE ECONOMICS OF HUMAN SERVICES

GERALD ROSENTHAL

Part III: DEVELOPING HUMAN SERVICES IN NEW COMMUNITIES

DONALD C. KLEIN

The Editors

Herbert C. Schulberg, Ph.D., M.S. Hyg. is Associate Executive Vice President of the United Community Planning Corporation in Boston, Massachusetts. He also is Associate Clinical Professor of Psychology in the Department of Psychiatry, Harvard Medical School. Dr. Schulberg's professional activities, and his more than 50 publications, have focused upon mental health and human services program development as well as program evaluation.

Frank Baker, Ph.D. is Professor of Psychology in the Department of Psychiatry and Director of the Division of Community Psychiatry at the School of Medicine of the State University of New York at Buffalo. Before coming to Buffalo, Dr. Baker had been a member of the faculty of the Department of Psychiatry of the Harvard Medical School for nine years and had headed the Program Research Unit of the Harvard Laboratory of Community Psychiatry. Dr. Baker received his Ph.D. in Social Psychology from Northwestern University in 1964.

The Contributors

Donald C. Klein, Ph.D. is a Former President of the Division of Community Psychology of the American Psychological Association and the author of numerous articles on community mental health and applied behavioral science, and of a book entitled, *Community Dynamics and Mental Health.* He is Program Manager of the Center for Macrosystem Change of NTL Institute for Applied Behavioral Science, Arlington, Virginia and Principal Investigator at the Community Research and Action Laboratory, located in the new town of Columbia, Maryland. He has been a consultant and human relations trainer for a variety of community change programs, federal agencies, and experimental communities.

Mark Lawrence, M.D. since 1971 has been Chief, Area A Community Mental Health Center in the District of Columbia. He also is an Assistant Professor of Psychiatry at Georgetown University. Dr. Lawrence has served as a staff psychiatrist at the National Institute of Mental Health and as a Fellow at the Laboratory of Community Psychiatry, Harvard Medical School.

Gerald Rosenthal, Ph.D. has been an Associate Professor of Economics and Social Welfare at Brandeis University. In 1973–1974, he was on leave as a Consultant to the Cost of Living Council dealing with health-wage policy. Dr. Rosenthal has recently been appointed Director of the Bureau of Health Services Research, U.S. Department of Health, Education, and Welfare.

Introduction

Social Values, Economic Influences and Integrated Human Services

Attempts to define the field of human services have highlighted the lengthy history, extensive domain, and still ambiguous nature of what now is one of the dominant factors in the American economy. Approximately one third of our gross national product already involves the many personal and social interventions subsumed within the field of human services, and this proportion is likely to rise as the country's defense budget is curtailed. Given the massive nature of the human services industry's expenditures and the millions of people who participate in it as providers and/or users, what trends can be discerned as affecting its immediate and long-range directions? Of what developments must human service planners, clinicians and administrators stay abreast if they are to exercise leadership and initiative during the coming years?

In searching for answers to these questions, it is important to recognize that man and his society through the centuries have devised ever changing ways to help those family members, neighbors, and even strangers confronting personal difficulties. The types of assistance

1

and manner in which they are provided reflect each period's social values, political ideologies, technological capability, economic level, organizational practices, and manpower availability. Each of these factors affects and is affected by all of the others so that the nature of man's helping actions at any given time is the product of complex systemic considerations and decisions.

As society has expanded its sanction for the range of human conditions requiring and deserving collective rather than personal solutions, it has traditionally established discrete programs to meet discrete needs. These programs, each with its particular technology, selected clientele along any or all of the following criteria: geographic residence, economic ability, attractiveness of the focal problem, etc. The more narrowly a caregiving agency defined its services and clientele, the more specialized the staffing pattern it needed. A great number of publicly and voluntarily supported caregivers has emerged as providers of expert help, and by the early 1970s most communities were liberally dotted with a multitude of health and social welfare experts. Although this proliferation of helping agents still continues unabated, a countertrend has also taken root during the past decade. Society and its caregivers have begun to emphasize the common rather than unique elements in the problems confronting troubled persons. The increasing tendency to designate a community's variety of health and social welfare interventions as human services reflects both a discontent with past procedures and a recognition of the common elements underlying the helping actions of diverse professional and nonprofessional caregivers.

In this series' initial review of the challenges confronting the human services (Schulberg, Baker, and Roen, 1973), we described the social and programmatic developments of the 1960s which seemed most immediately responsible for the current high level of interest in this field. Examples of emerging human services endeavors were presented along with their anticipated advantages and disadvantages. Speculative thoughts were also ventured about the implications of these service developments for manpower patterns, training programs, administrative practices, and research interests.

Developments in the past few years make it possible to consider here in greater detail some of the issues and dilemmas reviewed previously in only a cursory way. This introductory chapter to Volume II will focus, therefore, on the dominant social values and organizational practices likely to shape human services during the next several years. These factors will be related to the subsequent contributions in this volume, i.e., Lawrence's overview of the systemic principles underlying service delivery (Part I); Rosenthal's analysis of the economic principles fundamental to program development (Part II); and Klein's suggestions for establishing human services in new communities (Part III).

SOCIAL VALUES AND HUMAN SERVICES IDEOLOGY

The fundamental characteristics of any society are evident in the values and assumptions through which it determines what is right and important for helping its citizens. Specific social values differ with regard to stability and degree of popular acceptance. Despite the homogenizing effects of increased mobility and improved means of communication and transportation, this country is still composed of heterogeneous populations retaining widely diverse values, interests, and lifestyles. It is not unusual for the preferences and assumptions of one societal segment to be in direct conflict with those of other segments, e.g., high and low income groups view governmental spending very differently. Consequently, human services program planning faces the problem of seeking to satisfy the value assumptions of one group while recognizing that such activities may contradict the fundamental premises guiding the desires of other community groups. The design of human services is further complicated by the fact that the values of various segments of the population often are not conscious or explicit. Finally, the value assumptions guiding decision making are likely to change with time in relation to the shifting dominance exercised by various societal subgroups.

The Myth of Value-Free Planning

A basic premise stemming from the Industrial Revolution is that scientific rationality and technology, when vigorously applied, can solve even the most complicated problems. When this premise was applied to our country's space program, it once again proved its merit, as inspiring successes were achieved in man's effort to reach the moon. Physical and social planning concerns also achieved considerable prominence during the 1960s, and much effort was directed to the creation of a "good society." It was only natural for the planning participants to assume that by utilizing rational scientific procedures and engaging in value-free analyses, their goals would be achieved.

It soon became evident, however, that major divisions separate segments of American society, and that program solutions could not be harmonized and integrated without consensus about relevant values. While many openly acknowledged the mythical nature of value-free planning, others argued that this situation emphasized all the more a need for rational planning and program development. For example, Rein (1970) observed that:

> Rational planning is a myth when the value consensus on which it must depend is illusory, and technology for eliminating arbitrary decisions is not available. But as the conditions of society become more complex and as each decision is a response to short-range expediencies and accommodations of conflicting vested interests, the need to protect society's long-term interests becomes more insistent and the demands for rational solutions grow more urgent (p. 212).

Along with this approach, there also were increasing demands for moral commitment among planners, and questioning of value-free decision making. Commenting on this attack against rationality, Gross (1971) suggested that:

> Rationality must be rescued from narrow considerations of mere feasibility and consistency, and must be oriented toward what is truly desirable. This approach recognizes that organized rationality in the form of the sciences and the professions is always the servant of *some* structure of power and *some* set of values (p. 290).

Gross's recommendation that value-free decision making be replaced in the human services by "value-creating" decision making is not totally new, since for decades public leaders have made selective use of contemporary social values. At times, the dominant values were acceptable and pursued; on other occasions, public leaders modified or disregarded the prevailing sentiments. Vickers (1963) noted that:

> American presidents, from Lincoln to Kennedy, do not speak with accents of inquirers seeking guidance about other people's preferences ... they *criticize* contemporary values, urge *re*valuation, and appeal not to what people are thinking now but to what they ought to be thinking and would be thinking if they expose themselves with sufficient sensitivity to the subject matter of the debate. A free society is one in which these initiatives spring up freely and in which men are free to espouse or resist them (p. 391).

Program Structures and Policies

Whether one agrees that professional planners and program developers should consciously reflect the values of particular community interest groups, as some advocacy planners and "radical therapists" have attempted to do, or whether one believes that professionals should remain scientifically objective, changes in society's values inevitably affect the professional's activities and scope of responsibilities. Lawrence (Part I) points out that the administrative supra-structure integrating and directing human services program components reflects community value systems through a variety of possible mechanisms. For example, budget control and priority setting can be vested in professionals, bureaucrats, or lay-consumers. Publicly-supported services can be provided through public agencies, prepaid group practice, or voucher mechanisms. The multiple organizational patterns that have evolved for providing human services reflect choices among these options and represent the diverse combinations of ways in which communities may assert their dominant social values.

A fuller analysis of the intrinsic relation of values to human services programs is provided by Rosenthal (Part II). He points out that the experience of the Depression created an altered role for government in meeting health and welfare needs, particularly at the federal level. Social Security legislation and other New Deal measures laid the groundwork for an expanded post-World War II allocation of resources to human services. Furthermore, public acceptance of the principle that veterans are *entitled* to receive services and that it is incumbent upon government to organize and provide them, greatly expanded the scope of governmental involvement. Burgeoning levels of service activity accelerated the pace of technological development, and treatment and rehabilitation replaced custodialism in such fields as mental illness. In turn, public expectations grew, and even more demands were imposed upon a less than adequate service delivery system.

In the 1960s, federal policies that sanctioned services only to those in the "worthy" category of need shifted their emphasis to altering the root causes of poverty and social malaise. Rosenthal notes that this new policy required that economic development strategies supersede individually oriented assistance, since the high social burden of poverty extends beyond those costs falling directly on the poor individual and his family. This policy shift also forced a recognition of the fact that while poor people had a greater than average need for health, education, and social welfare services, they had only minimal access to such services. The existing service delivery system imposed excessive costs in terms of time, money, and inconvenience upon low-income consumers. More importantly, the lack of services was seen as related to poverty itself, and the notion of a "circle of poverty" provided the rationale for spending public funds on what were previously viewed as private responsibilities. Thus, sociopolitical changes in the United States during the 1960s were reflected in changing community values, which in turn affected the particular bureaucratic structures for planning and developing health and welfare services.

Professional Ideologies

How do human services professionals cope with the fluctuating social values directly and indirectly impacting upon their caregiving efforts? This issue is of more than fleeting concern since human services are as frequently rooted in the personal beliefs of their staff as in hard scientific theory and technical expertise. It is clear from many studies that when faced with a variety of social and professional pressures for change, those charged with the design and development of human services are likely to turn to professional ideologies for guidance.

Ideology may be defined as a commonly adhered to system of ideas or beliefs that serves to justify the position of a person or group and establish a rationale for behavior. By defining ideology as a system, we are emphasizing a framework of interrelated beliefs which may or may not be organized in a logical manner but which, nevertheless, are interdependent. The concept of a belief system as a basis for self-definition and guide to behavior can be useful for understanding the actions of various kinds of caregivers as they affect the type and quality of helping services offered to clients.

In the mental health field, several ideologies have developed in the last 25 years. A rebirth of popular support for humanism during the 1950s led to its replacing custodialism as the prevalent ideological orientation in the mental hospital (Gilbert and Levinson, 1957). Later, psychotherapeutic and sociotherapeutic ideologies competed with each other and with somatotherapeutic ideology for support among the country's mental health professionals (Strauss, *et al.*, 1964). During the second half of the 1960s, a new ideological movement arose in the mental health field which Baker and Schulberg (1967) described as focusing on the following elements: primary prevention of mental illness through the amelioration of harmful environmental conditions; assumption of responsibility by professionals for an entire population rather than for individual patients only; treating patients with the goal of social rehabilitation rather than personality reorganization; comprehensive continuity of care and concern for the mentally ill; and total involvement of both professional and nonprofessional helpers in caring for the mentally ill. This newly evolved mental health belief system was labeled "community mental health ideology," and Baker and Schulberg (1967) developed a reliable and valid scale for measuring people's positions on these ideas.

Adherence to community mental health ideology has been empirically related to support for expanding roles for mental health personnel, within professional settings as well as in the larger society. Baker and Schulberg (1969) also found that strong support for community mental health principles is inversely related to dogmatism and political-economic conservatism. In a similar analysis, Hersch (1972) has tied the community mental health movement and its underlying ideology to historical changes in the United States. He asserts that it is not accidental that the community mental health movement reached its fruition in this country during the decade of the 1960s. On the contrary, the fruition occurred because of this period's spirit of social-political reform and its emphasis on a revitalized humanistic concern for the disadvantaged, the oppressed, and the powerless.

Human Service Ideology

New beliefs continue to evolve about the best ways to help troubled persons. Baker (in press) suggests that the most current idea system of "human services ideology" extends community mental health concepts and is characterized by the following five major themes:

1. Systemic integration of services—comprehensive services can be provided only through the forging of systemic linkages which bring together the various caregiving agencies needed to provide a complex array of resources, technologies, and skills.

2. Accessibility—services in a total system of care should be accessible in terms of fiscal ability and geographic location.

3. Client troubles defined as problems in living — human distress stems from the difficulties individuals and populations have in coping with unresponsive environments.

4. Generalized characteristics of helping activities — there are common qualities integral to the activities of helpers which are not dependent upon specific professional training.

5. Accountability of service providers to clients — providers of service are responsible to the users and potential consumers of service as well as to the public at large.

Growing out of the community mental health ideology prominent in the late 1960s, the human services orientation is seen as potentially playing a major role in rationalizing and justifying an even more expanded pattern of organized, comprehensive, and integrated programs during the 1970s.

ECONOMIC INFLUENCES

Social values, technological capability, and organizational practices long have been recognized as significant forces in the design of human services, but only in recent years have economic influences received the explicit attention which they require. Increased public concern about the high costs and questionable efficiency of human services agencies has catapulted the economic dimension into prominence, particularly as the public's fiscal investment in services for the poor expanded geometrically. However, problems of cost and the gap between the demand for and the availability of services have implications beyond help for the poor alone. Our country is being painfully reminded that not all desirable ends are attainable, and that scarcity is a condition of human existence. Since resources are limited, committing them in a particular manner incurs opportunity costs; i.e., other, perhaps equally desirable, goals will not be achieved. Even though many of us deem human services to be inherently good, economists insist that they must produce more benefits than the alternatives which could be generated by the same resources. This principle is evident in Klein's (Part III) portrayal of the subtleties associated with developing model plans for meeting the personal needs of residents of new towns. He notes that even though human services must be treated as key modules in the design of these communities, their priority is low relative to other amenities, since they add little to the developer's profit margin. The social planner's bright but costly suggestions thus receive less consideration than the income-generating ideas of economic and physical planners.

Rosenthal's overview (Part II) is intended to

familiarize human services practitioners with the fact that their system has many attributes that are best understood and managed within an economic perspective. A brief description of economic concepts and analytic tools will help illustrate their application in a community's choice of strategies for resolving people's needs.

Every society must make basic economic decisions about the *nature* of the goods and services it will produce, the *manner* in which they will be produced, and the *recipients* of these products. The options for deciding these questions include the command, tradition, and market strategies. Rosenthal notes that in the field of human services we utilize all three to determine resource use and distribution patterns. The command strategy employs a central decision making authority, e.g., government mandates educational and immunization programs. The traditional strategy utilizes earlier societal commitments to given resource utilization patterns, e.g., professionals are permitted to select clients on the basis of personal and guild concerns rather than potential benefits to clients. The market strategy requires providers to compete for societal resources and permits consumers to demonstrate their own service preferences, e.g., the Medicaid voucher system enables clients to shop, within limits, for their choice of service provider. Each of these strategies yields differing degrees of economic efficiency, depending upon given societal conditions. Rosenthal points out that the market strategy works best under conditions of perfect competition. However, as we will note later, these conditions are lacking in the human services field, and public intervention through the command strategy is required to insure certain necessary programs.

The economic perspective also focuses upon efficient resource use relative to benefits. The two common approaches for determining this principle's application are

(a) cost-benefit analysis, i.e., assessing the relationship between the value of benefits and the costs incurred to obtain them; and (b) cost-effectiveness analysis, i.e., assessing the relative costs of differing services producing a given benefit.

How extensively have these economic analyses been utilized in the planning and operating of human services? In point of fact very little. Human services traditionally were viewed as personal activities to be performed within the family setting. Since technology was underdeveloped, the services primarily involved maintenance activities incurring minimal professional costs. However, as the high social costs of these maintenance services became evident, publicly supported custodial facilities were established for relief to the family. Public services were guided by the policy of minimizing fiscal expenditures and relieving society of undesirable persons. Only in recent years, under the pressure of changing social values, have we begun to recognize that this cost-benefit policy has not optimally benefited all concerned, and that profound alterations are needed in the service delivery system (Schulberg and Baker, 1974). As a corollary of this shift, more detailed cost-benefit and cost-effectiveness data are being introduced into the political decision making process, and professionals must now grapple with these variables even though they previously were deemed irrelevant to their concerns (Panzetta, 1973).

A similar reassessment of the relationship between costs and benefits has been undertaken in the voluntary sector of human services. Agencies supported by charitable donations and endowment income functioned for many years within an insulated marketplace, and they established operational practices with little regard for economic influences. Since the resources expended in the voluntary sector were small relative to public outlays, there was minimal pressure to consider alternative utilization patterns producing improved cost-benefit ratios. However, as mounting pressures were exerted by minority groups and other underserved populations, United Ways and the various foundations have been forced to reconsider their priorities and programs. Nevertheless, it is clear that human services of both the public and nonpublic type continue to operate within a marketplace largely devoid of the usual economic constraints and limitations.

What, then, are the unique characteristics of the human services marketplace, and how do they affect the help provided to distressed persons? Rosenthal, from an economist's perspective (Part II), and Klein, from the psychologist's vantage point (Part III), suggest that a key feature of the human services environment is its lack of perfect competition. This condition exists for the following reasons:

1. There are too few suppliers, and, as a result, they can restrict buyer's choices. The manpower shortages in most human services have created situations where generally only a single supply source is available to potential users, making market preference tests inoperable. Guild-oriented standards have maintained this situation. Interestingly enough, human services planners have also reinforced noncompetition by stressing that duplication of services is inherently inefficient and wasteful. Rosenthal suggests that the absence of competition and economic market tests may lead to even greater waste and inefficiency.

2. Service users have limited and imperfect information about even the few options available to them. In recent years, we have resorted to the concept of consumer "participation" as an alternative to the "sovereignty" which users hold in a competitive marketplace. It was hoped that increased consumer involvement in ad-

visory capacities would produce better utilization decisions. However, this approach is far from perfect, since the distinction between the consumer's role as a quasi-service provider and his role as service user is at best vague; in some instances, these roles have in fact been antithetical. Klein describes the fine distinction that the developer of a new town must maintain between (a) insufficiently involving the residents and generating anger or frustration, and (b) being overly responsive to residents' wishes and creating overdependence.

3. Many human services are interrelated and, therefore, produced and distributed in such a way that the users of one must obtain others as well. For example, youngsters being educated in public school systems must obtain physical examinations, and men receiving welfare benefits must obtain vocational counseling. Consequently, even though consumers may demonstrate high levels of demand for only one service, the supply levels of related ones will be inflated by mandated utilization requirements.

4. Human services often are financed by neither the producer nor the buyer but rather by a third party with its own view of appropriate resource utilization. For example, insurance carriers typically have determined that it is fiscally more desirable to reimburse providers for the remedial health services administered to identified clients (secondary prevention) than for preventive interventions to defined populations at risk (primary prevention). As an alternative, Klein (Part III) and Chu and Trotter (1972) advocate the establishment of new insurance programs which go beyond traditional coverage for medical illness. These programs would provide greater consumer protection by covering a variety of potential adverse conditions requiring the professional assistance of lawyers, psychologists, social workers, homemakers, etc. However, the values and preferences of users are

rarely injected into these decisions, and it is unlikely that such novel proposals will be adopted in the near future.

Another unique characteristic of the human services from the economic perspective is the ambiguity of their costs and benefits, since these assessments must include the impact upon indirect as well as direct service users. The benefits of such public health efforts as immunization programs become virtually incalculable since they accrue to society as a whole as well as to those individuals who have been personally vaccinated. Furthermore, benefits may not become evident until long after the expenses have been incurred. Determining the costs of human services becomes similarly complex when expenditures are incurred over extended time periods and by others than the focal user and provider. Thus, in determining the expenses of a phenylketonuria (PKU) screening program, we must include not only the initial laboratory costs for testing the infant's metabolic functioning, but also costs for the child's long-term dietary supplements, medical examinations, and parental counseling.

The ambiguity of an economic analysis is heightened even further when it is unclear whether a given human service constitutes a cost or a benefit. The growing practice of treating disturbed psychiatric patients in home settings rather than in institutions may be classified as a benefit, since per diem fiscal expenses are reduced, and the person does not lose his familial and social ties. However, this treatment pattern has also been deemed a cost because of the profound social burden which it imposes upon the disturbed person's relatives.

Despite the unique complexities of the human services marketplace and the difficulties inherent in cost-effectiveness and cost-benefit assessments, economic principles have become increasingly vital in the organizing and producing of human services. Given a constant shortage of resources, it is essential that human services benefit both users and society as a whole. Rosenthal suggests that decision making about the design of human services requires that we step back from the ideologically based advocacy stance so frequently assumed in recent years. Only then will we be able to clarify more rationally the specific relationships upon which each new service delivery strategy is dependent, and make the optimal choices needed for the future.

PROGRAM PATTERNS

Human services agencies have long shared common service goals and clients. Nevertheless, interactions and cooperative ventures to insure comprehensive care usually are minimal since organizational concerns rather than client benefits are paramount. One of the most pressing problems facing planners, clinicians, and administrators, therefore, is that of linking the many caregiving elements comprising the human services field. Since no single agency can provide the total array of help required to meet the diverse problems confronting people, organizational and administrative barriers to care must be minimized.

If accountability is to be imposed upon the human services field, how should the field's operations be streamlined so that client needs will be met more fully and efficiently? Obviously, an idealized service model must be consistent with the previously described sociopolitical factors dominating the contemporary scene, and it must build upon the economic considerations now being injected into the priority setting process. The service model most specifically should create integrative mechanisms to ease the flow of clients, resources, and information among service subsystems. What options are available for meeting this goal, and how are they related to the previously described ideologies?

Each of the themes contained in the "human service ideology" (Baker, in press) carries specific implications for the design of a service delivery system. For example, if a person's troubles are defined as stemming from an unresponsive environment rather than from internal pathology, it would be best to alter destructive societal influences rather than "blaming the victim" (Ryan, 1972). The "problems in living" approach leads to what Lawrence (Part I) describes as the community organization model; it assumes that the quality of life can be optimized through improved social institutions and agencies. The view that maladjustment is personally caused or determined is integral to the medical model, which emphasizes the remediation of pathology through medication and/or psychotherapy.

Two additional program options related to ideological orientations are the educational and self-help models. Lawrence describes the educational model as focusing upon an individual's capacity to grow and learn, and thus being proactive by offering services which facilitate normal development rather than being reactive and remedial in character. The self-help service model assumes that persons with similar needs can help each other as much or more than can professionals; self-help groups are increasingly being recognized as an alternative support system to the professionally dominated one.

Despite the proliferation of alternative program models, all the models incorporate several common conceptual principles. Perhaps the most fundamental is that human services must operate as a system of resources with linked and interlocking activities. Participating agencies and their personnel are coming to recognize that personal success is dependent in many ways upon the actions and cooperation of other caregivers. Thus, in a shifting and unsettled milieu. general systems concepts are viewed as particularly relevant for bringing the community's collective helping actions into greater harmony (Lawrence. Part I; Baker. 1974). The systems perspective emphasizes the need to remove the bastion-like domain boundaries surrounding organizations and professional disciplines. so that clients and services can move more easily across them.

We suggest that the period of the early and mid-1970s ultimately will be recalled for its efforts to insure continuity of care. The community mental health movement. for example. has been characterized by Dinitz and Beron (1971) as a "boundary-busting" effort since much of its energy is directed towards dissolving the barriers which impede a patient's flow among needed services. Baker and Broskowski (in press) stress that boundary changes can be of two types — boundary spanning and boundary expansion. The first emphasizes the coordination of independent professionals and caregiving agencies; the second. a single organization's movement into a wider variety of functions. Since the boundary-spanning strategy is more complex and fraught with greater pitfalls. we will consider it here in greater detail.

In recent years. numerous actions at the national. state. and local levels have been directed towards human services integration. which may be defined as "the linking together by various means of . . . two or more service providers to allow treatment of an individual's or family's needs in a more coordinated and comprehensive manner" (DHEW. 1973). The Federal Government has been experimenting with demonstration projects through which local agencies are induced to reassign functions and enter into new cooperative arrangements for service delivery. Similarly. many state governments have been reorganized so that traditionally independent departments like mental health. public health. public welfare.

rehabilitation, and corrections are now administratively subsumed within a single executive office of human services. An even greater impetus for this trend towards integration would be the "Allied Services" legislation which Congress has been reviewing for the past several years. Among its key provisions are grants to state, local, and nonprofit private agencies to develop and implement plans for coordinated human services delivery systems. States with approved allied services plans would be authorized to transfer up to 30% of their federal categorical funds from one program activity to another in accordance with local priorities.

Strategies for Services Integration

How can organizational boundaries be spanned and integrated human services achieved? Lawrence (Part I) suggests that organizations sharing common missions, ideologies, and service technologies tend to be more linkable than those lacking these affinities. However, even if client movement across agency boundaries can be arranged, this may be insufficient to insure adequate services unless information and personnel exchanges are also possible. These interorganizational activities and tasks are very time-consuming, and specialized boundary-spanning mechanisms have been developed for such purposes. For example, agencies may assign liaison workers to link their staffs with those of other caregivers, and expediters may be used to insure that clients are easily moved among services in keeping with their clinical needs (Hansell, et al., 1968). Several organizations may organize a centralized "client assignment unit" responsible for funneling persons to the most appropriate service subsystem. This unit could also perform such monitoring functions as determining why some cases consistently frustrate and stress the existing caregiving network.

The goal of better linking clients and services has led many communities to establish neighborhood multi-service centers which provide a range of life-supporting services under one roof. A client may receive employment counseling, housing assistance, health care, legal help, social services, etc. in the facility, which can be operated under single or multiple organizational auspices. Accessibility is enhanced, fragmentation is reduced, and administrative economies are maximized. A logical extension of integrated physical facilities for the human services is through the community school, a complex within which educational and other programs are offered to people of all ages and not just school-age children. Klein (Part III) describes the growth of community schools and notes that as the concept of multiple facility use becomes widely accepted, educational plants are being designed for many purposes.

It is necessary to realize that services integration efforts are designed to achieve various goals, including those of effectiveness, efficiency, and accountability. Some goals may compete or conflict with each other; the pattern for services integration in a given community, therefore, must be carefully selected. Boundary spanning may be formal or informal, limited or extensive; the various possibilities are described by Lawrence in Part I as the consultative, confederated, and federated strategies of achieving interorganizational linkages.

1. *Consultation.* A consultant and consultee agree jointly to explore program issues and problems confronting the consultee and his organization. The exchange of clients and staff collaboration are not required to implement the consultant's recommendations; the final responsibility for accepting or rejecting the recommendations remains that of the consultee. This pattern's use in furthering interorganizational cooperation has been stimulated by chronic shortages of specialists, and it is now a common one in the mental health field. The model

remains constrained, however, by the unwillingness of many fiscal policy setters and third-party insurers to agree that such indirect agency services as consultation should be reimbursable.

2. *Confederated Linkages.* Organizations are linked through mutual agreements and memoranda of understanding to engage in specified patterns of patient, staff, and/or information exchange, with each participant retaining its own fiscal and policy-making authority. Many confederated linkages have resulted from the National Institute of Mental Health's requirement that federally funded community mental health centers not directly providing all essential services insure continuity of client care by developing agreements with local resources. As fiscal and programmatic interdependence grows among the confederation's participants, greater central control is implicitly exerted upon its members. Nevertheless, even explicit controls can be diluted by unsympathetic staff exercising traditional prejudices against the interorganizational movement of clients. Leopold's (1973) description of the opportunities and dilemmas encountered by the West Philadelphia Mental Health Consortium illustrates the issues confronting confederated linkages.

3. *Federated Linkages.* Super-departments of human services have proliferated in recent years at all levels of government as well as in the voluntary sector. Agencies are linked by statute or charter as members of a larger system whose central authority can impose operating standards and practices upon all component subsystems. It is fair to state, however, that the resulting integration has been most evident at the highest administrative levels and least demonstrable at the grass-root levels of actual service delivery. Although member components of a federated system are mandated to comply with central policy directives and program standards, top echelon

administrators rarely impose the necessary controls and sanctions upon local program directors.

Given the widespread, albeit unproved, assertion that services integration utilizing the previously described strategies will improve client care, what do we know about the factors which facilitate or inhibit boundary-spanning efforts? A federally supported study of 29 programs identified as "emphasizing" human services integration revealed that linkages develop slowly and in a basically evolutionary manner (DHEW, 1973). Administrators must be comfortable with each other before integration can attain legitimacy in their eyes. Even after the linkages are forged, they need continued attention and support lest erosion set in.

The federally supported study found that services integration is optimized when: (a) the local sociopolitical leadership desires that it occur; (b) integration is a high priority of the participating agencies; (c) the project director aggressively pursues coordination and has good contacts with key participants; and (d) service providers have strong incentives to cooperate. Conversely, services integration was found less likely to occur when: (a) the local leadership opposes change; (b) the integrator is so burdened by service delivery responsibilities and internal operations that he has no time to pursue coordination; (c) the project fails to define its mission as the development of integrative linkages; and (d) service providers actively protect the status quo, jealously guarding their prerogatives.

Community Mental Health Programs

The programmatic and administrative principles cited thus far as affecting services integration can be better understood by analyzing the efforts of community mental health centers to establish the range of program linkages needed for comprehensive client care. The more such facilities view their mission as extending beyond narrowly defined psychiatric care, the more far-reaching must be the human services network with which they interact. Lawrence (Part I) describes various patterns for arranging necessary ties. It should be emphasized again that the community's choice among several options depends upon a combination of contemporary social values and priorities, fiscal requirements, manpower availability, etc. What, then, are the program linkages which community mental health centers are developing to relevant human services systems?

A mental health center's linkages to the health care system are vital regardless of its staff's degree of commitment to the social and political components of community mental health ideology. Varied patterns, therefore, have emerged for arranging continuity of medical services. For example, centers located in general hospitals may function as free-standing or integrated subsystems; in either instance, psychiatric patients requiring medical care can readily obtain it. However, fiscal payment mechanisms can significantly affect the nature of services available through a general hospital-based mental health center. Persons lacking adequate insurance or personal resources often will not be admitted for care. Furthermore, since most insurance plans cover only inpatient care, this treatment modality is overutilized, while partial hospitalization and outpatient services are underutilized. Conversely, mental health services provided through a comprehensive group health plan financed by advance per capita payments maximize ambulatory care and minimize inpatient hospitalization.

A second human services system vital to the community mental health center's effectiveness is the rehabilitation-vocational network. Many of the persons receiving mental health care need the diverse occupational and vocational training opportunities available in sheltered workshops, the social rehabilitation provided in day care centers, etc. All too often, however, the mental health system is unaware of these already existing resources, or inadequately tries to emulate them. The growing national trend towards community-based rather than institutional care for severely impaired persons makes it all the more imperative that the mental health and rehabilitation systems ally themselves.

Further examples of the mental health center's extended linkages are evident in relation to the judicial-correctional system, the educational system, and the public welfare system. Each of these related human services fields has unique characteristics and functional requirements; the mental health program must be sensitive to them if relationships are to take root and flourish.

Special Education Programs

The challenges and opportunities associated with providing comprehensive, integrated human services can also be portrayed through an analysis of a community's procedures for insuring the educational and social development of school-age children with special needs. The significance of this issue is evident in the fact that nationwide, over 50 million children, teachers, and administrators participate in the public school system, of which a substantial proportion are directly involved in special education programs.

Who are the children requiring special assistance and how have communities usually dealt with their needs? We have stressed previously that society's determination of who should receive publicly supported human services is very much linked to contemporary values and economic factors. This principle applies in public education as well. Most communities agreed many years ago that the educational and social development of blind, deaf, and physically handicapped children should be maximized despite their profound impairment; costly arrangements have been undertaken to fulfill this public objective. On the other hand, it is only within the past two decades that society has agreed that retarded and emotionally disturbed children have similar developmental needs and that appropriate public resources must be expended for these groups as well. Most recently, youngsters with learning disabilities and bilingual backgrounds have moved into the forefront of the public's attention, and in many parts of the country specialized programs are now being developed for these groups as well.

What are the results of society's evolving concern for the human services needs of children suffering various impairments? It is fair to conclude that considerable progress has been made in furthering their educational and social development. However, the success pattern is mixed and often even discriminatory. Most special education activities stem from legislation responsive to the legitimate but limited interests of persons concerned with the needs of children with a given handicap; hence, such education usually is categorical in nature. However, it also is set apart from the mainstream of public education and often is used by teachers and administrators as a dumping ground for students unresponsive to traditional classroom environments. It is not surprising then that the youngsters included in special classes are stigmatized and extruded even from normal opportunities well within their competence. In an equally distressing way, the categorical special education structure has isolated itself from those children whose needs and abilities fall between the gaps of this regulatorily demarcated subsystem of the public schools.

The pitfalls of this program pattern have become increasingly evident, and in recent years attempts have been made to break down the excessively rigid boundaries of special education. The challenges in doing so can be illustrated through the present Massachusetts effort to transform its overly narrow, categorical special education network into a more integrated one concerned with the education of any "child with special needs." Legislation enacted in 1972 to be effective in September, 1974 has among its goals the provision of a flexible and uniform system of special education for all children between ages 3 and 21 who require it, and the insuring of equal educational opportunity regardless of national origin, sex, economic status, race, religion, and physical and mental handicap. Recognizing that certain professional resources must be made available regionally if the Act is to be successfully implemented, provisions are made for meaningful cooperation among all agencies concerned with children having special needs. Recognizing, finally, that many of the inequities in the present special education system are the result of the lack of significant parent and lay involvement, the Act creates regional and state advisory committees with powerful review and evaluation responsibilities.

Among the Act's key features is the replacing of statutorily defined labels such as "mentally retarded" and "emotionally disturbed" with the designation "children with special needs." This change was made to reduce the lifelong stigmata associated with affect-laden labels, and to emphasize the child's educational and developmental potential rather than his limitations. Furthermore, the more generic designation, "children with special needs," insures that no youngsters are left without programs simply because they cannot be neatly categorized. This change does not mean that all such children will be lumped together in the same classrooms. On the contrary, the Act underlines the crucial role of *appropriate* education. Thus, a local school system must design or participate in a comprehensive network of human services including 11 program options, ranging from regular class placement or special instruction that supplements regular classroom activities, through self-contained classes in the public school or special day school, to residential programs. The Act contains complex fiscal provisions. The present inadequate state aid for special education is to be replaced by a formula which encourages school districts to develop adequate programs within a reasonable period of time.

Given the laudable, even lofty, public policy aims contained in this fresh approach to educating children with special needs, what problems must be resolved if the legislation is to be successfully implemented? For more than a year, hundreds of knowledgeable persons have been grappling with the following issues as the State Department of Education in collaboration with the Departments of Mental Health and Public Health, strives to formulate necessary regulations:

1. *Attitudinal Change.* Categorical, segregated human services fulfill many purposes, among them society's need to extrude persons with undesirable characteristics. Removing the barriers between regular and special education will require that school personnel and students modify their fear of the unknown, i.e., those children traditionally isolated and avoided because of real and imagined handicaps. Classroom teachers and special education staff can further the process of attitudinal change by personally accentuating the common denominators among these children rather than by stressing their unique limitations.

2. *Program Standards.* The Act clearly is based upon the principle of "normalization," i.e., emphasizing the child's assets and potentialities while remedying his limitations. However, program prototypes are lacking for

such a large scale, statewide effort to afford every handicapped youngster the maximally normal education possible for him or her. Even the evaluation procedure, intended to be as comprehensive and relevant as possible, generates anxiety among educators since it may lead to a doubling of the present special education caseload, i.e., from 6% to 12% of the total student body. Private schools operating sophisticated categorical programs are also uneasy, fearing a drop in referrals as more children are maintained in less segregated educational alternatives. Despite the uncertain impact of whatever program standards and practices are adopted, it is clear that responsibility for every child now resides with the local school system. This is the case even for those youngsters transferred to regional and statewide facilities.

3. *Financing Patterns.* A state or community's fiscal resources are finite. Increasing the expenditures for some services generally reduces the funds available for others. This is particularly the case when the public policy established during periods of economic affluence and heightened social consciousness is actually implemented during an economic recession. The expanded special education efforts in Massachusetts typify this all too frequent phenomenon. Rather than significantly increasing the sums to be allocated for its progressive public policy, the Massachusetts Legislature decided that the financing of expanded special education programs will occur by taking necessary funds "off the top" of the state's local aid contribution, paying them directly into the school committee account rather than a town's general fund. This strategy is certain to arouse the ire of all other special interest groups, who now will be competing for diminished sums of money. Furthermore, parts of the new special education effort, e.g., evaluation and treatment services provided by private practitioners, will require

fee for service reimbursements from the state to the town. Given the state's notoriously long lag-time in processing such invoices, the anticipated cash flow problems are but a further stimulus for ambivalent, if not negative, attitudes among politicians and school committees towards new special education ventures.

4. *Phasing Processes.* How quickly and efficiently can a local school system meet the legislative aim of establishing optimal combinations of integrated and specialized public and private educational services customized to each child's potential? Many factors influence this process. Among the most basic is the retraining of current teaching personnel to assume new roles and duties, and the recruiting of new staff so that program gaps will be filled. Solutions to this need can perhaps best be developed via linkages with university programs having the capacity to generate newly trained educators as well as to "retread" experienced ones.

We had indicated earlier that the success of public policy as complex and far-reaching as that affecting the educational and social development of children with special needs depends upon careful analysis of the systemic implications of program change. Hundreds of citizens and professionals have carefully scrutinized successive drafts of regulations, each person paying particular attention to the impact upon his agency and its particular function. Although such a process is quite protracted, it also is very democratic and productive. At the least, the review process has permitted scores of persons to become highly knowledgeable about the key factors involved in the education of children with special needs. Hopefully, this cadre of sophisticated citizen leaders will remain involved in this and other human services during the coming years.

MANPOWER UTILIZATION

Our preceding analysis of evolving human services program patterns has implicitly considered the manpower requirements associated with varying organizational structures and technological advances. Since optimal manpower utilization is such a key determinant of program success, it is appropriate that we conclude our review of developments in human services with a discussion of this issue. Space limitations permit us, however, to deal only with the question of specialists and generalists despite the multifaceted and complex nature of manpower utilization choices.

There is little need to emphasize the crucial implications to human services of wise decisions about personnel selection and deployment. Manpower and training costs consume the greatest part of most human services budgets, and administrators strive to minimize waste and optimize the use of high-priced professionals. However, this effort generally is impeded by intra- and extra-organizational constraints which limit the design of innovative approaches and reinforce antiquated patterns. What, then, are the factors affecting present manpower utilization in the human services, and what solutions can be considered for the future?

We had noted earlier in this chapter that a basic impetus for developing generalized, comprehensive human services systems was growing consumer dissatisfaction with specialized agencies focusing on segmented problems rather than the total person. Service fragmentation and the lack of continuity of care stem from many factors, but surely a key one in any community is the ever expanding array of highly specialized professionals supported by powerful universities and adminstrative bureaucracies, guild-oriented licensing regulations, and expensive technologies. Elite professional training programs annually produce new cadres of workers committed to this categorical approach, which is easily maintained in the absence of skilled generalists possessing a broader perspective on client needs. Moreover, strong citizen lobbyists have insisted that separate systems be established for clientele against whom human services caregivers discriminate. Thus, developmentally disabled and non-English speaking persons, for example, are often served within agencies specializing solely in their needs. Professionals desiring a personal power-base have, of course, supported parallel rather than integrated human services systems.

Various solutions have been proposed to this dilemma. Among the most promising are efforts in several states such as Utah and Maine to define far more precisely the objectives for which clients seek assistance and the job tasks required to fulfill these objectives. In reviewing this development, Broskowski and Smith (1974) recognize that the ambiguity of many human services functions makes it difficult to develop a coherent classification scheme which would then permit the aggregating of meaningful job roles. Thus, most jobs currently are based upon professional requirements or idiosyncratic frameworks. However, Broskowski and Smith suggest that if the total array of tasks performed by human services agencies are accurately categorized and computerized, a comprehensive system can be redesigned with specific service units provided by the most relevant personnel. For example, the "functional job analysis" conducted within Utah's social services agencies identified staff as performing over 600 discrete tasks. Having this information, manpower experts could determine whether to design new jobs by recombining tasks, or whether existing roles should be modified only as new service tasks are identified.

What are the implications of functional job analyses for optimal utilization of specialists and generalists? This question must be considered from many perspectives, including those of administrative accountability, specific client needs, manpower training opportunities, technological requirements, funding mechanisms, etc. Lawrence (Part II) suggests that functional job analyses be related to a systemic perspective which maintains a proper balance of specialists and generalists lest improper overloads strain the total network. Difficulties in achieving this balance are exacerbated, however, by antiquated fiscal policies. Thus, a community mental health center supported by third-party payments may enjoy a surplus of highly trained specialist inpatient staff for whose services insurance reimbursements can be collected, while suffering from a dearth of generalist outreach workers whose services are ineligible for such payments.

More specifically, Lawrence urges that ultimate responsibility for a client be vested in a staff person performing a generalist role. This staff member would see the client initially, assess his problem, determine objectives, and contract with the client to provide specific units of service over a defined time period. Specialists would be requested to consult or collaborate as needed, a process which would occur most clearly and frequently when the job task requires highly sophisticated technological skills, e.g., open heart surgery. Since elaborate technical tasks are performed less frequently than common interpersonal ones such as counseling, the specialist would be responsible for serving a population numerically greater and more geographically dispersed than that served by a generalist.

Some human services personnel can play a generalist as well as specialist role in accordance with client needs and personal skills. Thus a physician specializing in internal medicine may conduct a general family practice while also dealing with specific disease entities. More often, however, human services practitioners are more comfortable with one role or the other, and a comprehensive system must, therefore, include generalists and specialists at both the basic and advanced skill levels. A paradigm of the tasks and skill levels required in such a system is presented in Table 1.

Table 1
HUMAN SERVICES TASKS AND PERSONNEL UTILIZATION

		Nature of Task	
		General	Special
Skill Level	Basic	(A) Educating normal children; counseling high school graduates.	(C) Tutoring poor achievers; testing for intelligence score.
	Advanced	(B) Educating children with special needs; testing for personality assessment.	(D) Educating autistic children; conducting psychotherapy with psychotic persons.

Tasks assigned to cell (A) most often would be performed by bachelors degree teachers, guidance counselors, social work assistants, etc. Cell (B) tasks would be performed by teachers with advanced training and doctoral level psychologists. Tasks in cell (C) might or might not require personnel with as much training as is deemed necessary for level (B) tasks. Finally, highly sophisticated personnel are required for level (D) tasks; most probably they would be persons with doctoral level training and extensive experience.

This paradigm implicitly points to the issue of career mobility which has received so much attention during the past decade. A central concern of manpower policy makers has been the insuring of procedures whereby personnel performing level (A) tasks can advance within the human services system to assume responsibility ultimately for more advanced and/or specialized tasks at levels B, C, and D. Pattison and Elpers (1972) note that in the mental health field there has been a gradual emergence of individuals whose roles and functions are not closely tied to any one of the traditional disciplines of psychiatry, psychology, social work, or nursing. Instead, these generic "mental health workers" have synthesized functions from each of the disciplines. Their career development is related to on-the-job acquisition of specific skills and not to further formal education within one of the traditional disciplines.

Vidaver's (1973) concept of a career lattice permitting movement in a variety of directions rather than in the vertical one only would be facilitated if agencies conducted functional job analyses. Inservice training efforts within larger human services agencies and the continuing education programs at academic centers could then utilize a modular building block approach, teaching materials geared to specific job functions. Modular education would be particularly valuable to the personal growth of individuals who when seeking initial training can perceive only dimly the career directions they ultimately wish to pursue.

SUMMARY

The field of human services continues to develop in a variety of directions, and this introductory chapter has reviewed selected factors affecting program growth. Social values significantly abet or constrain public support of professional efforts, and the already existing rudiments of a human services ideology were considered as the principles guiding current ventures. Systems concepts are fundamental to this ideology, and we have stressed the economic elements upon which planners and clinicians must build their programs. The fact that human services lack perfect competition has led to unique market conditions in which providers and revenue sources dominate consumer preferences. Integrated comprehensive services have, however, become a high priority of both consumers and providers, and program patterns for achieving this goal are described. The several options currently being utilized have profound implications for such manpower utilization decisions as the roles of generalists and specialists, and they are best determined in relation to the job tasks of a comprehensive human services system. As functional job analyses become common, modular training efforts teaching specific skills will receive increasing attention.

REFERENCES

Baker, F. The living human service organization: Applications of general systems theory and research. In H. Demone and D. Harshbarger (Eds.), *A handbook of human service organizations.* New York: Behavioral Publications, 1974, pp.442–474.

Baker, F. From community mental health to human service ideology. *Amer. J. Pub. Hlth.*, in press.

Baker, F. & Broskowski, A. The search for integrality: New organizational forms for human services systems. In D. Harshbarger and R. Maley (Eds.), *Behavior analysis and systems analysis: An integrative approach to mental health programs.* Kalamazoo, Mich.: Behaviordelia, in press.

Baker, F. & Schulberg, H. The development of a community mental health ideology scale. *Comm. Ment. Hlth. J.*, 1967, **3**, 216–225.

Baker, F. & Schulberg, H. Community mental health, ideology, dogmatism, and political-economic conservatism. *Comm. Ment. Hlth. J.*, 1969, **5**, 433–436.

Broskowski, A. & Smith, T. Manpower development for human services. In D. Harshbarger and R. Maley (Eds.), *Behavior analysis and systems analysis: An integrative approach to mental health programs.* Kalamazoo, Mich.: Behaviordelia, 1974.

Chu, F. & Trotter, S. *The mental health complex. Part I: Community mental health centers.* Washington, D.C.: Center for Study of Responsive Law, 1972.

Department of Health, Education, and Welfare, Social Rehabilitation Service. *Integration of human services in HEW: An evaluation of services integration projects.* Volume I. Washington, D.C.: (SRS) 73-02012.

Dinitz, S. & Beron, N. Community mental health as a boundaryless and boundary-busting system. *J. Hlth. & Soc. Beh.*, 1971, **12**, 99–107.

Gilbert, D. & Levinson, D. "Custodialism" and "humanism" in staff ideology. In M. Greenblatt, D. Levinson & R. Williams (Eds.), *The patient and the mental hospital.* Glencoe, Ill.: The Free Press, 1957, pp. 20–35.

Gross, B. Planning in an era of social revolution. *Public Administration Review*, 1971, **31**, 259–297.

Hansell, N., Wodarczyk, M., & Visotsky, H. The mental health expediter. *Arch. gen. Psychiat.*, 1968, **18**, 392–399.

Hersch, C. Social history, mental health, and community control. *Amer. Psychologist*, 1972, **27**, 749–754.

Leopold, R. The consortium revisited. *Admin. in Ment. Hlth.*, 1973 (Fall), 92–95.

Panzetta, A. Cost-benefit studies in psychiatry. *Comp. Psychiat.*, 1973, **14**, 451–455.

Pattison, E. & Elpers, J. A developmental view of mental health manpower trends. *Hosp. & Comm. Psychiat.*, 1972, **23**, 325–328.

Rein, M. *Social policy: Issues of choice and change.* New York: Random House, 1970.

Ryan, W. *Blaming the victim.* New York: Vintage Books, 1972.

Schulberg, H. & Baker, F. *The mental hospital and human services.* New York: Behavioral Publications, 1974.

Schulberg, H., Baker, F., & Roen, S. (Eds.) *Developments in human services,* Vol. I, New York: Behavioral Publications, 1973.

Strauss, A., Schatzman, L., Bucher, R., Ehrlich, D., Sabshin, M. *Psychiatric ideologies and institutions.* New York: The Free Press of Glencoe, 1964.

Vickers, G. Ecology, planning, and the American dream. In L. Duhl (Ed.), *The urban condition: People and power in the metropolis.* New York: Basic Books, 1963, pp. 374–395.

Vidaver, R. Developments in human services education and manpower. In H. Schulberg, F. Baker, & S. Roen (Eds.), *Developments in human services,* Vol. I. New York: Behavioral Publications, 1973, pp. 363–524.

DEVELOPING PROGRAM MODELS FOR THE HUMAN SERVICES

by

Mark A. Lawrence, M.D.

Part 1 of *Developments in Human Services*, Volume II
Edited by
Herbert C. Schulberg, Ph.D.
and Frank Baker, Ph.D.

Library of Congress Catalog Number 74–9692
ISBN: 0–87705–170–4
Copyright © 1975 by Behavioral Publications, Inc.

BEHAVIORAL PUBLICATIONS, Inc.
72 Fifth Avenue
New York, New York 10011

Printed in the United States of America
56789   987654321

Library of Congress Cataloging in Publication Data

Lawrence, Mark A.
  Developing program models for the human services.

  (Developments in human services, v. 2, pt. 1)
  Includes bibliographical references.
  1. Social services.   2. Mental health services.
I. Title.   II. Series.   [DNLM: 1. Community mental health
services—Models, Theoretical—Social service.
WM30 L422d 1974]
[HV41. L33]   361   74–9692.

Contents

Preface

Widespread inadequacies in the human condition and concern for the difficulties and complexities of existing social arrangements have resulted in urgent pressures on professionals to revise present care giving mechanisms. Human service programs such as multi-service centers, which incorporate a wide variety of relevant services, are emerging as an alternative framework to the existing pattern of rigid, categorical services for meeting the bio-psycho-social needs of individuals and populations.

The editors of this series are developing materials which can serve as guideposts for those newly entering or already engaged in the field of human services. A flexible approach to the production and distribution of these materials has been devised. The series periodically publishes indepth discussions and reviews on the following human service topics:

> Emerging conceptual frameworks of human services such as systems and ecological principles.
>
> Administrative and planning tools such as information systems, economic strategies, and legal mechanisms.
>
> Innovative service programs within new organizational models and new communities.
>
> Educational programs for changing professional roles and new manpower requirements.

After several years, those who are standing-order subscribers will possess an encyclopedic library of human

services in either hardbound volumes or softcover separates.

Volumes I and II contain an introductory overview by the editors, substantive sections on different human service topics, and a comprehensive index. Each of the substantive sections, without introductory overview and index, is available as a separate.

Volume I

Teaching Health and Human Services Administration by the Case Method—Linda G. Sprague, Alan Sheldon, M.D., and Curtis P. McLaughlin, D.B.A.

The Planning and Administration of Human Services—Harold W. Demone, Jr., Ph.D. and Dwight Harshbarger, Ph.D.

Strategies in Innovative Human Service Programs —Harry Gottesfeld, Ph.D., Florence Lieberman, D.S.W., Sheldon R. Roen, Ph.D., and Sol Gordon, Ph.D.

Developments in Human Services Education and Manpower—Robert M. Vidaver, M.D.

Volume II

Developing Program Models for the Human Services —Mark Lawrence, M.D.

Economics of Human Services—Gerald Rosenthal, Ph.D.

Developing Human Services in New Communities —Donald Klein, Ph.D.

The Editors

1. The Tasks of a Human Services Program Model

The potential permutations and combinations of program models for the human services are myriad. The actual number of combinations of human services program models is less extensive, but still varied. My objective in this study is to make a partial summary of these varied program models to highlight what appear to me to be the most salient organizational and programmatic issues facing those of us trying to organize human services systems today. To synthesize my understanding of these issues, I have formulated a "super-model," based on general systems theory concepts and principles. The systems theory model is "super" only in that it is formulated at a high level of abstraction, not in its presumption of completeness or finality.

The program descriptions here are based on three years of observations as a program consultant to community mental health centers from the National Institute of Mental Health and as director of a community mental health center in the District of Columbia.[1] Hence the discussion of program models in this study will be to a large degree from the perspective of the mental health

[1]Since human services programs are generally in continual flux, the programs described here may have changed since my last exposure to them, and perhaps even since this study has gone to press. Hence, these descriptions are intended primarily to demonstrate models or approaches; they are not intended to be definitive summaries of the specific programs.

45

program or programmer in a human services system. I shall discuss the models and linkages between mental health components of a human services system and other health and social components of the human services system. Since mental health services are a key interface between health and social services, an examination of human services program models from the mental health perspective is a particularly useful approach. Furthermore, because mental health services are in themselves so diverse and aimed at such diverse population subgroups, e.g., the young, the old, the alcoholic, the schizophrenic, the neurotic, etc., the issues and problems presented in the organization and delivery of mental health services to a large degree parallel the issues and problems presented in organizing and delivering more generic human services. While mental health service programs may serve as a miniature model for the delivery of human services, and although mental health services programs include many professionals who are advocates of the human services approach, mental health programs also reveal many of the resistances to more comprehensive service delivery programs that are found among other components of the human services systems.

If I may make a partial digression, I will share with you some of the thoughts and considerations that were instrumental to my choosing my career path; this brief review should highlight some of the biases and basic assumptions that I have made throughout this study. For many years I have been impressed by the obvious multidimensionality of the problems presented by patients or by clients coming to various components of the health, mental health, or social service systems. Generally, although the patient-client seeks assistance with regard to all dimensions of his problem, he, in collaboration with the caretaker he first selects, tends to overly define the problem in one or two dimensions familiar to the client and his caretaker, to the exclusion of other dimensions, which are generally out of the purview of the caretaker and beyond the sophistication of the client. Such over-focusing may fortuitously alleviate other dimensions of the problem; often, however, the patient-client will be forced to get help elsewhere or to endure these other unresolved problems. It seemed to me that what was necessary was a human services worker in a human services system. But ten years ago there was no direct professional entry into the human services system as a human services worker. One had to enter as a health worker, mental health worker, social worker, vocational rehabilitation counselor, etc. Each of these entries had— and still has — its own limitations. The mental health worker, however, had the advantage of linking with both health workers and social workers by virtue of the physical and social aspects of emotional disability. Thus I decided to use the mental health delivery system as the entry route for development of comprehensive human services. Hence my perspective is not limited to that of a physician specializing in a certain kind of illness, i.e., mental, nor to that of a social worker, concerned with the social placement of his client in the community.

To integrate these various perspectives, I needed a conceptual model that could include the coexistence of a variety of different and separate, but complementary, objectives, pursued simultaneously by perhaps several different workers, or perhaps by the same worker in a variety of different roles. The basic concepts of general systems theory seemed to suit this need. With general systems theory concepts it is possible to talk about various subsystems in the human services delivery system, all sharing some common goals, but each having some goals, functions, and roles specific to itself. The various subsystems are interdependent with regard to shared resources and transfer of information, clients, and resources across organizational boundaries, etc. It is possible simultaneously to analyze the patient-client's problems with regard to the various social systems of which he is a member and with regard to the difficulties he has within each of these various social systems. Thus the general systems theory model can serve to analyze the problems both of the patient-client and of the human services system in meeting the patient-client's needs.

PARAMETERS OF A GENERAL SYSTEMS THEORY MODEL

A system or subsystem may be defined with regard to a variety of dimensions. The boundaries of the system may be delineated by its goals and by criteria as to which clientele will be served. The acquisition, transferability, and use of personnel and other resources define the system in another dimension. The locus and domain of decision-making has a key impact on the integrity of the system. Relative freedom of information exchange provides still another definition of the extent of the system. While the above dimensions relate to the internal operation of a system, a system may also be defined from without by the community-at-large through its view or lack of a view of the system, or by various organizational or bureaucratic suprastructures.

These various dimensions may define a system to a very similar or a very dissimilar extent. Boundaries between some subsystems may be so relatively closed with regard to a specific dimension that the subsystems may for all practical purposes be considered as separate systems with limited interdependence. The goals of one subsystem, for example, may be so different from those of another subsystem that the two subsystems may be in virtually continual conflict. When the boundaries of the system as a whole and of the various subsystems are relatively congruous with regard to most dimensions, we can say that the system has general "integrity." If a system is well defined with regard to only one dimension, then we may say that it has integrity with regard to that dimension. For example, if a system shares a common pool of funds and must operate within a common budget, then we might say that the system has "fiscal integrity." The same system on the other hand, may have relatively closed boundaries between subsystems with regard to the transfer of clients, information, and staff; then we would say that it does not have "program integrity." Many of the problems encountered in the development of human services systems may be attributed to the lack of general integrity, i.e., a lack of congruity in defining the boundaries of the system with regard to the several dimensions of a system that are essential to its effective operation.

The present study may be viewed as an analysis of the various incongruities that occur in human services systems, as evidenced both within the mental health subsystem and between the mental health subsystem and the other human services subsystems. We shall examine in a variety of programs various issues and conflicts and their attempted resolutions, and the advantages and limitations of these various approaches to these issues.

There are varying views as to the objectives of a human services system. Is it a system to provide direct remedial service to specific clients who have suffered a medical or social disability; or is it a system to prevent the development of such disabilities? Is the system to serve specific individuals who request help; or is the system to direct itself toward the needs of the community-at-large? For the mental health subsystem the additional question occurs as to whether resources should be directed primarily to medical or traditionally psychiatric needs or whether energy should be directed to social or general community problems. Some mental health programs may view their mission so as to include provision of assistance to individuals with regard to the social complications of their emotional difficulties, but so as to exclude attempts to eliminate what may be the underlying social causes of the client's problems.

Another group of fundamental issues pertains to the definition of the criteria for selection of the clientele to be served. Most community mental health systems now serve anyone who lives within certain geographic boundaries; anyone who is a member of that geographic population is eligible for services. Health maintenance organizations also serve anyone who is a member of a general group, but the criterion for membership is not geographic, but rather prepayment of a specific fee. Eligibility to become a member and to make a prepayment fee may be open, or it may in turn be determined by membership in another group, e.g., a labor union or a place of employment. These membership criteria have an important impact on the characteristics of the population to be served—whether they will be poor or wealthy, unemployed or employed, etc.

Some human services subsystems are not interested in population membership criteria, but prefer to define their clientele according to some internally determined factors. A program may be interested, for example, in serving only one type of client problem, e.g., children, alcoholics, narcotic addicts, etc. Or a program may be designed to sell a specific type of service, such as, psychoanalytically-oriented one-to-one psychotherapy, vocational rehabilitation, income maintenance, health remediation, etc. These kinds of criteria force the programs to put considerable energy into selecting out ineligible applicants for service, and they may leave some of these ineligible applicants without any resource for service at all. These problem-oriented service organizations also present special difficulties for clients whose problems may span the missions of more than one problem-oriented program.

The nature of these objectives and clientele of a human services system will largely determine its staffing pattern and functions. A specialized subsystem, such as an alcoholism program, will have to be staffed primarily with specialists in alcoholism, as opposed to a neighborhood center, which may be staffed with both generalists and specialists. The specialized subsystem will require elaborate arrangements for referring clients to and from the program. The neighborhood center, by contrast, may require very few referrals; the generalist and specialist may relate to each other through a team structure, which simplifies the referral process tremendously. A preventively-oriented program, on the other hand, will require staff to perform different functions from those of both the clinical generalist or specialist.

Staff organizational and functional patterns have a most crucial impact on the nature and quality of services provided. A general program may provide adequate continuity of care, but may suffer in quality with regard to certain specialized problems. Or some special needs may be well served in a specialized program, but with considerable redundancy in some areas and a lack of services in other areas. Or the services of another program may be comprehensive, but not readily accessible. The next chapter provides an elaboration of these issues.

The objectives, clientele, and staffing patterns of human services programs are generally determined by the administrative and fiscal context in which the programs operate. The source of funds and the locus of financial accountability are generally the loci for policy-making and administrative decisions. A human services system whose components are united by a common, single source of funds and authority may be called a "federated" human services system. A "confederated" human services system, on the other hand, is one in which the various subsystems are linked by mutual agreements, which leave intact the fiscal and decision-making authorities of each component. These agreements limit the "sovereignty," so to speak, of each subsystem insofar as they describe certain patterns of patient referral, information exchange, and staff collaboration; the agreements may or may not be extensive enough to provide effective linkages between the various subsystems. In general each subsystem remains free, however, to redefine its mission, its clientele, or its staffing pattern. A federated suprastructure, on the other hand, has the authority to impose prescribed patterns from above upon the various subsystems; by the same token a subsystem is generally not free to pursue an objective or a clientele problem that is not sanctioned by the suprastructure. It should be noted, however, that many federated human services systems do not invoke their full authority to develop an operationally integrated human services program.

The human services suprastructure may reflect the wishes of the community it serves through a variety of mechanisms. If the human services system is a federated governmental agency, then the governmental bureaucrats express their interpretation of the community's needs and wishes. On the other hand, a community citizens board will express the needs of those citizens they represent; the board may represent most of the community, or, as is often the case, only certain special interest groups from the community. The nature and extent of community input into the design of a human services system, will, of course, affect the general integrity of the system. The relative influence of the community and the consumers of human services, on the one hand, and the professional service providers, on the other hand, will affect the degree to which the human services programs remain responsive to community needs.

Community input into the objectives for human services programs, accompanied by a chronic lack of sufficient resources to meet all the needs for human services, have tended to force human services professionals to pay attention to the economics of human services programs. Many programs have tried to increase total productivity by the use of less expensive staff, e.g., paraprofessionals, and through the use of more economical intervention modalities, e.g., group therapy in mental health, consultation, etc. The community has been able to indirectly influence the objectives and quality of human services programs through the use of a variety of funding mechanisms. Federal funding programs, for example, have influenced the development of community mental health centers, and now health maintenance organizations. Services for children and senior citizens are currently top priorities. The medical expense prepayment system, using third-party intermediaries, has influenced the shape of health services programs tremendously. In a few areas a voucher system has been used, e.g., in education, to provide incentives for increased quality of services.

The organization of mental health services reflects the full variety of organizational patterns suggested by the above issues. Some mental health programs are organizationally and fiscally free-standing with their own community boards; they may or may not relate to health and social services programs in their communities. Mental health programs may be loosely tied to other human services programs through a confederated structure or closely tied through a federated administration. The third chapter of this study discusses the relationship patterns and linkages between mental health programs and other human services programs, and the fourth chapter describes examples of some of these patterns involving mental health and human services programs other than health. Of all human services subsystems, health programs are most often tied to mental health systems. The mental health and health systems may be linked through a general hospital or a neighborhood health center. Or more recently, they may be tied through a free clinic or a health maintenance organization. The fifth chapter expands on the relationship between the mental health and health subsystems.

2. *Comprehensive vs. Categorical Services*

Over the past fifty years human services have become increasingly specialized for good reason. Elaboration of technical knowledge, on the one hand, and of governmentally-funded highly regulated bureaucracies, on the other hand, have necessitated the development of a myriad of specialists with the substantive and bureaucratic know-how essential to bringing services to their clients. During the past decade this specialization has advanced to the point that we are now suffering the consequences of not knowing how to relate these specialists to each other. The consequences of this increasing specialization have prompted a movement for reestablishing the role of the generalist. Hence we are now faced with the problem of relating the generalists to the specialists and of relating general comprehensive service programs to specialized service programs. This problem is a basic impetus for current interest in development of human services systems.

IN FAVOR OF SPECIALIZATION

The case for continued use of specialists is so strong that it is irrefutable. The case is strongest in the technical medical area, where it takes four or five years of postgraduate training to learn specialized surgical skills and where it takes at least two or three years to learn specialized medical, neurological, or psychiatric skills. Clearly the generalist cannot be well informed in all of these areas, as well as in the social and psychological service areas. Furthermore, although the generalist may have a wide range of interests, he may often lack interest in areas of specific relevance to his client; a general practitioner, for example, may have only limited interest in diseases of the skin, or a mental health worker may be uninspired by the details of welfare eligibility.

Once it is acknowledged that specialists are here to stay, the next question is how to define the population to be served by the specialist. Clearly it is not economical to have an open-heart surgical specialist for every neighborhood center. As the degree of specialization increases, the size of the population base necessary to support the specialist also increases. Often a group of such highly specialized persons may band together to form a specialized program, such as a university teaching hospital or a school for autistic children. Thus specialized services come to be.

Although the technical training requirements of the specialists provide a strong rationale for the development of specialized services, the special needs of certain population subgroups also form the basis for a strong case for specialized categorical services. It is often argued, for example, that the alcoholic needs to be treated separately from other clients suffering from emotional difficulties; the alcoholic himself often does not want to be considered "mental." Those who treat drug addicts often go even further, saying that the subculture from which the addict comes is so different from that of the alcoholic that separate programs are necessary in order to be effective with the drug addict. Some professionals would even separate the heroin addict from the soft-drug addict. The legal aspects of psychiatric intervention with the drug addict, or others accused of a crime, often require the services of a mental health specialist in forensic psychiatry. The case for specialized services is similarly made for the retarded, children, the aged, the vocationally handicapped, etc. Each of these groups do indeed have special needs which should be understood and provided for. A similar case has been made for the needs of various ethnic subgroups—blacks, Spanish-speaking persons—who clearly need help from professionals who understand the specifics of their cultural and social class backgrounds. It is commonplace that middle-class professionals often have difficulty understanding the problems associated with poverty culture.

If these arguments were not enough to justify the continued existence of specialized human services programs, various political and social forces in the community would make sure that these specialized programs continue. Powerful lobby groups represent the interests of the mentally ill, the retarded, the epileptic, the alcoholic, the narcotic addict, the paralytic, the unwed mother, the cancerous, the heart diseased, etc. These groups want to be sure that services for their constituencies are provided and that funds they generate are used entirely as they are intended. To be sure that these objectives are obtained, these groups generally insist that clearly definable special services are formed for their client groups. To these citizens' lobby groups we must add the forces of the professionals and bureaucrats who have been in the business of serving special client groups for most of their careers. These professionals can present a very strong case for specialized services for their client group; in addition they often have the power and authority to prove that other service patterns just will not work, since they have operational control over the resources that would be necessary in any new service delivery pattern. It is very understandable why the specialized professionals would not want to give up their separate specialized programs, because such a change would mean not only a considerable loss of power and influence in the total delivery system, but also may require the development of new skills and approaches to the client population they are serving.

The strength of these citizen lobby groups and of the specialized professionals is augmented and continually rejuvenated by the professional training programs. Ten years ago there were virtually no training programs in the human services that were not devoted to training specialists with specific technical skills or special approaches to deal with specific types of problems. We now have junior colleges throughout the country that give an Associate in Arts degree for human services generalists. There are a few undergraduate programs providing a similar four-year curriculum. There are still no postgraduate noncategorical training programs, although some of the social work Master's degree training programs which focus on community organization come close to meeting this need. Most of the current postgraduate training is still oriented towards training professionals with special skills in meeting the needs of special client groups, i.e., professionals are trained to deal with medical problems, or psychiatric problems, or social problems, or vocational problems, etc. These training programs continue to add to the pool of professionals trained to deal with special problems, providing continually renewed resources for staffing these specialized services, as well as additional resources to oppose the development of new models for providing human services. These categorical training programs provide a strong force for maintaining funding and service delivery patterns of a highly specialized categorical nature.

IN FAVOR OF COMPREHENSIVE SERVICES

In spite of these cogent arguments and strong social and political forces in support of a specialized service system, the last few years have seen an increasing movement away from specialized services to general, comprehensive service programs. This new movement has resulted from some very real shortcomings in the specialized service system. One of the most basic and significant difficulties with the specialist service system is a lack of continuity of care, or, to put it another way, the fragmentation of the services. The specialist generally does not consider it his responsibility to explore and examine problems other than those within his limited purview. He may inadvertently overlook factors which are in fact very relevant to his specialized area, for example, the impact of personal or family problems upon a patient's adherence to a regimen prescribed by a physician. A person may have to see several different specialists, or to visit several different facilities, to have all of his problems dealt with. None of these specialists may be interested in taking an overview of the patient-client's problems. Prescriptions or recommendations may be in partial conflict. Or, there may be dimensions of the patient-client's problem for which he can find no specialist; this problem may go unresolved and may have an important impact on the other difficulties of the patient-client. A patient may fail to keep follow-up appointments with a physician because of some personal or psychological difficulties; the physician-specialist, however, may be too busy to determine why his patient did not return. Besides, dealing with personal or psychological problems is not his responsibility anyway. Because the patient-client's basic or general needs may fall outside the arena of each of the specialists he sees, each specialist may in turn pass the buck to another specialist, and so on; and the patient-client is left without adequate services.

In the meantime, as the patient-client goes from specialist to specialist, or from specialized program to specialized program, he may have to repeat his story several times, to fill out countless forms, and to undergo an array of duplicated tests and procedures. This redundancy in the provision of services is not only inconvenient and cumbersome for the patient-client, particularly for the poor client who may have to devote an entire day for each visit to a public clinic or service, but it is also expensive and inefficient for the specialized professionals. Add to that the number of patient-clients who visit specialists for problems that don't really require the technical know-how of the highly trained specialist; these visits are in effect a waste of the specialist's time. The patient-client, however, may not be aware of alternative resources for help (such alternative resources may in fact not exist), and hence he may be forced into inappropriate overutilization of specialized resources. Add the redundancy and the inevitable overutilization of specialists in a specialized service system to the general scarcity of specialists and you get an excess of demand over supply, resulting in long waiting lists, with often harmful delays and rushed, abbreviated service.

The patient-client may be inconvenienced in still other ways by a specialized service system. Since the specialists or specialized program must serve a large geographic area to support themselves, the patient-client may have to travel a considerable distance to obtain specialized services. Furthermore, he may have to seek the assistance of a number of different specialists located in different places. Then, once he finally arrives at the specialist's location, he may discover that the specialist or the staff of a specialized program may not adequately know the nature of local resources which may be an essential component of the treatment or services being provided.

Clearly, a specialized service system faces a serious dilemma. On the one hand, the patient-client is in jeopardy of receiving fragmented services, lacking in comprehensiveness, continuity of care, and follow-up. On the other hand, to avert these shortcomings, the specialized service system may become redundant, over-utilized, inefficient, and geographically cumbersome. As the specialized service system attempts to overcome the fragmentation consequences of specialization, an increasingly large number of linkages between the various system components needs to be developed. As more linkages are developed, the system becomes more complex, acquiring more bureaucratic procedures, more redundancy, repetition, and inefficiency.

AN ATTEMPT TO COMBINE SPECIALIZED AND COMPREHENSIVE SERVICES: A CASE EXAMPLE

We can conclude that a system of purely specialized services is no more effective in providing quality services for its clients than would be a system without specialists. We need a system of both general and specialized services so as to obtain the advantages of specialized services without acquiring their disadvantages. The design of such a mixed system, however, does not follow automatically. A system combining general and specialized services may be as cumbersome and inefficient as a system of totally specialized services.

The District of Columbia mental health service program illustrates some of the difficulties encountered in attempting to combine general and categorical programs.[2] In 1971 the District of Columbia Mental Health Administration had a budget of approximately $10 million, not including reimbursements paid to St. Elizabeth's hospital, a federally-run hospital serving D. C. residents.

The $10 million budget was approximately evenly divided between the support of three comprehensive community mental health centers and support of several categorical programs, providing services primarily for alcoholics, in forensic psychiatry, and for the retarded. It was generally felt that there were serious inadequacies with both the comprehensive community mental health centers and the specialized categorical programs. The reasons for these shortcomings are complex, and it is not the intention of this study to provide a comprehensive analysis of these difficulties. The following description, however, is designed to illustrate some of the pitfalls in combining general and specialized human services in one system.

Prior to 1965, District of Columbia mental health services consisted primarily of a large, centralized short-term psychiatric inpatient unit and a small, centralized outpatient unit for child and adult services. In 1965 a comprehensive mental health plan was developed in response to the Community Mental Health Centers Act. This plan proposed a tri-level system, providing comprehensive geographically-oriented health and mental health services to the entire city through the vehicle of

[2]Although the District of Columbia Mental Health Administration is part of the Department of Human Resources, which has the authority to integrate all the District of Columbia human service programs, mental health programs are nevertheless operated as a categorical program, virtually independent of all other human service program activities, including services to narcotic addicts. The difficulties attendant to such an administrative structure are similar to those described above for a purely specialized service system. We shall discuss some of these specifics in the next chapter.

neighborhood health centers. These primary ambulatory programs were to be backed up by more specialized health and mental health services for each of four catchment areas covering several neighborhood health centers. D. C. General and St. Elizabeth's hospitals were then to be city-wide back-up resources for the catchment area programs. This comprehensive, geographically-based system should have been able to provide both basic health and mental health services as well as the necessary specialized services.

This plan was initiated by dividing the large general psychiatric unit into three separate programs, each to receive patients on a geographic basis. At the same time, the first (Area C Community Mental Health Center) of the three community mental health centers was initiated, largely with Federal funds. In 1967 the second (Area B Community Mental Health Center) community mental health program was begun. During the first few years only about ten of the planned two dozen comprehensive health centers were started; none of these initially had a mental health component.

In the meantime, the Hagan Act was passed. This legislation in effect defined alcoholism as a medical, not a legal, problem, requiring that the city provide appropriate medical services for the publicly intoxicated and for all other alcoholics who need such assistance. The law did not specify the form of such services, but the health department elected to develop highly specialized programs for alcoholics. A large 48–72 hour detoxification center was established in a high-risk area. A 90-day, 700-bed "rehabilitation center" was established 25 miles out of town in facilities formerly occupied by the District of Columbia reformatory. A single alcoholic outpatient clinic was provided in conjunction with Area B CMHC; this clinic served only a few of the clients discharged from the detoxification or rehabilitation centers. Virtually no efforts were made to link these categorical services for alcoholics to other services of the community mental health centers, even though many of the patients being served by the other programs also had alcohol-related problems.

This separate, highly categorical service system for alcoholics was consistent with the development of services within the Area C and B community mental health centers. Area C had separate inpatient units for adults, children, adolescents, alcoholics, and geriatric patients. This resulted in a very large number of inpatient beds, considerable duplication of inpatient services, and very minimal ambulatory and outreach services. Area B had separate ambulatory facilities for adults, children, adolescents, and alcoholics. All of these separate programs had very limited communication with each other. Although alcoholism services comprised the largest portion of the clearly categorical programs, centralized specialized programs were also developed in the areas of forensic psychiatry, suicide prevention, foster care, and retardation.

The fragmentation, duplication, and inefficiency of services were so great that none of the programs felt they were able to provide adequate service, in spite of a reasonably adequate per capita budget. Follow-up services in the alcoholism program were very poor and the recidivism rate was extremely high. Foster care follow-up has been similarly poor, and the readmission rate to the inpatient units and to St. Elizabeth's Hospital has also been very high. At one point, for example, Area B CMHC had to close its emergency and outpatient intake services for adults for lack of sufficient staff resources, in spite of a total budget of over $2,000,000 for that center for that year! In 1970, a group of staff persons at the Area C Community Mental Health Center became sufficiently frustrated that they developed their own outreach programs in the community linked to neighbor-hood health centers. Two of the three satellites that were formed, however, were so poorly linked to the central inpatient unit that referrals to and from the inpatient unit were poorly managed.

The shortcomings of the District of Columbia mental health programs are due primarily to the fairly rigid, closed boundaries between the various subsystems. Movement of patients between the community mental health centers and the categorical programs is rare, and cumbersome when it does occur. Thus the specialized service programs, particularly those for alcoholics, pro-vide general, nonspecialized services to their clients, along with the more specialized services they were de-signed to provide. The community mental health cen-ters, in turn, are short on general mental health workers. The system is designed so that the redeployment of staff resources to correct staffing inequities cannot be readily accomplished. Thus the general mental health workers do not have ready access to the systems' mental health specialists, who themselves feel overburdened, because they are performing both generalist's and specialist's functions. The isolation of the generalists from the rest of the system reduces their effectiveness considerably and renders them, for all practical purposes, like anoth-er categorical component of the total system. In short, al-though the District of Columbia mental health system appears to contain a mixture of comprehensive and specialized services, in actual operation it resembles more a system of highly separated, categorical services with all the shortcomings described earlier of such a fragmented specialized system.

Hence, the nature of the linkages and interactions between the various subsystems of a human services sys-tem is crucial for the development of a comprehensive system containing both comprehensive general and specialized categorical programs. The specialist in a comprehensive system must be closely related to the generalist that he serves. Often he will serve in the role of consultant to the generalist, who will continue with the case. Or he may assume responsibility for providing "definitive treatment" or service in the case, leaving the generalist to continue with other aspects of the patient-client's problems. In addition, an effective system needs to monitor itself regularly to assure that these linkages and interactions between specialist and generalist are properly and appropriately carried out. Then, continuing in-service training must be provided to develop staff skills and to facilitate proper use of the resources of the system.

The next three chapters examine specific models and examples of the linkages and interactions (or lack of them) between mental health subsystems and other subsystems of the human services system. We shall examine these examples with regard to their advantages and disadvantages. In the sixth chapter we shall attempt to formulate a more abstract conceptual model, defining the principles of an ideal human services system, based on what we learn from the programs described in the next three chapters.

3. Patterns of Relationships Between Human Services Programs

PROGRAM IDEOLOGIES

The relationship between mental health and other programs in the human services system will be determined by several variables introduced in Chapter 1. Of critical importance to the pattern of relationships between mental health and other human service programs are the program's basic objectives and basic assumptions as to style and methodology. An organization will operate under one or more sets of basic premises, which may be complementary or, in some cases, mutually exclusive. Each set of basic premises makes certain assumptions about the causation of various human service problems and about the relative effectiveness of various problem-solving approaches.

Probably the most common model among service programs assumes that the problem at hand is caused by a defect within the individual. This model, often labelled the *medical model,* is most relevant in health programs, where an etiological difficulty can often be located within the individual, and where the defect, or pathology, is treated with medication or surgery, and the patient is "cured." Psychoanalytically-oriented psychotherapy is a derivative of this model; although it is not prescriptive or directive in approach, it places the source of difficulties within the individual in the area of conflicted feelings. The supportive therapies also place the client's difficulty

67

within himself, but in the area of his ability to negotiate with the outside world, e.g., employment, housing, welfare, etc.; in these cases, the client is helped to deal with those tasks he cannot manage on his own.

In contrast to the defect-within-the-individual model, the *community organizational model* places the defect within society — its institutions, practices, and organizational patterns. According to this model, the quality of human life services to people can be optimized most effectively by intervening at the level of social institutions and organizations. A human services program, and the human services worker, thus assume a social change agent role. This role may take a variety of forms. It may be one of community advocacy, an open confrontational approach directed to change specific social defects, e.g., obtaining services and rights for welfare mothers, changing police or penal practices through prison rioting, etc. The advocacy approach may use nonviolent approaches, such as the sit-ins and marches of the 1960's, or the legal challenges of the NAACP, Civil Liberties Union, or consumer advocacy groups. These confrontational advocacy approaches have generally been led by consumers of services or by lawyers. Mental health workers have not generally assumed a leadership role in such activities, except on an occasional individual basis without mental health organizational sanction. Mental health workers have occasionally taken a confrontational advocacy approach within their own organization, such as the "revolt" at Lincoln Hospital, following which the Director, Dr. Harris Peck, resigned.

Mental health programs are more likely to take a more moderate posture, through a mediator or consultative role. Bill Bolman describes an incident at the West Side Community Mental Health Center in San Francisco, in which community members came to the Center and were helped with regard to an incident in which a little black girl was sexually molested by a white former state hospital patient. The Mental Health Center convened meetings with all of the relevant institutions — the police, a medical hospital, and a foster care home. These meetings probably averted some violent protestation and probably facilitated improved interagency collaboration and may prevent recurrences of similar incidents (Bolman, 1972). Similarly, the Laboratory of Community Psychiatry, Harvard Medical School, has been asked to consult with the Boston school administration at times of school rioting. Many mental health programs throughout the country are engaged in noncrisis-oriented ongoing consultation to community agencies to help them become more responsive to the needs of their clients.

Ongoing community consultation is an example of an evolutionary social change strategy, in contrast to the confrontational advocacy style. Many human services programs have been attempting to change the social fabric of their communities by helping relatively deprived neighborhoods to develop more competency and strength. This social change approach tends to focus on the development of indigenous leadership capacity or on the promotion of economic activity within the deprived communities. This social change approach is generally not stimulated by mental health programs, although an occasional mental health worker, usually an indigenous worker, may become involved in promoting a specific local cause. For the most part, this approach has been prompted by OEO Community Action Projects (CAP) or by Model Cities programs. These projects are generally led by representatives from the communities to be served and involve mental health programs and mental health workers as contributors to the overall planning project.

The Area A Community Mental Health Center in Washington, D. C. is attempting to take this approach to help the Spanish-speaking minority in its community to develop itself more effectively. This project, Project Puente, is designed to develop indigenous Spanish-speaking leaders, using English language learning as a key point of intervention. American volunteers are recruited from the community to teach English to the Spanish-speaking community. Spanish-speaking persons with leadership potential are recruited and offered training in group leadership skills. These Spanish-speaking leaders then recruit additional Spanish-speaking persons from their neighborhoods to learn English from the American volunteers. Hopefully, this larger group will, in turn, be able to assume a leadership role with the larger Spanish-speaking community. Although learning the English language is the explicit activity of the project, the underlying goal is to help the Spanish-speaking community to organize itself and to become more effective in meeting its own needs.

The *educational model* shares some aspects of the two previous models. Although this model focuses on the individual need and capacity to grow and learn, it may or may not be remedial in its orientation. Whereas the medical model is generally applied to treat a client's "pathology," the educational model is often proactive, rather than reactive, and facilitates the development of normal growth potential. Elementary, secondary, and higher liberal arts education are, ideally, examples of this approach. Within the mental health arena, sensitivity training and encounter groups are examples of attempts to promote normal psychological growth and development.

Like the community organizational approach, the educational model often attempts to make its impact upon the individual by placing him in small social groups which have been organized to optimize individual growth and development. The use of group process to promote individual growth is often aimed at remediating specific disabilities. Therapeutic communities are designed to help clients with emotional disability to assume more active responsibility in coping with their feelings and their interpersonal relationships. The group learns to share responsibility with regard to group issues and to encourage individuals to assume personal responsibility for their own decisions and behavior. This model is being increasingly used in mental health programs throughout the country.

Another educationally-oriented group program for emotionally disabled clients is based on the principles of behavior modification. By careful and systematic administration of reward, and occasionally punishment, clients are taught to develop new personal, interpersonal, social, and vocational skills. A number of closed, inpatient units now use "a token economy" as a vehicle for implementing a reward system.

Another model, the *self-help group*, often combines aspects of the first two models. This model presumes difficulties or problems within the individual, but also presumes that a group of persons with similar needs and difficulties can help as much or more than professionals can. This model shares similar premises to the community organizational model, but the objectives are limited to meeting the needs of a very specific group, who comprise the total membership of the organization. Professionals are generally specifically excluded. There are a number of such self-help groups designed to assist persons with emotional difficulties, e.g., Alcoholics Anonymous, Neurotics Anonymous, and Recovery, Inc. Weight Watchers, Inc., is an example of a self-help group in the health field. Welfare mothers in many areas have grouped together to meet their needs, although their activities are generally aimed at getting additional resources from the government. Cooperative neighborhood nursery schools or day care centers are also commonplace. Senior Citizens groups are formed to meet the general needs of older persons. PTA groups are designed to meet the needs of parents and school children. Community neighborhood associations may be considered as examples of either the self-help model or the community organizational model, since membership is open to anyone in a certain geographic area, regardless of specific human service needs or problems.

Unlike many of the other human services, mental health programs often combine two or more of these models at once. Many times these models are combined within the very same service element. For example, a client may be a member of a therapeutic community or a token economy and at the same time may receive medication or even individual psychotherapy. Family therapy may, on the one hand, resemble an extension of the clinical medical model or, on the other hand, may resemble the community organizational model, in that the professional may serve as a consultant to help the family organize itself so as to become more effective in resolving its own difficulties. Or, to combine three models at once, family systems intervention may be offered to a family participating in a therapeutic community, while one of the family members is also receiving psychotropic medication.

More often, each service element within a program is designed around a specific model. The clinician who treats a case of gonorrhea, for example, is not likely to have the responsibility for locating the patient's sexual contacts so as to prevent further spread of the disease in the community. A school teacher or school principal will not generally assume the responsibility of helping the school's neighborhood organize itself to obtain better social or health services. These separate program elements, therefore, must be linked together just as a group of specialists and generalists must be linked, if they are to work together as an integrated system.

INTERORGANIZATIONAL AGREEMENTS

The administrative and contractual relationships between the various service elements are crucial in defining the linkages between the various subsystems and the roles of staff who cross these subsystem boundaries. These administrative and contractual relationships may be very limited or extensive in scope. Although these formal agreements may often restrict subsystem relationships, at times informal relationships and patterns of interaction develop to the point of exceeding the original limitations. Conversely, some systems with very extensive formal sanction for interprogram relationships have in actuality very limited subsystem interaction because of highly rigid informal boundaries.

Perhaps the most limited contractual arrangement is one in which one community organization, for example, a community mental health center, offers *consultation* to another community agency, e.g., the public school system. The consultation contract is limited to an agreement to explore jointly some problems of interest to both organizations. The consultant offers to bring to bear his specialized know-how to the problems presented by the consultee. As a consequence of the consultation process, the consultee may redefine his problem, or he may acquire new technical information which may permit him to develop new options to deal with his task. The final decision as to which option to apply remains with the consultee and his organization. The consultant has no power or authority, and in fact his lack of power may enhance his effectiveness, because the consultee is free to discuss his problems without defensiveness (Caplan, 1971). The consultation contract in no way commits either program to an exchange of records or clients or to staff collaboration. Although medical consultants generally do case consultation, thus requiring them to see specific cases for evaluation, mental health consultants

frequently try to limit case consultation to especially difficult cases or to the early stages of a new consultation
relationship.

The consultation model may be used in response to a
severe manpower shortage, or it may reflect a proactive
attempt to change the community by affecting its organizational structure. Mental health programs in several
rural areas, which generally have mental health manpower shortages, have decided to put more than half of
their mental health resources into consultation services,
e.g., Tullahoma, Tennessee, several counties in northern
Minnesota, and Columbus, Georgia. Leonard Maholick
(1972) describes how the Bradley Center in Columbus,
Georgia provides case consultation to public health
nurses in order to leverage the limited time availability of
consulting psychiatrists. The Multi-County Mental
Health Center in Tullahoma provides both case- and
program-centered consultation to virtually all other
caretaker and human services groups within its five
county catchment area, including family physicians, public schools, courts and probation agencies, clergy, and
welfare and rehabilitation agencies. Although crisis intervention direct services are also provided, the mental
health consultants attempt to prevent the classification of
social system failures as mental health problems. This
tends to force the community agencies to assume responsibility to become effective in dealing with problems that
might otherwise go unresolved.

Ironically, while the economics of manpower shortages have stimulated many rural programs to develop
extensive consultation services, the economics of financial reimbursement have prompted most programs to
concentrate on direct clinical services rather than indirect consultative services. Third-party payments and tax
funds are readily made available for direct clinical services, which are easily counted and assumed to be easily

evaluated. Consultation services are not so readily evaluated, and it is often difficult to obtain financial reimbursement for these services. Thus even programs which are very aware of the social needs of their clients, such as Central City Community Mental Health Center in Los Angeles, offer very minimal consultation services to their communities. Consequently the consultation model is underdeveloped in most community mental health programs in the United States.

Although the consultation contract is in itself very limited in scope, the consultation relationship may lead to much more extensive formal or informal interrelationships between various community programs. Even though mental health consultants will discourage premature referral for diagnostic evaluation and direct service, consultation activities may in fact become a source for case finding and for referrals for direct service. The Area A Community Mental Health Center in Washington, D. C., for example, receives over two-thirds of the referrals to its Youth Services program through the public schools to which it consults; the Center now consults at all 17 elementary and secondary public schools in the catchment area. Similarly, the consultation relationship may lead to the development of collaborative activities with other community agencies with regard to various community problems. Individual mental health workers, in addition, may extend their role beyond that of consultant to become an advocate or ombudsman for social change in specific areas.

Confederated agreements tend to bind participating agencies more closely than do consultation agreements; however, these agreements may also be quite limited. Most metropolitan areas have Health and Welfare Councils which were originally formed as community planning vehicles two, three, and four decades ago. Many of these planning councils, e.g., United Community Services of Boston and the Health and Welfare Council of Washington, D.C., still influence interagency relationships through their control of the disbursement of Community Chest and United Fund contributions. These superorganizations may influence the development of new priorities among community agencies, such as services to ethnic minorities, by refusing to provide new funds without the development of such new services. These metropolitan agencies may also serve as an information and referral clearinghouse.

These planning councils are limited, however, in the amount of money they can shift from year to year as program priorities change. Furthermore, many programs are not so dependent upon Health and Welfare Council funds that they would feel compelled to respond to major shifts in community priorities. In addition, the Health and Welfare Councils generally impose themselves only upon the policy formulation aspects of organizational behavior; for the most part, they do not formulate standards or expectations with regard to exchange of clients, records, staff, etc.

The National Institute of Mental Health, through its community mental health centers program, has required more detailed affiliation agreements from programs receiving Federal funds. These affiliation agreements generally preserve a confederated administrative structure, but provide explicitly for exchange of clients, records, and staff, as appropriate, between the various participating programs. These affiliation agreements, in their most limited form, provide only for exchange of patients and records, and when necessary, of staff, for the sake of continuity of care. This type of agreement is often made between community programs and their back-up state hospital or community hospital, e.g., between Northwest San Antonio Community Mental Health Center and San

Antonio State Hospital, or between Huntington Mental Health Center (Huntington, West Virginia) and the local general hospital.

Many affiliation agreements provide for or develop into a vehicle for joint program planning. These planning activities generally go beyond the Health and Welfare Planning Councils in that not only are program priorities established, but also specific collaborative procedures and programs are often developed. The Northcoast Regional Mental Health Center in Ventura, California and the Pennsylvania Hospital Community Mental Health Center in Philadelphia are examples of this type of affiliation pattern. The Pennsylvania Hospital has worked with its affiliates to obtain needed services in the educational, health, mental health, and welfare areas for ethnic minorities in its catchment area.

Affiliated organizations may agree to plan together with or without financial ties. However, as the degree of financial interdependence increases, other aspects of the program tend to become more interdependent; thus the program is likely to become increasingly integrated. Such a program is often called a *consortium*. The San Fernando Valley Community Mental Health Center in California is an example of a program with six affiliates which share funds from the National Institute of Mental Health; this program demonstrates a system with limited financial interdependence and considerable system incongruity. Each of the six affiliates maintains its own board, which receives funds from other sources in addition to the National Institute of Mental Health. Each board continues to make policy and set priorities for its program. Consequently, the child guidance clinic continues to serve the entire San Fernando Valley, not just the local catchment area; a special educational program serves the metropolitan Los Angeles area; a vocational rehabilitation program serves an adjacent catchment area. The board of the center is composed primarily of representatives of each of the six affiliates. Hence the center's board is more inclined to preserve the autonomy of the separate affiliates than it is inclined to strengthen the authority of the center over the participating programs. In short, the financial interdependence of this center is not sufficient to facilitate the development of other program linkages.

In contrast, the Westside Community Mental Health Center in San Francisco is considerably more integrated because the community has a major voice in the planning process. The board of the center consists of representatives of the fifteen, or more, participating agencies and an equal number of community representatives. Community board members are selected by quarterly community forums. The board determines the center's priorities, and participating agencies are reimbursed for services according to these priorities. This financial reimbursement system tends to force participating programs to move in the direction of the center's priorities.

It is clear that affiliation agreements in a confederated system can lead to a very integrated program, if the affiliation agreements provide a mechanism for financial and decision-making interdependence. On the other hand, an affiliate is always free to withdraw from affiliation should its priorities or style come in conflict with that of the overall program. As the financial dependence upon the supersystem decreases, the affiliate increases its freedom to withdraw from the agreement.

An agreement to permit something, for example, exchange of clients, does not in itself ensure that such an exchange of clients will in fact occur. The implementation of such an agreement really depends upon the commitment and interest of the program chiefs and their staffs to work together and to use each other's resources appropriately. The Huntington Community Mental Health Center, for example, was permitted to follow patients referred to the psychiatric unit of a community hospital, but for a couple of years staff declined to take advantage of this option. The alcoholism programs in the District of Columbia have agreed to exchange patients with the community mental health centers, but with the exception of one center this rarely occurs. These examples demonstrate how informal boundaries continue to separate subsystems even though they are formally linked.

The previous administrative arrangements provide for financial, planning, and loose programmatic linkages between components of a human services system. However, even Westside Community Mental Health Center in San Francisco has entirely separate programs at the service delivery level. Some communities have been able to develop integrated programs at the delivery level, even though participating organizations may continue to be administratively separate. The Mid-Houston (St. Joseph Hospital) Community Mental Health Center in Houston has developed a common intake-referral service in each of three separate communities. In collaboration with vocational rehabilitation, probation, state and county public welfare departments, and the public health department, the community mental health center has developed a program in which clients may receive a comprehensive evaluation in their own community with a smooth referral for remedial services. Records are shared, and staff contiguity facilitates collaboration.

Some communities have developed comprehensive neighborhood service centers for both evaluation and ongoing service. The Malcolm-Bliss Mental Health Center in St. Louis has placed some of its staff in an OEO neighborhood health service center. The staff in this program assume several roles. They provide direct service to clients from the neighborhood, and they consult with nonmental health staff in the neighborhood health service center. They also assume an advocacy role to help their clients to obtain needed services from other human services programs in the community. Although the mental health workers are part of a separate administrative structure from the staff of the neighborhood health services center, they are very closely linked both to the other staff and to the community, because they are recruited from the neighborhoods that they serve.

The Franklin Mental Health Center in Boston has joined with the Model Cities program to develop a Family Life Center to provide a wide range of services — medical; mental health; speech, hearing, and language; mental retardation; drug addiction; and information and evaluation. Again, the mental health staff provide both direct service to clients and indirect service through consultation to the nonmental health workers. The most common programmatic vehicle for direct collaboration at the service delivery level between mental health programs and other human services programs are the OEO-funded or Model Cities-funded neighborhood service centers. Although the mental health staff generally remain administratively independent, they tend to collaborate very closely with the nonmental health staff because of their common close ties to the community being served. However, even though the mental health workers may influence the establishment of the priorities of the neighborhood center, they do not directly participate in that process. Furthermore, the neighborhood center's director is not free to shift resources between the mental health area and other functions of the program.

Examples of a single administrative authority over all types of service at the program service delivery level are hard to come by. Turner, Smith, and Medley (1967) describe a combined health and mental health program in Santa Clara County, California under the auspices of a single department of public health and mental health. The authors feel that such an integrated program promotes better staff cooperation and much less distrust. In addition, they feel that the community more readily accepts mental health staff because they are part of a larger, nonthreatening unit. The authors feel that the integrated program facilitates the kind of interdisciplinary collaboration that Maholick (1972) attempts to achieve in Columbus, Georgia through the use of case consultation.

Although more and more states, counties, and cities are developing departments of human services, these departments are generally not exercising the full authority of such a federated system to develop integrated programs at the service delivery level. The Department of Human Resources in the District of Columbia, for example, has jurisdiction over health, mental health, narcotics, welfare, and vocational rehabilitation services. This department was formed out of several separate departments, each with independent jurisdiction over its own service area. Although priorities and policy are now made at the superagency level, so that funds can be transferred from one service area to another, e.g., from mental health to welfare, the several subsystems continue to operate virtually independently at the program service level. Thus in the District of Columbia there are virtually no collaborative neighborhood programs which include health, mental health, narcotics, welfare, and vocational rehabilitation. In fact, in some instances separate subsystems continue to operate preexisting programs which overlap in function, and which in effect are now competitors for financial resources. For example, both the mental health subsystem and the welfare subsystem evaluate and attend to the needs of families at risk of dissolution; in the one subsystem, the client may be admitted into an inpatient unit or offered psychotherapy, while in the other subsystem the client may be offered financial assistance, or a child may be placed in a foster care home. The evaluations and potential solutions are rarely jointly made, although the staff in both subsystems are employed by the same department.

There are a few neighborhood health centers in the District working with staff from the mental health centers. But these collaborative efforts for the most part predated the formation of the superagency and have not been facilitated by its formation. Thus, the development of a federated administrative structure does not in itself assure program integrity. We shall examine some of the possible reasons for this failure later on.

Program Linkage

These administrative and contractual arrangements define, permit, and facilitate a variety of linkages between the various subsystems of a human services system. These linkages serve to enhance the interactions and interdependencies of the several subsystems. The various types of linkages that may occur within human services systems may be described and categorized according to the system properties identified in Chapter 1.

Systems which share a common mission, ideology, methodological model, or other basic premises will tend to be more closely linked with regard to other properties of the system. This generalization is probably so commonplace that we take it for granted. A mental health program is more likely to work well with another mental health program than with an adoption agency. Furthermore, a community mental health center is more likely to work closely with another one than with a psychoanalytic institute.

Patient-client flow patterns are a key link in a human services system, because it is they who are being served by the system. If there is to be a system at all, patient-clients must be able to move freely from one component to another. Each component must be willing to accept some degree of responsibility for service for the patient-client.

However, patient movement without movement of any other resources or products of the system will not benefit the patient-client very much; that is what happens when a patient-client goes to a series of specialists, none of whom know about the other. Personnel movement is a major method for augmentation of the linkages between various subsystems and to enhance the quality of services for the patient-clients. There are a variety of models for accomplishing this. Joint staff appointments is a familiar method; in this way a single staff person may work with two or more subsystems simultaneously, bringing with him specific skills, information, and knowledge about the rest of the system. This is useful when there are a limited number of subsystems. However, when the number of subsystems becomes large, joint appointments become insufficient to span all the separate boundaries. In this case, a team is often established with representatives from all the separate subsystems. Such teams (or task forces) are useful for planning purposes in larger organizations. At the service delivery level such teams are generally multidisciplinary and provide a way of linking the resources of the various professional disciplinary sybsystems; thus a physician, nurse, social worker, psychologist, etc. are linked together through shared team responsibility. Such a team structure, however, may become very time consuming. Furthermore, although a team may link persons of different disciplines, it does not generally serve to link one functional service unit with another. In other words, it would be difficult to design a team that would effectively link on an ongoing basis a neighborhood health center, a psychiatric inpatient unit, a sheltered workshop, a surgical ward, and a public school.

Hence, many functional units develop the role of the "liaison worker," who is responsible for linking the staff of that functional unit with the staff of one or more other functional units, presumably through a comparable liaison worker in the other unit. One person may perform the entire liaison function for the functional unit, or that liaison function may be divided among the staff, so that several staff persons may each have responsibility for relating to other subsystems. The *expediter* has a similar role, but his task is to link the patient-clients in his subsystem to staff of other subsystems. Again, this role may be performed by only one person, or it may be shared by a number of different persons, each with his own case-load.

The *program coordinator's* role is still different. He is not necessarily a member of a functional unit, linking that unit or a patient-client from that unit to other functional units. Instead, he transcends all the functional subsystems, although he may be very closely attached to them, and he is responsible for overseeing all of the various linkages among the various subsystems. In some ways, he assumes the functions of a total system team or of a team of liaison workers. The program coordinator may work with or without such additional linkage.

Personnel may also relate to each other through a consultative role. Specialists from one subsystem may consult with one or more staff from another subsystem. Consultation may be around a specific case, or it may be more general, in which case it may begin to resemble in-service training.

Staff movement will bring with it movement in the technical support systems. Records, for example, must go with the patient-client from staff person to staff person, carrying with them information and evaluations from one staff person to another. Just as the telephone has allowed us to move our voices across subsystem boundaries, the computer has facilitated the movement of other functions across subsystem boundaries. Meharry Medical College in Nashville, Tennessee has instituted a computer which can arrange appointments, process bloods, and automatically coordinate a medical work-up for a patient, thus serving a generalist expediter function. Eventually, the computer's capacity to move information across boundaries may simplify some of the cross-boundary tasks currently assumed by staff.

The above programmatic linkages can be enhanced by a variety of administrative linkages. These linkages may be defined by affiliation agreements or memoranda of understanding, if the organizations are linked in a confederated structure, or they may be linked by charters, by-laws, legislation, or administrative orders, if they compose a federated structure.

Subsystems may share a common source of funds, either through governmental appropriations, or through shared fund raising, lobbying, etc. Since funds are the life-blood of any human services program, such a shared resource certainly necessitates active collaboration. When funds are shared, decisions about their distribution must also be shared, although in a federated system this responsibility may be assumed by a limited number of persons.

Funds may be distributed by allotting a flat total to each of the subsystems. Or, as at the Westside Community Mental Health Center in San Francisco, each program may receive reimbursements on a fee-for-service basis. The fee-for-service type of model is now being extended on an experimental basis to service areas previously budgeted on a flat allotment basis. Some school systems, for example, provide consumers with vouchers, entitling them to "purchase" educational services at any of a variety of eligible programs. This extension of the fee-for-service model tends to provide an incentive for programs to develop good quality services. The system has the disadvantage of making the annual budget formulation more difficult. The per capita prepayment model, used by health maintenance organizations, also provides a financial incentive for good quality of services, but permits somewhat more advance budgeting.

Human services systems also need mechanisms for joint decision-making. In a confederated system the appointment of a program chief, whose scope of responsibility may impact upon programs which are administratively separate, is often made with the concurrence of both organizations. Similarly, ongoing policy decisions may be made by a steering committee, composed of representatives of two or more administratively separate organizations; such a steering committee would be equivalent to the team task force described earlier. Decisions with regard to recommendations for patient-clients can be made in a large system through case conferences, which are jointly staffed by representatives from the several involved programs.

All of these administrative decisions should be made with as much information as possible with regard to the impact of previous decisions. Thus one crucial link in a human services system is provided by the monitoring or evaluation function, which should ideally continually examine the effectiveness of all the various linkages within the system — the patterns of patient-client flow, staff flow, etc. — to determine what patterns may need to be changed.

Finally, the various human services subsystems may be linked together by their common ties to the community-at-large and to other organizations and institutions. This link may be provided administratively by a board of directors, or it may be provided by a common constituency, represented by an advisory board. The components of a human services system may also be linked through shared gatekeepers, e.g., police, clergy, etc. Of basic importance is the view that the community-at-large has of the human services system and its subsystems. If the community wants the human services system to be integrated and expects the system to assume the responsibility for effecting system integrity, then the system is likely to move in that direction. If, on the other hand, the community sees the human services system as fragmented, and offers no clear expectation or mandate for the elimination of that fragmentation, then the various subsystems are likely to continue to operate with only very limited linkages between them. In the next two chapters we shall examine what types of linkages various communities have developed in their human services systems.

4. *Mental Health and Other Human Services Programs*

The administrative and contractual arrangements described in the previous chapter and their associated operational linkages are reflected in a variety of human services systems in which mental health services are linked to other human services subsystems. These human services programs range from general multiservice centers to specific medical services, recreational and social service activities, programs providing graduated living arrangements, vocational counseling and rehabilitation, education, and corrections.

Neighborhood Service Centers

Other than health services (which will be discussed in the next chapter) mental health programs are most frequently linked to neighborhood services centers. These programs, variously titled, are basically multiservice centers focusing primarily on the basic life-supporting services, e.g., employment counseling, housing, income maintenance (welfare), health, and mental health. These programs generally serve poverty-area clients, whose needs for such life-supporting social services are great. The programs are generally funded through OEO or Model Cities. These neighborhood centers tend to be oriented toward either health or social services. In the neighborhood health centers social services are a necessary, but nevertheless auxiliary, service. In the neighborhood services centers referrals are made for health services, but mental health services are often provided on location.

The Bernalillo County Mental Health Center in Albuquerque, New Mexico demonstrates a neighborhood service center composed of OEO-supported community workers and NIMH-supported mental health workers. The center has five "sustained contact teams," each associated with an OEO neighborhood center. Each team consists of several mental health workers (new careerists or other indigenous workers), one or two nurses and/or psychiatric social workers, and a part-time psychiatrist or psychologist. These teams are the core of the outpatient and the outreach program of the community mental health center. They manage crises presenting in the community either in their community setting or by making a referral to the center for an intake evaluation or for admission. If a patient is referred centrally for initial treatment, the staff maintain contact with him, providing for continuity of care when he is able to return to his neighborhood service center for follow-up treatment.

Although the mental health staff collaborate very closely with the OEO staff, the functions of the two groups remain separate, with the mental health staff concentrating on assisting clients with emotional disability. This is not to say that the mental health staff are not involved in community organizational activities; the sustained contact teams do provide consultation and education to the community agencies with whom they work, although this consultation is generally case-oriented.

This program is an example of a confederated, decentralized program in which staff linkages are developed on an informal basis as a result of geographic proximity.

Although all the staff of the neighborhood center perform generalist functions to a large degree, they also
retain a considerable measure of specialized functions.
Successful generalist-specialist linkages are achieved
through the development of informal collaborative relationships.

This kind of administrative and programmatic structure is common. The Family Life Center of the Franklin
Mental Health Center in Boston is similar. The Area B
Community Mental Health Center in Washington, D. C.
has mental health staff working with CHANGE, Inc., an
OEO-funded neighborhood center. The Area C Community Mental Health Center in Washington, D. C. has
mental health staff working in a similar collaborative
relationship with neighborhood health center staff; in
this case the mental health staff assist their clients with
their welfare, housing, and employment needs because
there are no OEO- or Model Cities-funded service staff
to perform these functions.

The Central City Community Mental Health Center in
Los Angeles is an example of a federated program functioning in a confederated style. In addition to its more
traditional mental health functions, the Central City
Community Mental Health Center has a staff of eight
nonprofessionals working in a "community service
center," which provides services in the following areas:
welfare, employment counseling, housing, development, senior citizens, youth services, and a friendship
club. Although the clinical staff and the community services staff are all on the same payroll and under the same
administrative structure, they work entirely independently and make formal referrals to each other. The
community services staff have little involvement with the
clinical psychotherapy staff and know little of what is
going on in these areas with their clients. The community
services staff and the clinical staff are centralized, serving

the entire catchment area from one location. This centralized structure has tended to encourage specialization, even among the nonprofessionals, such that one staff person focuses on housing, and another on employment, etc. The community services center staff functions collectively as a generalist, but separately as specialists. This centralized and specialized staffing pattern seems to contribute to the development of more formal relationships between staff members and program units, making the program resemble a confederation of separate specialized service programs.

RECREATION PROGRAMS

Service centers which are closely tied to the community often develop recreational and social services for its residents. The community service center of Central City Community Mental Health Center, for example, has both a senior citizens' club and a friendship club for chronically disabled clients. These clubs provide both recreational activities and a supportive social network for their members. A similar program is available for teenagers, who arrange their own community activities, e.g., street dances, lectures, weekend camping trips, field trips, and a black arts festival. Similarly, CHANGE, Inc. in Washington, D. C. operates a day-care center for chronically disabled clients in its area; the program is relatively unstructured, but offers an opportunity for people to get together informally during the day as they wish and to engage in a variety of social and recreational activities.

The San Fernando Valley Community Mental Health Center has developed an interesting recreational program for teenagers, called REC. This program was developed in response to a felt community need for special services for teenagers who seemed to be at loose ends. Staffed only with a recreational director and a secretary, the program functions like a therapeutic community and uses the youngsters themselves to plan and organize desired services. The teenagers have developed a variety of special interest clubs, e.g., gardening, photography, ham radios, etc., in addition to dances and other social activities. The youngsters learn to develop skills in meeting their own needs. The program provides structured meaningful activities for teenagers who otherwise might develop antisocial behavior patterns for lack of anything better to do.

REC may be described as a prevention-oriented program, based on the educational, growth-oriented model and emphasizing the self-help capacities of the teenagers. As a part of a very loosely confederated community mental health center, however, it operates very independently from the clinical direct service programs of the center. Referral of clients needing remedial clinical services to and from REC is not regularly accomplished, and mental health consultation to the sole professional in the program is not provided. REC has its own board of directors, and with the exception of its dependence upon the community mental health center for funds, the program operates virtually as an independent human services program.

REC, in aiming to provide services for relatively normal youngsters, is different from most of the recreational services sponsored by mental health programs; these programs (except for services for senior citizens), tend to be designed for emotionally disabled clients, e.g., chronic schizophrenics. Most recreational services for the "normal" population are operated entirely independently of the mental health system. The main tie between the two systems, if there is any at all, is consultative. The Area A Community Mental Health Center, for example, consults with the staff of a neighborhood recreation center with regard to group process, specific clinical problems, and a growing drug addiction epidemic in the area. This linkage is based primarily upon the community organizational model.

Most recreational groups which are composed primarily of nonemotionally disabled clients do not need the services of mental health professionals and in effect operate as self-help groups, e.g., senior citizens' clubs. Ideally, such self-help groups would have available to them a variety of consultants who could bring to them the specialized resources of a human services system. Thus, not only mental health consultants, but also nutritional, recreational, and health consultants would be available to these groups. This kind of programmatic linkage should suffice for the group to handle its own human services needs in most cases, and for identification of those cases which would need specific referral for remedial services. This range of consultative services is not generally provided to self-help groups, although there is an increasing interest in developing such resources for senior citizens' groups.

REHABILITATION: SOCIAL AND VOCATIONAL

Recreationally-oriented groups are sometimes associated with programs designed to promote social and/or vocational rehabilitation among emotionally disabled clients. The Soundview-Throgs Neck Community Mental Health Center in New York City has a very large rehabilitative program for chronically disabled clients. This program provides a large number of day-time activities, ranging from sewing, arts and crafts, woodwork, and clerical skills to the operation of a canteen and a thrift shop. Clients may participate in these activities primarily with a recreational interest or primarily with a desire to learn skills that will enhance their capacity to function successfully in the community. Although clients may move freely between this program and other clinical services of the center, this service tends to operate fairly independently of the other programs, largely because the clients remain there for long periods of time. The rehabilitation program, however, is closely linked with a housing program, which will be discussed in more detail later; this linkage facilitates the provision of this essential service to clients in the rehabilitation program.

State hospitals have had "industrial therapy" and sheltered workshops for a very long time. These programs are designed to develop good job habits and work skills among patients who are severely limited in these areas. Unlike the Soundview-Throgs Neck program, however, these services are often not well linked to other community human services programs. Hence, little assistance may be provided to the patients in finding housing or jobs in the community. Or, little effort is made to help these patients develop a social support network in the community. Hence these patients often remain institutionalized, or they return frequently for rehospitalization. The industrial therapy and vocational rehabilitation programs thus become in effect another activity project for institutionalized patients. The Alcoholic Rehabilitation Center, a 700-bed institution for severe alcoholics in Washington, D. C., is an example of how institutionally-based rehabilitation programs often fail because of a lack of sufficient linkages to other community human services programs. Aside from a small community work release project, most of the clients discharged from the Alcoholic Rehabilitation Center return to the community without adequate assistance in finding housing and employment, in establishing a healthy social network, or even in entering an ongoing psychotherapeutic program. As a consequence, the readmission rate to the Alcoholic Rehabilitation Center is over 60 percent and the number of persons who are really benefited over the long run by the rehabilitation program is very limited.

Community-based sheltered workshops tend to operate outside of the mental health system. They tend to receive funds from state departments of vocational rehabilitation on a per capita basis for each client who is evaluated and found to have good prospects for successful vocational rehabilitation. These sheltered workshops serve clients with a variety of disabilities, both physical and mental. Although the linkages from the sheltered workshops to the community, specifically to community employment, are generally well developed through vocational job counselors, the linkages between referring programs and the sheltered workshops are often more complex and cumbersome. Because of the per capita funding system each potential client must be thoroughly evaluated. This evaluation often results in a considerable delay for the client, who is without appropriate services in the meantime. Furthermore, clients whose prognoses are less favorable are often rejected, leaving them without an alternative option. Relationships between sheltered workshops and mental health programs with regard to shared clients tend to be distant and formal, so that the sheltered workshop staff do not generally fully appreciate the psychiatric difficulties of an emotionally disabled client, and the mental health staff are generally not aware of the task or problems facing the sheltered workshop's staff in trying to help emotionally disturbed clients.

When vocationally-oriented programs are tied to a mental health system, they generally are low key and only moderately structured, such as the Soundview-Throgs Neck rehabilitation program. The sheltered workshops, which often use behavior modification principles, or a token economy, are designed around a schedule of tasks which require gradually increasing skills; these workshops are more generally freestanding. However, there have been a couple of vocational rehabilitation projects tied to a mental health system. The Seattle Mental Health Institute, when it was fully operational, had a vocational rehabilitation program which first helped its clients to develop basic job skills, e.g., how to dress, how to behave on the job, etc. Then they placed their clients in one of several community job "samples," such as a cooking school, or an automobile service station. Clients were paid from 50c to 70c per hour, according to their productivity. Hopefully clients would eventually find independent employment in the community. As a part of the community mental health program, referrals came smoothly from other components of the center, particularly the inpatient unit.

The San Fernando Valley Community Mental Health Center includes a transitional workshop, called BUILD, among its six affiliated programs. BUILD is a well-developed, sophisticated workshop, training its clients in a variety of skills which help most of them to become successfully employed. Although referrals can come smoothly from other components of the center, only 25 percent of BUILD's clients come from the catchment area. This low percentage partly reflects the clientele of the catchment area and partly the loose linkages between BUILD and the other service units of the mental health center. BUILD has its own board and operates virtually independently of the other center components, which are probably not fully aware of this resource.

HOUSING SERVICES

Mental health programs have variable ties to the housing-shelter provision system. We have already discussed the role of the mental health worker in a neighborhood service center as an ombudsman or expediter to help his client find adequate housing. The role of an ombudsman or expediter has tended to develop in these settings because, short of the expediter, there are rarely any formal links between mental health programs and the housing system, thus providing no formal mechanism for moving the client from the mental health subsystem to the housing subsystem.

There are, however, a few kinds of situations in which the mental health subsystem is linked to the housing subsystem. Halfway houses are often loosely tied to other mental health programs. But they are generally independently operated, so that mental health program operators do not have much influence over admission or discharge policies. Thus many clients are rejected for admission to a halfway house as inappropriate, and other appropriate clients are not able to be admitted for lack of sufficient beds, because the duration of stay tends to be very long. This very loose linkage between halfway houses and mental health programs tends to reduce the utility of halfway houses considerably.

Mental health programs have had a more active involvement in the development of foster care homes, small homes in which the operators are paid a certain amount per month per client to provide room, board, and minimal supervision, e.g., administration of medication. Boston State Hospital, for example, recruited former practical nurses to operate foster care homes, thus providing a large community living resource to which patients from the hospital could be discharged. Funds for paying foster care operators, however, often come from the welfare budget, thus requiring approval by the welfare system. Ties between the mental health subsystem and the welfare subsystem may be so poor that long delays may ensue before a client is placed on foster care status. In the District of Columbia, even though both mental health and welfare subsystems are part of the same department of human resources, such long delays regularly occur because there are virtually no linkages between the two separate subsystems, except at the very highest administrative levels.

Some programs have innovated the development of more independent living arrangements for their clients. Soundview-Throgs Neck Community Mental Health Center has acquired an apartment building across the street from its mental health facility; apartments are leased to groups of clients, most of whom are participating in the rehabilitation program, but who are capable of living independently without supervision. This permits clients to move from foster care status to relatively independent living. These clients may have difficulty in obtaining a lease on their own because of their welfare status, or in finding roommates to live with. The mental health program is able to facilitate the resolution of these difficulties, thus permitting its clients to live in the community and to continue in a community-based rehabilitation program. San Mateo County in California has a similar apartment project.

Emergency shelter resources are even less frequently tied to mental health programs than are long-term housing services. The St. Luke's Community Mental Health Center in Phoenix, Arizona has an affiliation agreement with a program providing emergency shelter services.

The emergency shelter program provides some matching money for a Federal NIMH staffing grant and receives some of the Federal money in return. Because of this financial tie, the emergency shelter service has become much more closely linked as a resource for the community mental health center to help clients who need short-term emergency housing assistance. Similarly, the mental health professionals of the center provide supervisory and consultative support to the staff of the emergency shelter service with regard to clients who present themselves directly to the emergency shelter service. This financial linkage has resulted in meaningful programmatic and staff collaboration.

Although most ties between mental health subsystems and housing systems are designed to provide a housing resource for mental health clients, there are fewer systems which have linkages designed to provide mental health resources to operators and residents of a housing project. Neighborhood service centers or mental health satellites are often based in housing projects. Some of these satellites, such as a satellite of the St. Luke's Community Mental Health Center in Phoenix, Arizona, are very closely tied to the management of the housing project. In this case, an indigenous Spanish-speaking mental health worker serves as an ombudsman for a variety of social service and mental health needs of the residents of the projects. Together with the housing project manager, the mental health worker attempts to deal with some of these problems at the organizational level. The Kissena project, described in a previous study in this series (Schulberg, 1973, pp. 317 – 326), illustrates the introduction of social and mental health services into a senior citizens' housing project. Sometimes consultative services are offered to housing project managers, nursing home operators, etc.

SCHOOLS

Mental health programs are most commonly linked to school subsystems through the provision of mental health consultation services to the schools. Of all community consultation activities, school consultation is probably the oldest and the most prevalent. These consultation activities meet with varying degrees of success because the public school systems tend to be very large, bureaucratic, and defensive. Often, however, an individual consultant is able to work successfully with an individual principal to help develop a more effective school milieu.

Mental health programs have only occasionally undertaken the development of their own school programs, and this is generally done only as a part of a residential treatment program or day treatment program for children. These programs, moreover, generally operate as highly specialized services with minimal relationships to both the mental health system they are in and the public school system. The Area A Community Mental Health Center in Washington, D. C. has developed a special education program for disturbed elementary age children, using a variety of intervention models. These various intervention approaches are videotaped and subsequently presented to area public school teachers as part of an in-service training and consultation program to enhance the ability of the public school teachers to manage such disturbed children in the public school classroom. In addition, some public school teachers will spend one-half day per week observing the special education program.

Central City Community Mental Health Center in Los Angeles has developed an innovative summer educational project, leveraging very limited professional resources. Professionals taught a cadre of college students, who in turn taught a group of high school students, who in turn supervised and taught elementary school children. Activities and courses consisted of regular school curriculum subjects, dance, fashion, art and music, African studies, writing, drama, clerical activities, and athletics. A preschool nursery was also provided. Other programs have used college students and community volunteers to tutor children who are having academic and emotional difficulties.

JUDICIAL-CORRECTIONAL SYSTEM

Links between the mental health subsystem and the judicial-correctional system are even less well-developed than the mental health-school linkages. Consultation to police, judges, probation officers, and correctional institutions is not frequently offered, and is even less frequently accepted. Police and correctional officials are often suspicious of mental health workers offering consultative assistance.

Corrections officials are a bit more ready to accept mental health participation in providing direct services to former prisoners. Central City Community Mental Health Center has developed an exfelon program for 10 former convicts who live in a halfway house under the supervision of three counselors and one secretary. The Psychiatric Institute, a private program in Washington, D. C., has been contracted with to operate a similar halfway house for former convicts from the D. C. reformatory. The Atlanta South Central Community Mental Health Center has also agreed to participate in a prison release program providing services for former convicts.

The Law Enforcement Assistance Administration of the Department of Justice has funded an innovative program in Wichita Falls, Texas. In addition to establishing an elaborate psychiatric evaluation center for persons charged with crimes, the center has developed a new training program for paraprofessionals. Psychiatric attendants are given training both as police sheriffs and as psychiatric aides. They work on the inpatient units of the psychiatric evaluation center and are available for emergency calls in the community. They respond to such calls wearing their psychiatric aide clothing, and they are generally able to handle their clients successfully without force. They have the ability, however, to use their police training if appropriate.

The general paucity of linkages between the mental health and correctional subsystems is certainly not a reflection of the need of former convicts for mental health and other human services. It is instead a reflection of the general lack of interest on the part of workers in both systems to cross these subsystem boundaries. The recent increase in collaboration between LEAA and NIMH has resulted in more availability of funds for such collaborative activities. Much further work, however, needs to be accomplished.

These various human services subsystems reflect a range of associations to the mental health subsystem. The impetus for the development of these linkages often comes from the mental health system and generally reflects the mental health system's perceptions of the needs of its clients. Mental health clients, both those who have been admitted to inpatient or day hospital units and those living in poverty areas, frequently need help with housing, employment, or welfare payments. Also, many community residents who are isolated, lonely, and inactive often tend to gravitate to a community mental health center, particularly if it is closely tied to its surrounding neighborhood — hence the development of recreational services. The need for educational services is apparent only to programs providing extensive services for children. However, the need for services for potential or former convicts is rarely apparent to mental health workers, because such clients rarely present themselves voluntarily to the mental health system.

It is a truism that a high percentage of persons with medical complaints have associated emotional difficulties. One would expect, therefore, that health and mental health service programs would be closely related. And that certainly is often the case. Yet there are some mental health programs with very minimal relationships to the health system. We shall explore this paradox in the next chapter.

5. Relationships Between the Health and Mental Health Subsystems

There are four major models for linking health and mental health services. We discuss each of them below.

THE SOLO PRIVATE PRACTICE MODEL

Solo private practice financed by fees for service, generally reimbursed by insurance, remains the most common model in current medical practice. Consequently, it remains as the basis for most health-mental health system interactions. In this model a medical or surgical physician will refer a patient to a privately practicing psychiatrist, or vice versa. This model encourages individual, one-to-one psychotherapy, although some psychiatrists with busy practices may recommend group therapy for their patients. Patients requiring more intensive treatment generally are hospitalized on a 24-hour basis, because insurance benefits rarely provide coverage for day hospitalization. This system does not encourage ongoing psychiatric consultation to medical physicians, because no insurance reimbursement is provided for this.

The quality of interaction between the psychiatrist and nonpsychiatrist is quite variable. Some family practitioners are very sensitive to the emotional aspects of their patients' problems. They often are very skillful at helping their patients resolve their difficulties, but they are able to make referrals to psychiatrists when appropriate. They are generally prepared to continue working with their patients with or without continued psychiatric intervention. Some specialists, on the other hand, can't be bothered by a patient's emotional difficulties; they may not even recognize such problems sufficiently to make an appropriate referral. When a referral is made, they may not be interested in feedback from the psychiatrist. Psychiatrists also vary in their willingness to work with nonpsychiatric physicians to help them understand the emotional aspects of their patient's difficulties. In this model both the psychiatrist and nonpsychiatric physician may ignore the patient's social problems. In short, the effectiveness of this model very much depends upon the individual practitioners involved.

THE GENERAL HOSPITAL WITH PSYCHIATRIC INPATIENT AND OUTPATIENT UNIT

This model is an organized extension of the solo private practice model, except that in some cases patients without the ability to pay the full fee will be accepted. Municipal hospitals and some private teaching hospitals will accept patients that the private practitioner cannot afford to treat. A very large number of the community mental health centers are tied to a general hospital. In many of these cases, the major portion of the community mental health program is based around the general hospital. These programs are likely to provide good consultative services to the inpatient medical and surgical wards, except when the service chief has strong prejudices against psychiatry. One difficulty, however, is that physicians often will not readily accept consultation from nonpsychiatrists, e.g., social workers or psychologists.

Psychiatric inpatient units in these programs are often very medically oriented, and day treatment programs are often nonexistent because there is little insurance reimbursement for these services. Electroconvulsive therapy is extensively used. The wards may be locked. Nurses often wear regular nursing uniforms, rather than street clothes. Activity on the ward may be very limited, with patients spending much of their time lying on their beds in their separate rooms. A therapeutic community program is very rare, although group therapy is somewhat more common. Occupational therapy may be provided.

Unless there is Federal or local tax-supported funding, the general hospital is not likely to accept patients who cannot pay and who do not have insurance. Even with funding from the National Institute of Mental Health, many general hospitals try to restrict the number of indigent inpatients. Furthermore, the private psychiatric units need to maintain full capacity to remain "profitable," thus preserving a waiting list of two to four weeks, leaving the real emergency without an adequate resource for treatment. The municipal psychiatric inpatient unit, on the other hand, is not likely to receive any patients who could afford private hospitalization (unless, of course, it is a real emergency, and there are no beds elsewhere). The municipal wards tended to be overcrowded and understaffed, putting pressure on the staff to maintain a high patient turnover rate.

The outpatient psychiatric units generally offer a standard range of services — evaluations, individual and group psychotherapy, and even some family therapy. Although without Federal funds these units tend to be closely tied to their home base, with the acquisition of staffing grant funds many of these programs have moved out into the community. The Rochester General Hospital Community Mental Health Center, for example, has a mental health worker affiliated with each of several health teams in a Model Cities neighborhood health center. St. Luke's Hospital Community Mental Health Center in Phoenix, Arizona has mental health workers in a variety of community settings.

Like outpatient services, consultation and community education services are provided if there is special funding and if the director of the program is oriented towards providing such services. Again, general hospitals historically are not oriented towards reaching out into the community; hence they become engaged in such activities only if there is adequate financial reimbursement.

COMPREHENSIVE GROUP HEALTH PRACTICES (HEALTH MAINTENANCE ORGANIZATIONS WITH COMPREHENSIVE MENTAL HEALTH SERVICES INCLUDED)

These groups consist of prepaid group practices and a few Federally-subsidized neighborhood health centers. Although superficially resembling general hospitals with outpatient facilities, these groups are significantly different in that they receive funds in advance on a per capita basis, rather than reimbursement on a fee-for-service basis. The financial incentive here is to use ambulatory services whenever possible, to minimize inpatient hospitalization, and to eliminate potentially expensive benefits; in short, these programs aim to keep their premiums as low as possible to remain competitive with fee-for-service insurance carriers.

Not surprisingly, the initial group health programs developed in the 1940s had no mental health benefits. The number of potential consumers wanting such benefits was not great enough to induce the plan organizers to add a benefit which they feared would raise the premium rates considerably. It was not until several large purchasers of group health services, i.e., the Federal Employee Health program and some unions, insisted on the inclusion of a mental health benefit that these services were provided. Most plans provide a limited number of free outpatient visits, ranging from 10 to 20, with additional visits often provided at a fee, $5 or $10. Many programs, however, severely restrict treatment services for certain types of problems, e.g., alcoholism or drug abuse. The larger programs are able to support an intramural psychiatric staff, who are able to develop ongoing consultative relationships with the nonpsychiatric physicians. Smaller programs, such as Group Health Association in Washington, D.C., rely heavily on part-time staff or outside psychiatrists, who, although they may make reports which are returned to the nonpsychiatric physicians, do not develop as close a relationship with the nonpsychiatric physicians as do full-time psychiatrists in other programs.

The even smaller neighborhood health centers, which serve at most 30,000 persons, are able to support only a small ambulatory mental health staff, not to mention an inpatient or day hospital unit. These mental health workers are likely to have a very close collaborative relationship with the other health workers of the center. Because these programs are generally Federally funded, the mental health workers are free to provide indirect consultative services to the community, as well as direct clinical services. Mental health staff in the prepaid group practices, however, only rarely provide community consultation, except on an individual case basis, because the prepaid premium does not cover such community services.

The organizers of group health prepaid plans have become aware of the need for and advantages of mental health services. Dr. Sidney Garfield (1970), of the

Kaiser-Permanente program, has noted that a large percentage of his staff's man hours go for providing services to the nonsick. He classifies persons coming for services into four categories: the well, worried-well, asymptomatic-sick, and sick. With the removal of a fee for service as a financial barrier to making an appointment with a physician, the prepaid group practices have seen a considerable increase in the number of visits by persons in the well or worried-well categories. Dr. Garfield proposes that these persons be screened out by paramedical staff using sophisticated technical equipment. He also proposes that the nonsick receive the services of paraprofessionals. Although he does not discuss the use of psychiatrists and other mental health workers, his proposed system could be appropriately expanded to provide mental health services to the nonsick, as well as to the sick category. In fact, the establishment of mental health services in group health practices has resulted in a decline in inappropriate utilization of medical services, thus contributing toward a reduced premium.

In addition, mental health benefits have not been overutilized. Only one to two percent of the subscriber population uses mental health services in any one year. Furthermore, the average number of visits is far less than the maximum permitted, indicating that most persons use mental health services for help in solving crises, rather than for long-term character analysis. Since mental health service benefits can currently be provided for a family for a premium of only $5 to $10 per year, the newer group health plans are recognizing the advantages of including mental health benefits and are providing broader coverage than the older plans.

In spite of these broader mental health benefits, however, the health-oriented nature of these financial vehicles does not permit them to provide genuinely comprehensive mental health services, particularly in the area of social and community services. In addition, these plans are designed around physicians' services, leaving social workers, psychologists, and psychiatric nurses at a disadvantage. The neighborhood health centers, on the other hand, although freer to use paraprofessionals and to engage in community and social services, are generally too small to provide a comprehensive range of direct services.

FREE-STANDING COMPREHENSIVE MENTAL HEALTH SERVICE PROGRAMS COLLABORATING WITH COMPREHENSIVE GROUP HEALTH PRACTICES OR SOLO PRIVATE PRACTITIONERS

There are a large number of free-standing comprehensive mental health programs, some of which are based at state mental hospitals, and a large number of partially free-standing mental health programs, which use general hospitals for their inpatient services. The degree of involvement of totally free-standing programs with medical services is quite variable. Programs which have developed extensive community consultation services, such as the Multi-County Mental Health Center in Tullahoma, Tennessee and the Bradley Clinic in Columbus, Georgia, provide extensive mental health consultation to the medical providers, particularly public health nurses, much less so to physicians. Programs which have neighborhood health centers in their communities, for example, the Area C Community Mental Health Center in Washington, D. C., often develop good collaborative working relationships and consultative relationships with the medical staff. On the other hand, community mental health centers which have large group health practices in their communities have not developed ongoing collaborative relationships with these medical programs and relate at most on an ad hoc basis around specific cases.

There are a large number of community mental health programs which have no consultative or collaborative relationships with the health system, leaving that responsibility to individual private psychiatric practitioners, who consult on an ad hoc fee-for-service basis around specific cases with their medical colleagues. This leaves the rest of the medical system, particularly nurses and hospital administrators, without benefit of ongoing psychiatric consultation. Although one might expect that community mental health programs using general hospitals for their inpatient units would have more extensive ties to the medical system, this generally does not occur. Sometimes referrals are made for inpatient hospitalization by the community mental health center without subsequent follow-up, for example, the Huntington Mental Health Center, in Huntington, West Virginia. In such a case, provision of ongoing mental health consultation is not even considered. Often there is a strong sense of mutual distrust, and even hostility, with each group feeling that the other group is not assuming its fair share of the responsibility. Furthermore, some community mental health programs do not have enough psychiatrists to provide consultation to other physicians; moreover, the nonpsychiatric physicians are often resistant to accepting consultation from nonpsychiatric mental health workers. In general, partially free-standing mental health programs with a general hospital inpatient unit have less well-developed relationships with the hospital as a whole than do mental health programs based in the general hospital itself.

Much of the tension and lack of communication between the health and mental health systems derives from presumed conflicts between the basic models that each system uses. The medical system, of course, is based on the medical model, i.e., the defect-within-the-individual model. The patient is defined as "sick," unable to help himself, and in need of a prescription from a physician. Mental health programs, on the other hand, often emphasize the community organizational, the educational, or self-help models. This is not to say that mental health programs do not use the medical model. However, when mental health programs do apply the medical model, they often exclude the other social models. Thus, for example, mental health programs based in general hospitals, e.g., Rochester General Community Mental Health Center, often have very medically-oriented inpatient units. Ironically, however, their outpatient programs may incorporate the social models. The difficulty, it would seem, is in the integration of these two sets of apparently different models, particularly within inpatient settings.

The free-standing mental health programs have the same difficulty in integrating medical and social models. Community-oriented mental health programs often are inattentive to the medical aspects of their clients' problems or to psychological factors involved in cases presenting to the health subsystem, e.g., alcoholics, psychosomatics, etc.

The barriers between the health and mental health subsystems, however, are based on more than the difficulty in integrating seemingly conflicting models. The financial bases of each system mandate different types of services. Both fee-for-service and prepayment systems require that funds be used to treat *medical* problems among a subscriber population. This excludes community consultation, although it would include case-oriented consultation by a psychiatrist to another physician. This mandate excludes provision of comprehensive social services, e.g., helping a patient-client find a place to live or to get on welfare rolls. Furthermore, a subscriber population is generally not geographically based, and persons who are not able to afford the insurance premium are not eligible for reimbursement services. Services to community agencies, which would generally serve only a small percentage of subscribers, would also be excluded. Finally, private medical organizations, whether profit-making or nonprofit-making, must remain in the black. They are generally conservative financially — particularly the older prepaid group practices. Program administrators want to avoid committing themselves to programs that may jeopardize their "profitability." Thus even though health maintenance or disease prevention is a part of the mission of prepaid group practices, only a small percentage of their resources are actually devoted to such preventive activities. This would preclude preventive mental health activities as well. Furthermore, the apparent low productivity of psychiatric intervention, which often takes 45 minutes to an hour per visit, adds to the argument in favor of restricted mental health benefits.

In addition to these financial constraints, the health and mental health subsystems are often kept apart because of sociological and political conflicts between the professionals in each group. The nonpsychiatric physicians, who control the general hospitals and the prepaid group practices, are often fearful of losing that political control to a growing mental health staff. They sometimes fantasize that unlimited growth of mental health services would result in an overwhelmingly large mental health staff, which might then control the organization.

Mental health workers, on the other hand, often feel alienated from medical workers. Some mental health professionals, for example, Dr. Thomas Szasz (1960), want to take services for emotional disability entirely out of the health system. Although many psychiatrists continue to remain identified with the medical profession, other psychiatrists feel quite alienated. Other mental health workers, e.g., social workers and psychologists, often feel hostile to the medical profession, which gives psychiatrists higher status than psychologists and social workers. These social, political, and psychological forces contribute to the tension between these subsystems.

In spite of these differences, there remain, as noted previously, strong reasons for linking the health and mental health subsystems. As many as two-thirds of the patients presenting to the medical system have important emotional difficulties in association with their physical complaints. Either direct or indirect psychiatric services to these patients will improve the overall effectiveness of the medical system, and inservice training and psychiatric consultation to physicians and public health nurses will, in effect, augment the limited staff resources of the mental health system. Such joint services also benefit the medical professionals, since they would have to spend less time dealing with emotional difficulties disguised as somatic complaints. This provides more time for the medical professionals to devote toward their primary areas of specialization.

Interestingly, the health and mental health systems are not in absolute ideological conflict; to the contrary, they each accept a version of the public health preventive model. The community organizational model may be seen as an analogue for the public health model, which attempts to prevent disease by the location and alteration of etiological factors in the community, e.g., sanitation. Similarly, the mental health educational model may be seen as an analogue to public health educational activities aimed at promoting healthy growth and development among children, e.g., nutritional guidance, use of fluoride, etc.

Clearly the health and mental health subsystems need not be in total conflict and in fact should benefit from their mutual interaction. The task is to design a system whereby the two programs can interact effectively. That is the subject of the next chapter.

6. An Idealized Systems Model

This chapter describes an idealized model for human service systems in response to the current tendencies toward fragmentation of services and the inadequacy of services for chronically troubled persons; the model is aimed at providing comprehensive integration of services. The model is designed to highlight the systems principles that ought to be implemented for the development of an effective human services program.

The difficulties and shortcomings of the human systems programs that we have described in the preceding chapters can be translated into a systems analysis. There are three major deficiencies in current human services systems as systems. First, there is a considerable deficiency in the integrative function of the system, i.e., the organization of the flow of information, personnel, resources, and products (patient-client services) through the system. Needless to say, human services programs do coordinate with each other, generally at an administrative or planning level. What is most often lacking, however, is a reliable vehicle for integrating the needs of the patient-client with the services of the system. Furthermore, the clinical direct-service functions of the human services system are often not integrated with the indirect community organizational services of the system.

Second, inefficient allocation of manpower resources results from the lack of sufficient integrative activity in the system. The system's most scarce resource is its most

117

highly trained specialists. Yet the specialist is often used to perform integrative functions (frequently poorly done), or to do tasks that a less skilled person could perform, or to deal with a problem totally inappropriate for his specialty because of a faulty referral. Misuse of manpower is most dramatic with chronic cases because specialists are readily overloaded with these cases. Furthermore, chronic cases may be poorly managed by a specialist who often treats only those symptoms related to his specialty because he does not have time to review the patient-client's overall situation.

Third, and most important, most human services programs fail to provide a major tool for the management of emotional distress, i.e., a continuing relationship between the patient-client and the helping person. A trusting, caring, empathetic relationship is the *sine qua non* for successful psychotherapy, and such a relationship between a doctor and his patient inevitably contributes to the emotional well-being of the patient. The importance of the general practitioner-patient relationship, although a cliché, nevertheless stands as testimony to the potential therapeutic usefulness of a sound relationship between a nonpsychiatrist and a patient. However, with the decline of the general practitioner and the relative disappearance of the integrative function in the human services system, this therapeutic tool has been lost.

From these deficiencies in the current human services system we can infer what features are necessary for an adequate human services program. To start, there must be a coordinating unit. This unit's function would be to define the relationships between subsystems and, when applicable, between the system as a whole and outside systems. This unit would, of course, include the coordinating functions which are currently a routine part of the administrative offices of a large system. In addition, however, this unit would be the ultimate resource for defining the relationship between the patient-client and appropriate components within the system. This function, which may by necessity have to be geographically decentralized, is generally absent from most human services systems.

The coordinating unit would have one or more subunits called *patient-client assignment units* which would be charged with the assignment of new persons to appropriate staff persons or subsystems, evaluation of past assignments when questioned, and making reassignments when appropriate. The functions of this unit may be performed by one staff person, or more likely, by a team of persons with complementary specialized skills. A patient-client may be evaluated and routed by one staff person or by a "committee of the whole" team, whichever approach is most relevant and effective for each specific situation.

Assignments could be made to one or both of two major types of subsystems. One is a subsystem of persons for performing specialist functions with specified roles. Specialized tasks must be graded according to degree of technical skills and competence required, so that the most scarce personnel will perform specialized tasks whenever possible.

A second subsystem of generalists, however, will receive most referrals. The generalist would have two major functions. First, as mediator (or advocate or ombudsman), he would help the patient-client relate to the system as a whole. Here he will be performing an integrative function for the patient-client, just as the coordinating unit would perform an integrative function for the total system. Second, as "caretaker," he would establish a relationship with the patient-client .

A key aspect of this system is the differentiation of generalist and specialist roles — the generalist assuming "ultimate responsibility" for the patient-client and the specialist consulting and/or collaborating with the generalist. The patient-client assignment unit would make this differentiation and, together with other subunits of the coordinating unit, would make sure that the generalist and specialist are satisfactorily linked together. The coordinating unit would aim to bring to the patient-client the resources of the specialist whenever appropriate, without excessive and inappropriate use of his time. By combining the integrative functions of the coordinating unit, linking separate components to each other, and of the generalist, linking the patient-client to the various subsystems, the system should maximize the potential development of the relationship between a patient-client and a generalist without the loss of specialist skills but with more efficient use of the specialist's time.

To complete its integrative task the coordinating unit will need to perform other functions, each possibly accomplished by a separate subunit. The coordinating unit, together with the specialists, generalists, and other subsystems, must define the roles and responsibilities of each specialist as precisely as possible. Since an entire program may function as a specialist, e.g., a day treatment program for children, the coordinating unit would need to help work out the functions of major programs and subsystems. The coordinating unit will define with the specialists and generalists appropriate uses of each by the other.

The coordinating unit will then need to monitor the way in which these relationships in fact do work out. Referral and utilization patterns will need to be observed and evaluated as to their effectiveness. The *monitoring unit* will be responsible for seeing that specialists are used when they should be and that they are not used when they should not be. The monitoring unit will watch for instances in which either generalists or specialists attempt to extrude a patient-client prematurely, for example by discharging the most "frustrating" cases. These frustrating cases will be examined to determine if they are frustrating for lack of appropriate services within the system.

In short, the monitoring unit will attempt to locate stress, overload, or failure points in the system, to identify the causes of these weaknesses, and to propose solutions to improve the effectiveness of the system. On the one hand, the system may require more generalists, or, it may on the other hand, require more technicians to relieve an excessive load upon the specialists. If the specialist subsystem is overloaded, then a functional job analysis must be done to break down the specialty skills in such a way that some of these tasks could be performed by more readily trained persons.

The coordinating unit must perform a *training and consultative function* for the entire system to alleviate the defects identified by the monitoring unit. If generalists are not appropriately using specialized resources, then they must receive training or consultation from the specialists so that they might use these resources more effectively. Generalists may fail to use specialized resources because of a failure to recognize situations in which the specialists might be of help. On the other hand, generalists may refer an excessive number of cases because of insufficient competence to handle a specific type of problem; for example, a generalist may refer an excessively large number of persons with alcohol problems to the specialists; this generalist may be able to handle a larger number of alcoholic patient-clients with the help of a minimal amount of inservice training and/or consultation.

If a group of specialists is overloaded by virtue of an excessively large caseload, then their task must be broken down into subcomponents, so that less expensively trained persons can fulfill these tasks. The training unit might then upgrade the skills of some generalists to make them technicians or subspecialists. This will alleviate some of the excessive workload of the more scarce specialists.

Some staff of the coordinating unit may assume both monitoring and training functions in certain specialized areas. For example, staff with well-developed skills in the evaluation and treatment of alcoholics may monitor the system to see that the generalists and specialists together are providing good quality services to alcoholics. When they identify deficiencies, they would then provide either ad hoc consultation or establish an inservice training program designed to alleviate the technical shortcomings of the staff. The specialized staff, in their role in the coordinating unit, might be considered as ombudsmen for services for these special target groups, e.g., alcoholics, Spanish-speaking persons, senior citizens, children, etc. They would serve as ombudsmen or advocates for these specialized groups in the same way that the generalist would serve as an ombudsman for his own individual clients. Such a central coordinating ombudsman role is particularly important for those types of clients that are difficult to help and whom it is often all too easy for a human services system to give up on.

Another function of the coordinating unit would be to link the human services system to the community they serve and to other community organizations. Just as the monitoring system must assess the needs of clients as presented to the human services system and the way that these needs are or are not being met, the community relations subunit must attempt to assess needs in the community that do not present themselves directly to the human services system. These needs must be assessed and responded to, if they are within the domain of the human services system. Community organizations, such as self-help groups, must be linked to the human services system so that clients who no longer need the help of professionals can be located in appropriate community support systems. If the human services system is overloaded, and if it must be redesigned to reflect new priorities, then these priorities must be determined in conjunction with the community that is to be served by the program. The community is also a source of valuable resources, aside from funds, such as volunteers; the community relations unit can facilitate the incorporation of these additional resources into the human services system.

This model can be applied to a variety of situations in which the elaboration of special skills has outpaced the system's ability to remain integrated. The principles elucidated here could be applied, for example, to a single human services organization, or to a confederation consisting of several organizations (some with generalist and some with specialist functions), or to a highly specialized industry or business. Thus an entire program may assume the role of the specialist, although it may have within it both generalists and specialists. An alcoholism program, for example, may have mental health workers perform a generalist-advocacy role for their clients as well as provide specialists, consisting of highly trained psychologists or psychiatrists. Similarly, a specialized program may restrict itself to direct client service, or a program may specialize in community organizational services, attempting to help the community get itself together.

The functions and relationships defined here in many ways seem obvious; yet many human services programs are deficient in one or more of these functional relationships. It is perhaps because of this obviousness that these integrative functions are often only partially developed in human services systems. This idealized model is in part a positive summary statement of the shortcomings of the programs described in previous chapters. The significance of this model is perhaps in its almost boringly repeated call for the development of integrative functions in human services systems. The call for linking the patient-client, with the assistance of a generalist, to the system as a whole is probably of greater significance than is the call to link the various subsystems together through a coordinating unit, because these latter functions are present to varying degrees at the administrative level of many human services programs.

The functions of the generalist, on the other hand, are sorely needed. Although the number of generalists in human services programs is increasing considerably, these generalists often lack sanction to extend significantly beyond the narrow boundaries of their own small program, usually a neighborhood health or service center. They often have little more luck in negotiating with the specialty subsystems than do their patient-clients.

The potential integrative effect of a generalist in this idealized system might be clarified by a path-analysis of a hypothetical patient-client, and by examining the associated referral process. A person would enter the human services system through the assignment unit. The function performed here is in itself a specialist function requiring the collective skills of persons of highly professional training, for example, physicians, social workers, etc. How staff persons in this unit would collaborate to make assignments and what combination of professional skills would be optimal would be subject to experimentation and would depend upon patient-client flow rates with respect to different kinds of problems and upon the skills and experience of the specific workers in the unit. This function might be performed by one person in cases in which it is relatively easy to make an initial dispositional decision. At other times, particularly when the information, resources, and skills of a number of persons are involved, it may be more expeditious to make the initial evaluation in a group setting. This latter type of operation would often be convenient in neighborhood center settings.

The contact of the patient-client with the assignment unit must be long enough for the diagnostician to make one of two possible types of referrals: 1) to the most appropriate *generalist*, or 2) directly to a *specialist*, for example, if the diagnosis is clear and/or the problem is urgent and in need of specialist skills. The essence of the initial assignment unit decision is not to make a definitive diagnosis, but rather to decide who is most likely to be able to help the person meet the majority of his needs, thus decreasing the probability and frequency of future referrals. Such a decision requires both an ability to assess complex situations and a thorough knowledge of the human services system. (Hence the assignment unit is located within the coordinating unit.) The objective of the assignment unit is to make a careful placement within the system, not to make a definitive diagnosis of the patient-client.

The generalist will function as both a *mediator* and *caretaker*. As a mediator or ombudsman, he may help the client plan and make various arrangements and contacts within the subsystem that he is most closely connected with, or in other subsystems of the human services system. If the patient-client is very competent, the mediator may merely suggest referral sources. On the other hand, if the patient-client's skills are limited, the mediator may actually negotiate directly with other subsystems on his client's behalf, e.g., helping him get on the welfare rolls.

In his "caretaker" role the generalist may try to support or control the patient-client's behavior for a short or long period of time, e.g., through counseling, directive advice, or patient understanding of the person, his family, and his emotional needs. The generalist might see his client frequently for a brief period, if the situation is acute, or infrequently for an extended period, if the problem is chronic. As "caretaker" the generalist shows *care for* his client, but he does not take *care of* him. He tries to encourage his client to care for himself as much as possible, and much of the generalist's success is a result of his clear concern and interest in his client.

The generalist will be chosen for a specific client according to the central problems of the client. Some generalists will work almost exclusively as generalists, e.g., family health workers, and some will also perform as specialists, e.g., physicians. A diabetic without other serious medical problems, for example, might be followed by a nurse, while an older person with many diseases would be seen by an internist. A social worker or social worker assistant might be the generalist for a healthy young person with social and economic problems, and a family health worker might work with a family with a variety of routine medical problems. A child with cerebral palsy might have a physical therapist as his generalist. If a person is assigned a generalist from the subsystem of specialists, he will be assigned to that specialist whose skills require the least amount of training, yet who can meet the bulk of the patient-client's needs. So, for example, although a diabetic would from time to time have to see a physician, he could be followed generally by the less skilled nurse.

The role of the specialist is to assist the generalist in the diagnosis and/or "treatment" intervention through either consultation or direct action, whichever might be most appropriate. In the case of the diabetic patient, the physician might periodically consult with the nurse as to recommended changes in the patient's regimen. But he might not take the time to explain the regimen to the patient, leaving that action to the nurse who has a good relationship with the patient and who can take the time for a thorough discussion. On the other hand, if a patient has a broken bone or an acute myocardial infarction, the physician would probably work closely with the generalist in both diagnosis and treatment throughout the acute phase. In this situation the physician would be collaboratively sharing responsibility with the generalist, who would continue working with the patient-client.

Some specialists, in addition to their client-related activities, would perform tasks related to the other models described in Chapter 3, e.g., the community organizational or educational models. They may assume a consultative, advocative, or educational role in the community. Health or sex education, homemaker services, or obtaining adequate housing facilities, would be examples of some of these activities. These specialists would be responding both to the needs of individually referred patient-clients and to the problems of the community.

The generalist and specialist are differentiated by role functions, not by who performs the role. The same staff person may serve as generalist to some patient-clients and as specialist to others. Hence virtually all persons serving in the generalist capacity will have some specialized skills. The essential difference in the two roles is that when a staff person is assigned to be the generalist for a given patient-client he has the "ultimate responsibility" for that person; that is, that patient-client will continue to return to him for further help if and when the generalist refers the client to a specialist for consultation. For example, in his capacity as mediator the generalist might decide that consultation with one or several specialists would be helpful, e.g., in the diagnosis or therapy of an acute medical problem. The generalist might make the referral directly, or he himself might get assistance from the assignment unit. In a complex case the generalist might collaborate and consult with two or more specialists. After consultation with the specialist, the client will return to the generalist for subsequent follow-up.

An advantage of this system of service delivery is that inappropriate referrals will be restricted, because a generalist will continue to be responsible for difficult chronic problems, even after consultation with specialists. It will be to his advantage to refer only when he feels he can help the patient-client more effectively with consultation; it will not be possible to "pass the buck." Obviously the generalist and specialist will need to maintain adequate communcation, both for the benefit of specific patient-clients and in order to improve the effectiveness of the referral process. The human services program will need to develop indicators and criteria to optimize the referral process, i.e., to minimize both unnecessary lags in referrals and inappropriate referrals. The monitoring and training functions of the coordinating unit should facilitate the development of a sophisticated referral process by noting its failures and shortcomings and by training both generalists and specialists to make more appropriate use of the system.

Clearly, the assignment unit may occasionally err in its choice of a generalist, and sometimes a patient-client's needs may change over the course of his affiliation with the center. The generalist would be free to discuss his assessment of the situation with the assignment unit so that hopefully a mutually agreeable approach to the management of the problem could be determined.

Generalists can be grouped into teams, sharing responsibility for a given locality. These teams can become the basis for services in satellite units. A single team might then serve all members in one family. Formal and informal channels of communication among team members will therefore facilitate the diagnosis and management of family problems.

This idealized system would probably be of least value to a person who has a single acute specialized problem. In this system, he would, as he could readily do now, proceed directly to a specialist, receive what help he needs, and then leave the human services system. This can be simply accomplished now, if he gets to the right specialist. This system would help avert errors in routing patient-clients to specialists.

As the number of problems increases, or as these problems increase in chronicity, this idealized system should become increasingly helpful in bringing appropriate specialized services to the patient-client in a relatively continuous, nonfragmented manner, offering him simultaneously the advantages of both specialized skills and a sustained trusting relationship with a human services worker. The maintenance of a relationship with a staff person should be of particular assistance to the chronically or recurrently troubled person in dealing with the emotional aspects of his difficulties. A generalist who has a thorough knowledge of a patient-client and his family is likely to be able to make a relatively precise evaluation of the patient-client's emotional problems. So, for example, such a generalist might be more useful to a person in a psychiatric emergency than would be a psychiatrist who sees that person for the first time alone in an emergency clinic. Or, a generalist might be much more likely to determine the etiology of a psychosomatic disorder in the psychodynamics or family dynamics of a patient than would a physician who would be busily focusing upon the physical aspect of the patient's complaints.

The development of a trusting, empathetic relationship between the generalist and patient-client would also contribute to the generalist's ability to help the patient-client with his emotional needs. He may be able to encourage the patient-client supportively to make appropriate changes in his life. Or, he may meet many of the patient-client's emotional needs more subtly, e.g., needs for dependency gratification. When patients are hospitalized and discharged, the maintenance of a relationship with the generalist should facilitate the patient's readjustment to his life responsibilities.

Although the generalist may often meet the dependency needs of his patient-client, his function is not to encourage such dependency needs. His task is not to take care of his client, but to help his client take better care of himself. Thus, for example, with clients who have strong dependency needs, the generalist's task would be to help him develop a social support system in the community, possibly through a self-help group. The responsibility of the coordinating unit would be to locate such self-help community support systems, or if they do not yet exist, to help develop them for clients who have major social dependency needs. The generalist, however, would remain as an available resource for his client in helping him obtain appropriate services from the human services system.

The beneficial results of the integrative and supportive aspects of the generalist's role for the client would be complemented by positive changes in the role of the specialist. There would be a considerable reduction in the need for specialized categorical services. Most alcoholics, for example, would not need a specialized alcoholic clinic. An alcoholic might be assigned to a nurse, a social worker, or a physician as his generalist, depending on the nature of other medical and social problems. He might be referred to a psychiatrist for specialty consultation, or he might be hospitalized for a while, returning to his generalist upon discharge. This system would reduce considerably duplication of efforts and would free the specialist to consult with more persons.

Specialized programs will, of course, continue to be necessary where the resources of several specialists must be combined in order to provide desired service, e.g., an intensive medical care unit, or where services are more effectively provided in small or large groups, e.g., group psychotherapy for alcoholics, or a sheltered workshop.

Probably the most critical test of this idealized human services system will be in its ability to handle the patient-client load presented to it. The boundaries of the system will be determined on geographic criteria, not on the basis of admission-discharge policies. Hence, all persons in a certain population would be considered as clientele of the human services system. This definition of boundaries is crucial, because in a system in which there is continued pressure of demand for services, there will be a tendency to try to reduce the pressure by extruding patient-clients prematurely or by discharging the most frustrating cases. In a geographically defined system such inappropriate extrusion cannot readily occur because there are no other human services systems in the area to pass the buck to.

Instead, this commitment to a population will encourage the human services system to respond to the demand pressure by attempting to find the most economical means of meeting the demands, without sacrificing quality. If quality is sacrificed, the pressure is certainly not likely to be reduced. Attempts to find economical service methods should lead to the formation of a human services system which will change patterns of utilization of services. An outreach program, for example, would recruit patient-clients in order to help them before their problems became more complex, requiring the assistance of a scarce specialist; a diabetic, for instance, can be helped more easily and with less expense before he develops acidosis. The use of technical assistants in the management of chronic disease will minimize the load on the more scarce, highly specialized personnel.

This geographical commitment forces the human services system to be accountable with regard to both the scope and quality of services it provides. If the system is properly linked to the community it serves, it will know when it is failing to respond to the needs of its client population. This accountability will also require the development of adequate internal monitoring, training, and staff development functions, so that proper adjustments in the system can be made to respond to changing needs.

Nevertheless, in spite of efforts to train personnel, the system may remain overloaded. However, such a system should be less overloaded than the fragmented, uneconomical programs currently in use. First of all, the generalist assigned to a person would have the least amount of technical training necessary to service that person, in contrast to the present system in which highly skilled specialists often serve unnecessarily as generalists. Second, the reduction in unnecessary referrals and in duplication of evaluations should allow the specialist to consult with more persons. Furthermore, the specialist will be assisted in his evaluations by the more comprehensive knowledge of the patient-client available to him from the generalist. The deployment of many technical assistants will also free-up specialist time. The preventive efforts made possible by the establishment of a relationship by the generalist with the patient-client should also reduce the demand for acute services and should shift the service demand from specialists to generalists.

As this model is applied to a variety of human services programs and community situations, a range of questions and specific issues will arise that need to be answered, often via trial and error. This idealized model is designed to point the way to the issues, tasks, and functions that an effective human services system will need to take into account. The questions not raised here are the practical ones. Ultimately, it is the practical realities that will determine the course of human services programs in the future.

7. *The Probable Realities of the Future*

We have just reviewed some of the ideal properties of human services systems, designed to optimize the probability of bringing relevant specialized knowledge to bear on behalf of a patient-client whose needs will be looked after by a generalist. The degree to which these principles will be applied will be determined by the social process of which this study is a part. This social process is a function of the professionals and paraprofessionals who provide these human services and of the training programs from which they come; of the public and private organizations which bring these human service workers together; of the sources of funds for these programs; and of the community which is supposed to receive these human services.

The idealized model of the previous chapter is premised on the necessity to maximize the use of scarce resources—personnel in general and specialists in particular — through the development of a system in which generalists provide basic services insofar as possible. This generalist role will often be filled by a paraprofessional, who will be supported in a variety of ways by a cadre of specialists. The specialists will leverage their skills by developing a variety of role relationships with the less highly trained generalists. The specialist may supervise a generalist directly in ongoing case work, or he may provide inservice training to the generalist or to the less trained specialist. Or, the specialist may provide consultation (case-oriented or consultee-oriented). Thus, for example, mental health specialists may provide mental health consultation to a range of persons serving as generalists in both the health and other human services subsystems.

It is clear that the use of paraprofessionals is here to stay. The extent and kinds of uses of paraprofessionals will depend in part upon their acceptance by the clients they serve. This in turn will be determined in part by the development of positive attitudes among clients, and in part by the development of a competent system in which the client can rely on the quality of service he receives from a generalist paraprofessional. The paraprofessional will have to have the resources of a specialist readily available. The role and task of the paraprofessional need to be well defined, consistent with his capabilities and specifying the situations and types of problems that he can or cannot handle and the ways in which supervision can be readily available. The specialists, on the other hand, need to learn that they are not being displaced by the paraprofessionals and that their function as specialists is enhanced by the assumption of their generalist functions by the paraprofessionals.

Paraprofessional generalists are likely to be most widely used in poverty areas where multiproblem situations requiring an ombudsman are most prevalent. Furthermore, the indigenous paraprofessional is more likely to understand the nature of the problems facing the poor family than is the middle-class professional. In addition, the higher prevalence of multiproblem situations in lower-class communities requires a higher concentration of human services workers and hence, because of manpower economics, a higher percentage of paraprofessionals.

The need to expand the role of the generalist paraprofessional among middle-class communities, although less dramatic, is nevertheless pressing. Acceptance of this role will depend both upon the middle-class clients and the middle-class professionals who currently serve them. These changes will occur over time as a result of changes in the training programs for professionals; professionals will become familiar with and learn how to work with paraprofessionals. Some professionals may even get training as generalists themselves.

Training programs will need to teach professionals how to work with subsystems other than their own and, hopefully, some programs will train professionals in how to span boundaries, i.e., to be an administrative or programmatic generalist. These changes, however, may take as long as a generation to be completed in order for new curricula to be developed and for the more traditional professionals to retire.

The expansion of the generalist paraprofessional and the professional boundary-spanner roles will be facilitated if the organizations that might use their services become more receptive. We have seen in the previous chapters that the development of human services departments in itself is not sufficient for the development of integrated programs at the service delivery level. The vested bureaucratic interests of those who control each of the several subsystems are such that they are reluctant to relinquish control for the sake of developing services which span several subsystems. These bureaucrats have considerable operational power, even though they may be officially under the authority of a director for an entire human services system. This continued operational authority can frustrate or retard the development of new integrated programs. Furthermore, the development of superagency human services departments generally results in an elaboration of bureaucratic and administrative procedures, rather than a simplification. This increase in centralization of authority adds to the number of levels from which approval for new programs must be obtained. The restrictiveness of the large governmental bureaucracy is probably most evident in the operation of the civil service system, which establishes a schedule of salaries and job descriptions which for the most part are inflexible and minimally relevant to the kinds of responsibilities required of general human services workers in the community. Although career ladders have been discussed now for several years, they are not generally worked out and applied.

These bureaucratic frustrations tend to have a serious impact upon the morale of the staff, so that many of the more competent paraprofessionals and professionals leave. Those who remain find it difficult to stay invested in the idealistic mission of the organization they work for and consequently develop secondary adjustment patterns, focusing their energies around lunchtime, time-off, and intraoffice or intraprogram social interaction.

In short, as a consequence of the vested interests of the authorities in charge of the large governmental human services programs, and as a consequence of the frustrations of the line workers in such a system, these governmental organizations often will become oriented towards perpetuating themselves and meeting their own needs, rather than meeting the needs of their clients or potential clients.

The smaller, privately-run organization offers an alternative approach for the delivery of human services. A system of decentralized service programs, providing all services which can economically be provided at a decentralized level, would increase the probability that service providers would be responsive to the needs of the citizens they serve. Services which are not economically provided at a decentralized level would, of course, be centralized; and each decentralized program would be able to contract with centralized program operators. If profits are permitted, then the use of contracts with both the decentralized and centralized operators will encourage both efficiency and quality, since contracts would not be renewed if adequate quality is not maintained. In addition, a system of centralized consulting specialists could be established, analogous in a public school system to the use of staff specialists who serve as resources to classroom teachers. Governmental agencies would continue to have the responsibility for monitoring the quality of performance of the various contractors to ensure that standards are maintained. They may also elect to offer inservice training to the staff of the various program operators. Such a system will increase the accountability of the program operators while at the same time permitting more opportunity for innovation and experimentation.

The development of health maintenance organizations is consistent with this model. In the social service area, however, funds are primarily routed through the governmental bureaucracy and are most likely to remain there, being used for programs operated directly by the bureaucracies. The recently enacted ceiling on contracts for social services under the Social Security Act will restrict the development of privately contracted services in this area.

The health insurance system, insofar as it is developed, seems to be the most reliable source of funding in the area of human services. Once a person pays his premium, he is sure that he can receive a certain range of services at a specified cost to himself. These services are not dependent upon Federal or local appropriations. His receipt of these services is dependent only upon his ability to find someone to perform them (which may be, as we have noted, no small task!). These insurance programs provide broad health benefits and, in some cases, broad mental health benefits. The stability of this financial reimbursement system is a strong incentive for mental health workers to align themselves with the health delivery system.

On the other hand, proposed legislation authorizing support for health maintenance organizations and for national health insurance limits the extent of mental health benefits. These restrictions may force mental health service providers to look elsewhere for funds.

There is no evidence to suggest that a social insurance system is likely to be considered in at least the next decade. Mental health and social service programs will continue then to be dependent upon Federal, state, and local appropriations. The Federal Community Mental Health Centers Program has permitted, although not actively encouraged, the development of linkages between mental health and other social systems. It is not certain, however, how long this funding source will continue to be available.

The future pattern in the delivery of human services will be very much dependent upon Federal priorities. At present, these are not clear. On the one hand, President Nixon has accomplished the passage of the revenue sharing bill, which has the potential of promoting non-categorical human services programs. At the same time noncategorical OEO projects are being cut back in funding, while new Federal programs for narcotics addicts, alcoholics, children, and the aged are being developed. It is conceivable, and in fact quite likely, that this conflicting funding pattern will continue indefinitely, so that both general, comprehensive programs will be developed simultaneously with specialized, categorical services with minimal efforts at linking the two types of services.

Whether and how these contradictions are to be resolved will depend upon the persons for whom these human services are being designed. Ultimately the community will shape the structure of the human services programs that serve them. Synanon is an example of a small community which uses educational, self-help, community organizational, and, to a lesser degree, medical models. It has also been able to integrate both generalist and specialist roles in serving its clientele. The linkages between the generalists and specialists are well developed because the Synanon community wants these linkages to be there. In short, if the community is committed to developing an integrated system of human services, so that people don't get passed from specialist to specialist, then an adequate administrative vehicle will follow. The community will monitor its adequacy, and it will be committed to changing it if and when it no longer serves to integrate the various functions that are needed. There is considerable evidence to suggest that the public prefers a categorical, specialized system. A considerable amount of energy goes into lobbying for special interests, in competition with the needs and interests of other groups. Mental health is as much, or more so, a party to such lobbying as any other special interest group. At the same time there is evidence to suggest that the community prefers to have certain persons labeled as "mentally sick." Such labelling permits society to extrude such sick persons and to relieve themselves of responsibility for contributing to or alleviating the "sick" person's problems. Furthermore, if the "mentally ill" person's difficulties are totally internal in origin, then society need not feel guilty for contributing to his problems by not providing him housing, employment, adequate schooling, sufficient social support, etc. Hence there is some psychological advantage to maintaining a categorical perspective on the problems presenting to human services programs.

On the other hand, an increasingly large number of persons are themselves suffering the consequences of our currently fragmented human services system. This group of consumers, along with a growing group of professionals identified with the noncategorical human services programs (OEO, Model Cities, and some community mental health centers) are developing into an expanding constituency for integrated human services programs. This constituency may be able to insist that at least planning for integrated human services be done, if nothing else. This planning process may serve as an effective strategy for social and organizational change in human services programming. Such planning can bring together the human services professionals, the trainers of the professionals, the bureaucrats who hire the professionals, and the community so that at least the relevant interorganizational questions and issues can be raised and examined. As long as the questions continue to be raised, the task cannot be forgotten. As long as the task is not forgotten, there is still hope.

REFERENCES

Bolman, W. M. Community control of the community mental health center, II: Case examples. *The The American Journal of Psychiatry,* August, 1972, **129**, 2, 181–183.

Caplan, G. *The theory and practice of mental health consultation.* New York: Basic Books, 1971.

Garfield, S. R. The delivery of medical care. *Scientific American,* April, 1970, **222**, 4, 15–23.

Maholick, L. T. A delivery system for local mental health services. *American Journal of Public Health,* March, 1972, **62**, 3, 364–369.

Schulberg, H. C., Baker, F. & Roen, S. R. *Developments in Human Services,* Vol. 1. New York: Behavioral Publications, 1973.

Szasz, T. S., *The Myth of Mental Illness.* New York: Harper & Row, 1961.

Turner, W. E., Smith, D. C., & Medley, P. Integration of mental health into public health programs—Advantages and disadvantages. *American Journal of Public Health,* August, 1967, **57**, 8, 1322–1326.

THE ECONOMICS OF HUMAN SERVICES

by

Gerald Rosenthal, Ph.D.

Part 2 of *Developments in Human Services,* Volume II
Edited by
Herbert C. Schulberg, Ph.D.
and Frank Baker, Ph.D.

Library of Congress Catalog Number 74-9694
ISBN: 0-87705-171-2
Copyright © 1975 by Behavioral Publications, Inc.

BEHAVIORAL PUBLICATIONS, Inc.
72 Fifth Avenue
New York, New York 10011

Printed in the United States of America
56789 987654321

Library of Congress Cataloging in Publication Data

Rosenthal, Gerald D
    The economics of human services.

    (Developments in human services, v. 2, pt. 2)
    Includes bibliographical references.
    1. Social services—United States.   2. Cost
effectiveness.   3. Social service—United States—
Finance.   I. Title.   II. Series. [DNLM: 1. Economics—Social services. HV40 R815e 1974]
[HV91.R68]   338.4'7'361   74-9694

Contents

Part II: THE ECONOMICS OF HUMAN SERVICES

GERALD ROSENTHAL

Preface

Widespread inadequacies in the human condition and concern for the difficulties and complexities of existing social arrangements have resulted in urgent pressures on professionals to revise present care giving mechanisms. Human service programs such as multi-service centers, which incorporate a wide variety of relevant services, are emerging as an alternative framework to the existing pattern of rigid, categorical services for meeting the bio-psycho-social needs of individuals and populations.

The editors of this series are developing materials which can serve as guideposts for those newly entering or already engaged in the field of human services. A flexible approach to the production and distribution of these materials has been devised. The series periodically publishes indepth discussions and reviews on the following human service topics:

> Emerging conceptual frameworks of human services such as systems and ecological principles.
>
> Administrative and planning tools such as information systems, economic strategies, and legal mechanisms.
>
> Innovative service programs within new organizational models and new communities.
>
> Educational programs for changing professional roles and new manpower requirements.

After several years, those who are standing-order subscribers will possess an encyclopedic library of human

services in either hardbound volumes or softcover separates.

Volumes I and II contain an introductory overview by the editors, substantive sections on different human service topics, and a comprehensive index. Each of the substantive sections, without introductory overview and index, is available as a separate.

Volume I

Teaching Health and Human Services Administration by the Case Method—Linda G. Sprague, Alan Sheldon, M.D., and Curtis P. McLaughlin, D.B.A.

The Planning and Administration of Human Services—Harold W. Demone, Jr., Ph.D. and Dwight Harshbarger, Ph.D.

Strategies in Innovative Human Service Programs —Harry Gottesfeld, Ph.D., Florence Lieberman, D.S.W., Sheldon R. Roen, Ph.D., and Sol Gordon, Ph.D.

Developments in Human Services Education and Manpower—Robert M. Vidaver, M.D.

Volume II

Developing Program Models for the Human Services —Mark Lawrence, M.D.

Economics of Human Services—Gerald Rosenthal, Ph.D.

Developing Human Services in New Communities —Donald Klein, Ph.D.

The Editors

1. Introduction

The notion of a study of the Economics of Human Services may seem, to some, improper. After all, economics has to do with buying and selling, with markets where goods and services go to the highest bidder, with emphasis on each individual serving his own selfish interests, with a world in which greed and aggrandizement are treated as desirable human attributes. Human services, on the other hand, are directed at enhancing the human condition, at providing life-facilitating and life-improving services to individuals needing them. The human service emphasis is beyond economics, its motivations are not market or profit based. Rather, the object is to make such services available to those for whom they might be beneficial as a matter of right, without regard to economics.

The observations above are clearly overstated but, nevertheless, represent perceptions which often color and influence discussion of policy in the area of human services. Too often, certain human services are viewed as having sufficient "absolute" value (particularly by the providers of such services) to have unlimited first claim on the resources of society. The establishment of a "right" to medical care, for example, means to some that every newly-available procedure and medical service ought immediately to become part of the "menu" of every service-providing setting, without regard to the cost to society (or often to individuals).

The economist, on the other hand, starts from a different position no matter what his values. He starts from an assumption that we live in a world of *scarcity* in which decisions to devote resources to a particular end imply that fewer resources will be available for other uses in society. Because of this, it is not enough to determine that a particular use of resources is *good* since there are more good things to do than there are resources to do them with. Rather, the issue of prime importance is to determine, given the limited resources available, how such resources may *best* be used. Such decisions involve not absolute worth, but relative worth. It is not sufficient that certain social ends are achievable; we need to know the costs of that achievement—most importantly in terms of the other desirable ends which we give up to get it.

All human activity is resource-using and, therefore, all human activity involves the making, either consciously or unconsciously, of economic decisions. Decisions about the way to spend a weekend embody all of the economic elements of a decision to build a new factory, to establish a national program of children's day care centers, or to establish a program of housing for the elderly. In each case, decisions must be made as to the use of scarce resources such as time, manpower, or money. Every resource can be used in a variety of ways, each of which may have different value. The desired end is to select a use that yields the most benefit to the decision-maker or to those whose interests the decision-maker serves. Even if one were to decide that a given objective were to take precedence over all others it would be necessary to decide how that objective was to be met. Other things being equal, it is always better to achieve an objective using fewer resources rather than more.

Economics is the discipline that examines resource-using decisions as a dimension of social behavior. It has as its object two major results:

1. Better understanding of the nature of such behavior.

2. The development of strategies to improve economic decision-making.

The first of these objectives is basically descriptive, but it is organized around theoretical structures which provide some guidance as to what to look for and how to organize such an inquiry. Economic concepts of Supply, Demand, and Markets are examples of concepts which serve to organize and structure descriptions of resource-using activities.

The second objective is pursued by generalizing from accumulated experience. The object is to develop general rules for decisions which can be applied to specific problems. Analytic strategies such as cost-benefit and cost-effectiveness analysis are examples of decision-making tools which emerge from the central perspectives of economics. While economic analysis has been focused on many dimensions of human behavior, the notion of human services as a separate area of economic activity in society is a relatively new one. There are a number of reasons for both the failure to consider these activities in the past and the growing interest in the economics of human services in the present.

THE DEVELOPMENT OF HUMAN SERVICES

In the earlier stages of economic development, many of the services which we consider human services were not generally a part of the developed market structure within which other goods and services were produced and distributed. Care for children, the aged and handicapped, the mentally ill, and the sick was provided within the family unit. The technology of care was not well developed and often required little more than maintenance, within the family, of a place for such people to live. Allocations of resources on their behalf were made within the economic decision-making unit (e.g., the extended family) and were usually limited to services provided by family members and friends.

As such problems were perceived to have social costs, public facilities, typically at the state and county level, developed to provide these same custodial services, freeing the individual families from the burden. Old peoples' homes, mental hospitals, poor farms, and schools for "wayward" children all reflect the public form of this "human service" activity. The trend toward a public setting was emphasized by changing social and economic influences. The increasing mobility of the American people and the associated breakup of the extended family made it ever more difficult for families to meet human service needs within their own households. The developing public form of "human services" emphasized the custodial and residential, partly to compensate for the inability of families to provide the services and partly as a reflection of the pervasive view that individuals needing such services were a burden to society which was best dealt with by removing them from it.

The emphasis on custodial and residential "services" also reflected the limited technical view of what appropriate services were. For the most part, the need for human services was seen as a reflection on the individual. Such services were required only when a person had failed or was "beyond help." Concepts of preventive mental health services, family counseling, and other human services appropriately used by "well" persons were not developed and such services were not sought by or considered a part of the consumption patterns of "normal" families. Only when individuals became incapable of functioning did responsibility shift to the service provider. Alcoholics were ignored or arrested for drunkenness; children with histories of chronic truancy were dealt with through the courts and parents either were fined or denied the right to raise their children; the aged often ended up in mental hospitals where "treatment" consisted primarily of food and shelter.

While the public efforts were largely custodial, there was, at the same time, a developing of various service-providing settings within the voluntary sector, motivated by personal philanthropic desires and dependent for financial support on private funds. While such services were often provided as a matter of charity to the poor, often the voluntary agencies were the only source of such care regardless of income. Many human services had not found their way yet into the private sector marketplace. Each agency was free to establish its own criteria for who could receive services, and often the availability of such services was restricted to a small proportion of those who might desire and benefit from them, often along regional or ethnic lines or the agencies' preference for "desirable" clients. For example, the system of blindness services, heavily dependent on voluntary agencies for the provision of services, still provides most of its services to employable adults and children who are not otherwise handicapped. The aged, who make up the largest proportion of the blind and visually impaired in the United States, receive little in the way of services (Scott, 1969). The Bureau of Labor Statistics estimated that in 1955, no more than 20–22 percent of the estimated total of blind persons were receiving services. This was true in spite of the fact that an examination of a number of such agencies in 1967 found considerable evidence of unused capacity to provide additional services (Organization for Social and Technical Innovation, 1971). The lack of "acceptable" clients reflects the providers' view as to who ought to receive services and a reluctance to make those services available to the large "potential market" now being unserved. The notion of a *user* interest or a *public* interest is often secondary to the provider interest in determining who receives services and how those services will be produced.

While such services were seen as being primarily relevant to those who were dependent on charity, the appropriateness of such a decision-making structure was not widely questioned. An agency providing a service might choose to limit its availability or limit itself to a single mode of service such as accepting only those delinquents who might be expected to respond to psychiatry (Teele & Levine, 1967). As long as such services did not visibly utilize resources of manpower and money in ways that *obviously* imposed burdens on other interests in society, the choice of services to be provided, who should receive those services, and how such services should be produced was clearly an issue to which most of society was indifferent. While such decisions were economic decisions, the criteria used to make them were not derived from economic analysis. Since the resources used in the production of these human services were relatively small and freely given by individuals who were satisfied with the way they were used, there was little incentive to consider alternative uses to which those resources could be devoted.

Many of the services which we consider as part of human services today were developed and provided through voluntary agencies supported neither by payments from the user nor by publicly-provided funds. The mix of such services and the forms in which they were provided reflected the preferences of the donors on whom they relied for funds. The mix of services in the first day care center in the United States was designed as much to meet the needs of the wealthy for wet nurses as to provide care for the children of working mothers (Rothman, 1973). The assurance of funding, often made secure by endowment, insulated such service providers from market influences and made evaluation of the relative worth of such services difficult.

The developing human services, then, reflected the two influences noted. The public effort was primarily developed around custodial and residential services, typically for needs which were reflected in socially undesirable behavior, mental illness, delinquency, and some phases of aging. The development of services outside of institutions was left to the efforts of private charitable agencies. Often such services were provided on a small scale, with each agency serving a limited number of clients and specializing in a limited set of services. Such agencies provided services of personal counseling, day care, rehabilitative services, referral, recreation, family planning, and child welfare as well as most other components of what has become human services. There existed a variety of models for dealing with human services needs. But the bulk of the service provision was developed within the voluntary sector without either public or private market direction and was supported primarily by charitable giving.

While the actual service-providing activities developed primarily within the private, voluntary sector, and the residential and custodial services evolved within the public sector at the state and local level, the experience of the depression of the 1930s stimulated a large increase in the role of the federal government in providing the fiscal resources for meeting human needs. The passage of the Social Security Act provided a basis for the development of an extensive and growing commitment to income maintenance as a vehicle for dealing with conditions that might generate increased requirements for services. A federal program of retirement benefits for the aged, the establishment of a program of grants to states for the poor and disabled, and the imposition of an unemployment tax to stimulate the development of state unemployment insurance programs were all components of that legislation. The federal role in the direct provision of services was small and largely restricted to groups for whom there was a special federal responsibility such as Indians, disabled veterans, and, for medical care services, merchant seamen.

The development of such programs established a federal responsibility for providing for the fiscal needs of the poor, the aged, and the unemployed and generated vehicles for broadly identifying the service needs for such groups in society. The program of grants to the states to provide income maintenance for the blind, disabled, aged, and some other categories of the poor also meant that federal funds were flowing on a significant scale to support, albeit often indirectly, the provision of social services and medical care to these groups.

While the aggregate economic impact of the resources devoted to human services was small prior to World War II, many of the basic forms for organizing, providing, and paying for such services had been developed. The depression years left us with a changed view of the potential federal role in what had been primarily a private or local matter. The experiences during the war years accentuated the pace of change and generated a vast expansion in both the desire for human service activities and in the development of resources to provide them. That experience also set the stage for a different perception of the appropriate role of public resources in the provision of human services.

THE POST-WAR DYNAMIC

Today the picture is quite different than it was prior to World War II. The experience of the post-war decades has been characterized by a large expansion in the amount of resources devoted to human services activities and in increasing dependency on public funds for their support. There are no simple arguments to account for these changes, but it is likely that a number of aspects of the developing American society contributed.

In an overview, Wilensky and Lebeaux (1965) argue that the form and structure of social services is related to the process of industrialization. They summarize their arguments as follows:

1. The problems the social worker deals with would not be matters for organized public attention if it were not for industrialization. Some of them— old age, unemployment, leisure time—have increased in importance with economic growth. Others, whether they have increased or decreased in frequency (and this is something we often do not know), are now visible, urgent subjects for public action—family breakup, delinquency, mental and physical illness, poverty, and so on. No social problems— no welfare services, no profession of social work.

2. Welfare expenditures on a scale which evokes the label "welfare state" could not be made if the resources were lacking. Industrialization so vastly increases the income of a society that it makes such expenditures possible. No industrialization—few welfare services, and few specialists to dispense them.

3. A major function of social work, its liaison function, derives from a major effect of industrialization: the specialization of modern life. The social worker is, among other things, a guide through a kind of civilized jungle, made up of specialized agencies and service functionaries the citizen can hardly name, let alone locate. From this fact stems another function many social workers and agency administrators perform: the planning and coordination of specialized services.

4. Changes in the clientele of social agencies derive from another major effect of industrialization: shifts in stratification. On the casework rolls the people of poverty and low status are dwindling and those from the middle class growing—with lasting effects on the services demanded, relations with clients, and the status of social work.

5. All industrial societies develop large numbers of "bureaucracies"—large scale formal organizations; all move toward central controls over many spheres of community life, including the welfare services. The specialized social agency and the central fund-raising body, both professionally staffed, are part of this general tendency —with important consequences for social service. The business elite, coupled with high-status lawyers and doctors, play a prominent role in the control of these bureaucracies. Working out a satisfactory relationship with these men in the formulation of welfare policy is a major problem for welfare professionals. Another major problem is that of resolving the conflict between professionalism and technique, on the one hand, and social reform, on the other.

6. American culture (especially those values shaping economic action—our individualism, our ideas about private property, the free market, and the role of government) affects not only the amount of cash we spend for welfare services, but also the kinds of services we assign to private versus public agencies, local and state versus federal agencies. In America alone among advanced societies has the voluntary, private welfare effort remained so large a part of the total; the very ambiguities of the term "social welfare" reflect these values in our culture. [Wilensky & Lebeaux, 1965].

While the Wilensky and Lebeaux arguments reflect a set of influences which operated over a much longer period than the post-war years, the decade of the 1940s accelerated some of those influences. The very high labor mobility of the war years and the frequent residence changes of military families generated even greater needs for services in those areas which had significant immigration. In some cases, communities were developed almost overnight to house wartime manufacturing workers in areas which had no services at all while other communities grew in population well beyond the capacity of existing services to meet the needs. The severe disruptions in previously developed family and community relationships necessitated the development of new services, typically as an element of public or industrial activity. The provision of such services was seen as a necessary element in a policy of labor attraction and essential to the economic objectives of society as part of the war effort.

The above circumstances also led to a breakdown of the existing formal and informal referral networks in society and placed a premium on the development of more visible and accessible means of entering the service-providing system. Obtaining housing assistance, medical care, educational services, and other services in a new community was a necessity for the majority, not a set of occasionally needed services. The limited and often restricted services developed in the voluntary sector were frequently not able, within their desires or resources, to meet these needs. Whether the response was to increase resources in the voluntary agencies or to develop public services, that experience nevertheless changed dramatically the view of many Americans as to the place of such services in their overall patterns of existence and provided real opportunities to experiment with new forms for the provision of such services.

The war also contributed to the development of large-scale new demands for services. Millions of returning veterans needed vocational and employment assistance for their reentry into civilian life. Every community was affected by the need to respond to the requirements of this population. For those veterans injured in the war, even greater service needs were manifest. The simple provision of income maintenance payments was not sufficient to meet the requirements of the injured veterans. Medical care and rehabilitation services together with counseling for personal and vocational needs had to be integrated in a way that was consistent with the nation's obligations to its wounded servicemen. The sheer scale of such requirements led to a significant expansion of federally funded and *operated* service-providing settings under the Veterans' Administration. What was of significance was the notion of entitlement to service where it was incumbent on the provider to organize and make available services. This contrasted greatly with the more prevalent view that services were provided by agencies at a certain level and that they would select clients to fit their available resource level. Once the notion of entitlement was accepted, the potential influence of high levels of "need" for services on the available supply was significantly increased. Because the veterans involved were numerous and because their need for services was generated as a result of service to the country, it was possible to find broad support for the expenditure of public funds to meet their service needs. The centralization of that responsibility in the Veterans' Administration made possible the development of new modes of service delivery and provided a "critical mass" for the development of new technology, particularly in the areas of medical care and rehabilitation.

The post-war period also saw the development of new means of financing various services as part of the employment relationship. The widespread growth of collective bargaining and the growing emphasis on incorporating health and welfare benefits into the labor agreement contributed to an expansion in the degree to which certain human services, particularly medical care, were financed through third parties, usually insurance companies. While the emphasis on fringe benefits was stimulated by the War Labor Board rulings on acceptable wage increases, post-war collective bargaining accelerated the trend. By 1949, the National Labor Relations Board had held that such subjects were "mandatory" for collective bargaining and had to be dealt with if either party to the bargain so desired. The increased health insurance coverage created, in a way, a large additional group for whom entitlement was assumed. Since the services were already paid for, either directly or in lieu of other benefits, the pressure was on suppliers of such services to respond to the demand. In this case, however, there were no central providers as there were for veterans. The financial incentives were private rather than public and each individual or group of insured had to make its own demand felt in the medical-care marketplace. Even so, the growth of health insurance generated a significant increase in the amounts of services available and stimulated peoples' expectations as to the availability of services and their appropriateness.

The increased demand for services was also accompanied by significant changes in the technology of service provision. The needs of returning veterans led providers to build on the wartime improvements in medical care and rehabilitative services. Not only did people demand more services, but the actual relevance of services to the human condition was expanded. New techniques in mental health and medical care services expanded the potential benefits which could be derived from their utilization. The refusal to accept simple custodial care led to many improvements in the technology of rehabilitation of the blind and the physically handicapped. The expectation of a return to normal or near-normal existence stimulated new techniques of vocational training and counseling and physical medicine. Within the Vetrans' Administration, the existence of many individuals with multiple service needs led to the development of new ways of coordinating services and changed some of the traditional views of appropriate referral patterns.

The development of improved medical technology also made possible significantly improved results from the provision of services and raised expectations with regard to the efficacy of care. By the mid-1950's, the development of chemotherapeutic technology in mental health, most notably the development of tranquilizers, made it possible to think in terms of treatment of many mental illnesses which had previously only led to the patients being "locked away." That initial experience in what has come to be called "deinstitutionalization" set the stage for a whole new perspective on mental health services as having general relevance to the needs of people who did not require or who would not have utilized public inpatient mental hospital services. While such changes had significant impact on the technology of mental health services (Schulberg, 1965, 1971), they also expanded significantly the demand for those services and required major changes in their organization, structure, and financial base (Albee, 1970; Kelly, 1968; Kiesler, 1965; Peck, Roman, & Kaplan, 1967).

The post-war changes in technology and demand for human services led to a significant increase in the amounts of resources devoted to the provision of these services. The pace of change and the scale of public involvement was considerably expanded in the 1960s with the "discovery" of widespread poverty within the "affluent society" and a growing public commitment to respond to this need (MacDonald, 1965). Prior to this time, most of the public effort in dealing with poverty took the form of income maintenance for specific categories of recipient: the aged, the blind, the disabled, certain veterans, and certain families with dependent children. The level of such income maintenance varied considerably from state to state and from category to category. The basic perspective, however, of almost all such public programs was focused on providing some minimal level of income to individuals who were unable to provide for themselves. Such individuals had to be in a "worthy" category, that is, one for which some public willingness to provide funds had been demonstrated. The circumstance of poverty was viewed as an attribute of individuals who were exceptions to the general form of income adequacy. The appropriate response was the provision of income.

The development of the federal programs and policies of the 1960s reflected a significant change in this perspective (Rosenthal, 1972). The first major change was a move toward economic development strategies, embodied in the Area Development Act of 1962, for dealing with areas characterized by high levels of unemployment, low levels of income, poor housing, and low scores on other general economic indicators. The establishment of the Appalachian Regional Commission in 1963 formally designated a section of the country, Appalachia, as an economically underdeveloped region. While the area had high poverty levels and a relative absence of services, the emphasis was on encouraging economic growth rather than dealing directly with individual needs. The regional approach emphasized construction of highways, industrial development, and, to a lesser extent, manpower training as investment in the overall improvement of the economic climate. It reflected a view that the relatively widespread poverty in the area reflected more the region's deficiencies than the individual's. Few of the expenditures made under these programs, other than the job training, went directly to the poor. Rather, they were directed at enhancing the ability of the area to generate employment and thereby increase the economic well-being of the region. Without evaluating the success of the programs, it is important to note that the view of poverty incorporated in these activities was quite different from the previous individually-oriented one. No distinctions were made between the deserving and the nondeserving poor. The program dealt with the poverty of the region, not the poverty of individuals, and utilized federal funds in an effort to improve the economic status of the area.

By the early 1960s, it was clear that poverty was a more widespread and general condition than the overall economic performance of the country would suggest (Harrington, 1962; MacDonald, 1965). The Council of Economic Advisors (1964) indicated that in 1961, 20 percent of the population had annual incomes below a poverty level of $3,000 per year. Although poverty was not restricted to any single group in the nation, among the poor were to be found disproportionate numbers of aged, blacks, rural residents, and female heads of families, all reflecting the results of unemployment, discrimination, the economic decline of labor-intensive agriculture, and the inadequacy of existing income maintenance programs.

The poor were characterized by high needs for human services reflected in higher rates of illness, family debility, and exclusion from the usual access to such services. Paradoxically, the growing availability of services in the previous decades did not spill over to the poor. Where poverty was most concentrated, services were often least available. The declining relative availability of medical care in the traditional form of personal physicians in rural areas and in the inner cities belied the relatively greater need for services in those populations (Rosenthal, 1970). Even within the public assistance programs which came in contact with many of the poor, the vast expansion of welfare caseloads eroded the ability of social workers and other case workers to provide services or to serve as effective referral points for their clients. Individual social worker caseloads often grew beyond 100 families and the rapidly expanding costs of welfare led to most of the effort of staff being devoted to eligibility determination and not service delivery. When services were sought, however, they were often not available to many who needed them.

Ferman, Kornbluh, and Haber (1965) have identified six major influences on the urgency of dealing with poverty:

1. The dislocation and erosion of manpower resources stemming from the changes in technology in the post-war period.
2. The challenges of the Cold War.
3. The Civil Rights Movement of the 1960's.
4. The increased financial costs of social welfare programs.
5. The increase in crime and juvenile delinquency.
6. The growing awareness of failures of the educational system in preparing youth for occupational (and even military) service.

Some of these influences began to make more clear the high social costs associated with poverty beyond the costs falling directly on the poor individual or family. Such influences set the stage for a major shift in the role of the federal government in influencing the delivery and financing of human services and stimulated significant changes in the view of the role of human services in the lives of the people.

As the interest in poverty grew, many arguments were offered to account for the persistence of poverty and its accompanying social and economic costs. The discovery of the intergenerational tenacity of poverty, particularly among the nonaged poor, led many to a belief that money alone would not solve the problem. There were those who argued that there existed a "culture of poverty," a set of responses to poverty which enabled individuals to survive but which also generated the conditions which ensured their continuation in that state (Lewis, 1968). The characteristics of these "societies" of poor reflected both economic adaptation and the development of perspectives on institutions in society which differed substantially from the perspectives of most Americans. Expectations about the role and function of many activities which were increasingly institutionalized as human services for the majority were not incorporated into the life circumstances of the poor. Nonmoney exchange was prevalent and extended families provided services that included income maintenance, child care, medicine, and counseling. At an extreme, the "culture of poverty" arguers often seemed to take the position that such arrangements were essential to the lives of the poor and reflected *more* than simply the absence of money. They argued that provision of money alone would not change many aspects of the lives of the poor.

While many disagreed with the extensions of this argument, it was clear that the lives of the poor incorporated many attributes which prevented their effective movement into the mainstream of economic and social participation in society. Low levels of education and inadequate transportation often prevented them from entering primary labor markets. The secondary labor markets in which the poor often worked were characterized by casual employment, lack of fringe benefits, no job tenure, and low wages (Piore, 1970). Such income as the poor obtained did not provide the same levels of consumption that equal amounts of money would provide others. The impact of housing discrimination, transportation inadequacy, lack of savings, and poor work experience all served to make the poor pay higher prices, face exorbitant credit costs, and receive poorer quality goods and services (Caplowitz, 1963; Rosenthal, 1968).

With regard to public services, the poor fared badly also. Poor neighborhoods had inadequate recreational facilities, libraries, and schools. Even within cities served by a single school system, the poorest school districts received the smallest per pupil expenditures. Access to medical care was difficult. Poor neighborhoods had few private physicians, many of whom were old and often not integrated into systems of services which made available to their patients the vastly improved medical technology of the past two decades. Services were often provided to the poor in outpatient departments and emergency services of municipal and large voluntary hospitals. Lack of public transportation often made it costly to get to such facilities and the clinics were characterized by long waits for care, fragmented services, and settings in which the needs of the patients often appeared considerably less important than the needs of the providers. The poor received little in the way of preventive services, family planning, followup, home care, and mental health services, particularly on an ambulatory basis. As noted before, even for those on welfare, inadequate staff and growing welfare loads made it difficult to obtain appropriate counseling and referral services.

In general, human services were organized in ways that made them particularly inaccessible, or accessible only at very high social and economic costs to the user. The organization of human services was clearly structured to serve the provider, and provider interests dictated the scope of services, the intensity of care, and the procedures by which users gained entry. While services for the nonpoor also evidenced some of the same characteristics, lack of choice on the part of the poor and generally greater need for many services generated greater dependence on large institutions and public programs which suffered most from these deficiencies.

The discussion regarding poverty in America led to widespread general agreement that the poor, while having greater than average needs for services, had little access to such services and that the forms in which they were available often discouraged their use by imposing great costs in terms of time, money, and inconvenience on the user. More important, the lack of human services was seen as being related to poverty itself. One typical line of reasoning might be as follows: The poor are sicker, therefore they cannot find employment, therefore they are poor, therefore they are likely to be sicker, etc. Similar arguments were made for educational services, housing, transportation, mental health, and general social services. This notion of a "circle of poverty" was incorporated into the developing public antipoverty policies. This view was particularly significant because it provided a rationale for spending public funds on what were basically viewed as private services in many cases.

The argument stems from the discovery of the social costs of poverty and the growing willingness of the nation to devote resources to a reduction of these social costs. To the extent that service deficiencies were seen as contributing to the extent and severity of poverty, investment in the development and provision of services to the poor could be justified as an essential part of an antipoverty strategy. Medical care, counseling services, housing assistance, job counseling and training, day care, family planning, consumer training, and health education were all seen as appropriate and useful human services which could enhance the effectiveness of such a strategy (Advisory Council on Public Welfare, 1966; Brown, 1968; Johnson, 1964; Task Force on the Organization of Social Services, 1968).

The growing evidence concerning the service needs and deficiencies of the poor supported a more intensive look at the delivery of services generally. The difficulties of availability, lack of access, and a growing concern with the quality of services and relationships between providers and users were not limited to the poor alone. Many services were equally difficult to obtain and possessed these same qualities for the nonpoor. At the same time that evidence was being assembled that encouraged the poor to increase their use of services, it was becoming evident that adequate services were often difficult to obtain even when the user was willing to pay. By the 1960s, increasing attention was being paid to the rapidly rising costs of medical care and the increasing difficulty of gaining access to those services. The widespread lack of mental health services on an ambulatory basis was emphasized as more and more people began to seek such services. Shortages of manpower, pernicious market influences, growing levels of demand stimulated by the development of insurance for services, both public and private, and shifts in population away from the central cities were all influential in broadening the gap between the demand for services on the one hand and the available supply of services on the other (Silver, 1969).

The public response took a variety of forms, all of which provided new public funds to stimulate the development and use of greater amounts of services. The increase in resources available for human services was accompanied by a reexamination of the ways such services were organized, produced, and delivered. Many of the existing structures for service delivery were seen as unresponsive to the needs and preferences of the populations they were being developed to serve. The increased demand placed a high premium on finding more effective and less costly ways of providing services. Scarcity of essential professional manpower encouraged different manpower and staffing configurations and the development of new classes of paraprofessionals.

The rapid increase in expenditures on human services is reflected in the fact that for medical care services alone, per capita expenditures rose from $28.83 in fiscal year 1940, to $141.63 in fiscal year 1960, to $358.05 in fiscal year 1971. This latter amount, $75.0 billion, was 7.4% of the Gross National Product; of it, $28.5 billion was public money. This was 37.9% of the total, as compared to a public share of 20.2% in fiscal year 1940 and 24.7% in fiscal year 1960. The actual amount of public funds almost quadrupled in the period 1960 to 1972. While the increase in medical care expenditures was perhaps greater than for other human services, by fiscal year 1970 expenditures of *public* programs of social welfare accounted for over 15% of the Gross National Product. While much of these funds represent income maintenance payments, probably more than half was expended for services.

The vast increases in the resources devoted to human services and the even greater increase in the use of public funds for that purpose provide considerable basis for the growing concern with the economic aspects of human services. The rapid changes in the technology of production of human services creates new demands for manpower and new requirements for training and education. Growing expectations as to the "right to services" and the benefits to be derived from their use impose new burdens on providers and lead to new forms of organization, financing, and distribution, each of which has implications for the use of resources and the costs of care.

The growing emphasis on services to communities of users and not just individuals has stimulated new forms of organization which go beyond the delivery of a single service to the point of taking responsibility for organizing a whole range of services. The Neighborhood Health Center, multiservices center, and the community mental health center all represent new structures for service delivery and present new opportunities and problems in the allocation of resources. Formal structures of user involvement in the planning and operation of the service delivery process have implications for the demand for services and the technology of production and imply a significant change in the market for human services.

ISSUES IN HUMAN SERVICES

It is clear that the production and distribution of human services has become a significant component of the economic as well as the social and political structure of the American society. Significant amounts of the nation's resources and a large and growing share of the nation's manpower are engaged in these activities. A growing share of incomes, both public and private, flow into the human services sector. It becomes increasingly obvious that our demands for services far exceed at present our abilities to respond to these demands. Not only the quantity of services, but also the quality is subject to more acute scrutiny by a public growing more aware of the nature of economic scarcity. As we discover that many "good" services are not available we confront the necessity of taking a more disciplined look at the services we do produce in an effort to make more effective use of resources. Central to this effort is the awareness that resources are not unlimited, that decisions to utilize scarce resources in a particular manner imply that other "good" things to do will not get done.

The preceding discussion is intended to provide an overview (albeit a superficial one) of the variety of influences that have shaped our present system of human service delivery. Its development has not been planned, but reflects a variety of responses to changing influences on expectations, technological developments in the production and distribution of services, changing public perceptions of the appropriate role of the government, economic growth in available resources, development of private insurance, and a host of other, nonplanned social and economic forces. It *is*, however, a system since each of its components influences and shapes both the form and effectiveness of all the others.

As we confront the necessity of choice, it becomes important to inquire in a more disciplined way as to the effectiveness with which resources are used. Clearly, more money alone will not automatically guarantee that the potential of human service delivery to enhance the human condition will be attained. Planning *per se* does not make the task easier since planning will not necessarily change the forces that shape and mold our current system. But understanding these forces is an essential element in improving the system.

While the system reflects social, political, and technological factors, it is also shaped by economic forces. An understanding of the economic dimensions of human service delivery can only enhance our ability to make more effective use of knowledge, people, and resources in seeking to improve the effectiveness with which human needs are met. This study is an attempt to provide such understanding by examining some contemporary aspects of the existing variety of human services in the context of an economic frame of reference. Such an effort can only give the "flavor" of economics without an overdose of the substance. However, it is intended to sensitize those interested in human service delivery to the extent to which the organization, production, and distribution of human services reflects economic influences and to the degree to which understanding these economic influences can enhance our understanding of the system as a whole.

The next section presents a brief overview of that economic frame of reference and attempts to identify its assumptions, limitations, and utility as an organizing perspective on human service delivery. The remaining chapters are devoted to examinations of specific elements of the economic structure of human services.

2. An Economic Perspective for Examining the Delivery of Human Services

Approaching any significant dimension of society from the perspective of a single discipline is always a risky business. In order to utilize a single disciplinary focus it is necessary to ignore, assume away, or hypothesize many other aspects of the activity being investigated. Often, the most important aspects are left out of the resulting analysis. While that is the risk, the reward comes from gaining further understanding about forms of human behavior.

Such a strategy is not necessarily either unrealistic or nonuseful. The world is a complicated setting and the need to know everything before one can know anything would preclude understanding anything at all. However, it is essential always to be aware that the specific aspects of behavior which are being studied (in this case *economic* behavior) operate in the context of a host of other influences. One can derive considerable insight about behavior from such a restricted perspective.

For example, it can be shown that *usually* more of a particular good will be bought at a lower price than at a higher price. This observation about economic behavior tells us nothing about the other influences on people's desires to utilize that good. Clearly, cultural, social, and environmental factors will influence their decision to consume. The economic principle stated above *assumes* that those influences, whatever they may be, are the same for both the higher price and the lower price. This is the type of assumption embodied in the "other things being equal" (*ceteris parabis*) qualifier typical of statements about economic behavior. The principle states a general tendency that will operate unless other things occur to modify that aspect of economic behavior.

To demonstrate that such qualified statements are not trivial, particularly in terms of shaping policy, it is only necessary to examine a number of policies designed to influence aspects of the market for human services that obviously incorporate (and depend for their impact on its validity) the espoused relationship between price and what economists call *effective demand*. That is, that higher prices will lead to lower utilization and vice versa. Consider the arguments that led to the development of the Medicare Program of health insurance for the aged. Many of the arguments in favor of the legislation were based on evidence that the aged were underutilizers of medical care services. While this was not the only argument, it was a major factor in the passage of the bill. The response to this underutilization was the passage of a program which *lowered* the costs of hospital and other medical care to the aged. It should be noted that the program did not lower the total cost of care, *only* the cost to the aged (the actual users). The assumption, proven in fact, was that this would lead to an increase in the use of such services by the over-65 population.

The use of the economic principle of demand also shows up in policies designed to reduce utilization. The addition of deductibles and coinsurance to medical care (and other) insurance is supported as a way of reducing "overutilization" and controlling costs. It does so by reducing the amounts of such services used by raising the price to the user and thereby *eliminating some potential users from the market*. This latter observation is important. From a welfare perspective, it makes quite a difference which users are discouraged. If they are those with the least immediate medical needs, we can argue that a deductible/coinsurance strategy enables us to use scarce medical resources in the way that best serves medical needs. If, on the other hand, such a strategy tends to restrict the use of the poorest user regardless of his relative medical need, then the policy may yield a use of medical care resources which serves a different end and which would be valued differently. In either case, less medical care resources will be used than would be the case without the deductibles and coinsurance. The actual impact of the increased price of medical care to the user in terms of who gets the care and who does not depends on a specific analysis of the nature of the demand for medical care (a subject taken up in the next chapter). It should be noted that the cost-reducing objective of the policy is served in any case.

This last point is important. It is rare that any policy has impact on only a single objective. *That* the policy works may not be as important as *how* the policy works since other objectives may be affected. Nevertheless, it must be emphasized that all of the issues raised around this last example are economic issues and a better understanding of the economic structure of the human services system is essential to the development and evaluation of policies designed to enhance the human condition through the provision of human services.

THE PERSPECTIVE OF ECONOMICS

The economic perspective on social behavior starts from a number of assumptions about the nature of the world.[1] Perhaps the most basic is the assumption of scar-

---

[1]Because the material discussed in this section is basic to all economics, no specific references are made. Further discussion can be found in any standard economics text.

city as a condition of human existence. The absence of unlimited resources establishes the need for choice in the use of resources since every commitment of resources for one purpose reduces the resources available for all other ends. In recent years, the assumption of scarcity as a guiding economic principle has been criticized. In the face of widespread waste and the devotion of resources to what appear, to some, as frivolous ends, the critics argue that our society has virtually unlimited resources to provide for the achievement of many unfulfilled social and economic goals.

Such a view reflects, not a rejection of scarcity as a fact of life, but rather a belief that the uses to which resources are being put are inappropriate. Indeed, the concern with waste of resources implies a recognition of scarcity. To argue that society could "afford" to deal with social problems through a different use of resources is very different from arguing that it could do so without having to forego any of the other ends to which resources are currently devoted.

The economic perspective imposes on the resource-using decisions in society an awareness of the opportunity costs embodied in those decisions. Among the costs of using resources a particular way are the loss of those benefits which could have been obtained from alternative uses. The concept of opportunity cost is essential and follows from the assumption, well substantiated by experience, that resources are not in infinite supply nor are they sufficient to meet all of the wants and desires that exist in society. Each time a decision is made to use resources in a certain way, the choices left to society are reduced. It should be emphasized that even with unlimited resources, societies would still have to make decisions about the use of resources. However, such decisions would not be economic decisions since there would be no opportunity costs associated with any use of resources.

A society's ability to meet the wants and desires that

exist in it are also limited by technology and knowledge. Many desires exist that would command resources even under the most limited conditions of supply if only we knew how to utilize resources to fulfill them. The limitations of technology always serve as constraints on choice, just as do limited resources. (However, when resources are scarce, reducing the limitations of technology is also a resource-using activity. It needs to be weighed against the other uses to which those resources could be put. Decisions to invest in research as opposed to service provision in human services embody this type of tradeoff between alternatives. Each time we devote medical manpower to research we reduce the supply of physicians for providing medical care services. Whether or not this is a good thing to do depends on our expectations with regard to the future benefit from the research as compared to the present opportunity cost in lessened availability of services.)

Basically, the economic perspective is directed at identifying the way that societies make resource-using decisions. It goes beyond this, however, in attempting to evaluate those decisions in terms of *economic* efficiency. It perceives all use of resources as an attempt to derive *benefits* and the resources used in that process as *costs*. The evaluative assumption is that, given scarcity, it is always preferable to obtain a given benefit at a lower cost than at a higher since more resources will then be left over for other uses. An efficient use of resources is one that generates the greatest amount of benefits from a given set of costs or one that produces a given benefit for the smallest amount of costs. Efficient use of resources maximizes societies' opportunities for satisfying human wants and desires.

It must be emphasized that the economic analysis cannot place the values on benefits or costs. Every society has its own strategies for valuing activities and different individuals will place different values on identical activities.

However, economic analysis can make obvious the opportunities in society to improve the allocation of resources within the context of given sets of valuations of costs and benefits. As part of the analysis, we study the implications of a society's economic decision-making process for the efficiency with which it makes use of its resources.

Every society needs to develop a means to make three basic economic decisions:

1. What goods and services are going to be produced?
2. How are those goods and services to be produced?
3. Who will get them?

Historically, three general economic decision-making strategies can be identified: command, tradition, and the market.

Command strategies are typified by the existence of a central decision-making authority that determines, for the society as a whole, how resources will be used and how the goods and services produced will be distributed. Ancient Egypt under the Pharoahs and contemporary nations such as China and many of the Eastern Bloc countries utilize command strategies to organize their eonomic activity.

Tradition strategies depend on the continued commitment to resource usage established in a society's past. Many primitive societies used tradition to assign jobs, organize the production process, and distribute resources. The caste system in India provides a large-scale example of a job structure determined by tradition. Such strategies are characterized by considerable lack of flexibility and often prove viable only under conditions of stable technology and "steady state" economic scope and scale.

Market strategies rely primarily on the creation of settings within which individuals in society can demonstrate their own preferences and compete for resources without central direction. The market is the basis for most economic decision-making in the United States and most industrialized Western nations. (Markets will be discussed more extensively below.)

In actuality, there are no "pure" systems for economic decision-making. Few countries are without some market arrangements for buying and selling goods and services. Even in a market-oriented economy such as the United States, union apprenticeship programs reflect more of tradition than of the market and the use of command to allocate manpower to the nation's military through conscription is well established.

Within the human services system itself, resource use and distributions reflect all three strategies. *Tradition* often establishes the "appropriateness" of clients for the services of particular agencies, the mix of services provided, and the manner in which such services are produced. Many of our uses of manpower reflect traditional commitments to particular production processes without specific reference to the impact of the output itself. For many years, only physicians could take blood pressure readings "officially" even though it is clear today that such tasks are equally well performed by other personnel. *Command* is often used to allocate by requiring welfare recipients to utilize certain services in order to retain eligibility for income maintenance. Children are required to go to school and further required to receive certain immunizations and preventive health services as part of that experience. *Market* strategies are exemplified by the Medicaid program which pays for medical care services rendered to eligible persons, but leaves it up to those people to obtain services in the context of the medical care marketplace.

The degree to which any of the general economic decision-making strategies is economically efficient depends on the degree to which the allocations of resources that it achieves maximize the benefits obtainable from the resources available to it. However, each strategy implies a different perspective on how those benefits are to be measured. Traditional strategies tend to establish distributions in a relatively inflexible way. Although an initial set of allocative decisions may be economically efficient, there is little assurance that either the costs or benefits associated with a particular use of resources will remain unchanged. The efficiency of such strategies tends to deteriorate in the face of new options provided by technology or new desires generated in society.

Command strategies depend on the ability of the decision-maker to ascertain appropriately the relevant benefits and costs associated with alternative uses of resources. What is needed is some vehicle for establishing consensus in society; such as by authority, where the preferences of the decision-makers are the only relevant preferences; by concessions to accede to some elite group's preferences through technocracy or, on a more limited scale, professional judgment, or through some societal weighing scheme such as voting.

Pure market strategies solve the problem of evaluating costs and benefits by allowing each individual to reflect his own preferences in the marketplace to the extent that his influence as reflected in his income will allow. It assumes that, within the limits of choice, individuals will direct their resources to those goods and services which they value most highly. No central direction is imposed.

Under different conditions, each of these strategies will yield different degrees of economic efficiency. Since the central economic decision-making strategy in the United States is the market modified by public involvement through command and direct market intervention, it is clear that the dynamics of market economics will have great influence on the organization, production, and distribution of human services. The discussion that follows of the basic dynamics of the market is intended to provide a basis for evaluating the potential of the market and its limitations in achieving an effective and efficient allocation of resources for human services.

The market economy is organized around two sets of decision-makers, households and firms. Households, which own the productive resources in society (land, labor, and capital) provide these resources to firms who use them to make goods and services. The firms, in turn, provide households with their incomes. At the same time, firms produce goods and services and provide them to households in exchange for money. The settings within which these exchanges occur are markets. It is in the markets that the prices of goods and services and their quantities are determined.

In the product markets, the firms *supply* the goods and the households *demand* them. In the market for productive resources (factor market), households are suppliers and firms are demanders. This model of a market economy can be depicted as in Figure 1.

The process whereby each of the participants in these markets influences the price and quantity of goods and services is based on each decision-maker undertaking his own evaluation of costs and benefits. It is assumed that all of the costs and benefits associated with each transaction fall upon the direct parties to it, the buyer and the seller. For the firm, the benefit-maximizing strategy entails maximizing the difference between the costs of production and the revenue accruing to the firm from the sale of its products (profit). It is in the interest of the firm to use as few resources as possible to produce a given output. Whether or not to produce the product at all is dependent on the willingness of buyers to pay a price for it that is greater than the costs of production. If there are no profits, the firm will cease using resources since it is clear that buyers do not value the product sufficiently to merit

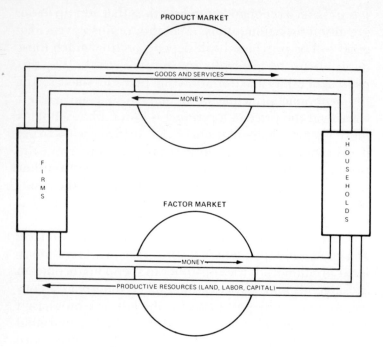

Figure 1. A market system model.

its resource cost. If, on the other hand, the product is highly valued by buyers, its scarcity will raise the price and concomitantly, the profits to the producer. The higher profits will attract resources to the production of the good through new firms entering the industry or expansion of existing firms. In sum, the workings of the supply side of the market are such that resources tend to be used where they are most highly valued and not used where they are little valued.

On the demand side, it is assumed that each household also wants to maximize the benefits it obtains from its income and the use of its time. (To some extent, time and income can be traded off.) Ideally, it wishes to spend its income in such a way that, given the prices that it faces, it purchases a set of goods and services that add up to the greatest satisfaction (utility). Whether or not a particular good will be purchased will depend on how much must be given up to get it (its opportunity cost). It is this process of utility maximization that provides the basis for the economic principle of demand discussed earlier. Clearly, if the price of a product is lower a household is more likely to demand it since it has to give up less to get it. The household that derives great benefit from the product will be willing to pay a higher price than another household with the same income which values the product less, but at a lower price they might both find it worth its cost.

Since the utility derived from an additional purchase of a good is independent of its price, the process of utility maximization leads the consumer to spend his income on those goods and services which make the greatest contribution to utility per dollar for the last unit purchased (the marginal unit). If one good has a higher marginal utility per dollar than another, spending a dollar more on the first and a dollar less on the second will increase total utility. The firm will also follow such a rule in seeking the most efficient method of production. It will buy resources (factors of production) in such a mix that the marginal product (benefit) of each factor per dollar of cost is the same for each factor.

Given certain attributes of the markets we can make some normative judgments as to the economic efficiency of the resulting resource-allocative decisions we have described. We assumed earlier that all of the costs and benefits in each decision were incurred by the parties to it. A number of other attributes must also be present:

1. full and free information about available choices, prices, profits, etc.;
2. mobility of resources;
3. free entry and exit from the market;

4. many buyers and sellers;
5. no discrimination—any seller will sell to any buyer and vice versa.

A market with these attributes is called a perfectly competitive market. Such markets have the property that, given the distribution of income and the tastes and preferences of households, these markets will result in an optimal (efficient) allocation of resources. In such a market, consumers exert their influence through the workings of demand (this is called consumer sovereignty) and producers, in a quest for profit, become ever more responsive to consumer preferences and the need for efficient use of resources.

The market system solves the problem of measuring benefits by letting each recipient of benefits place his own value on them and indicate that value to producers in the marketplace by his willingness to pay for the good or service. If there is insufficient willingness to pay to justify the use of resources relative to other uses, it is assumed that the benefits generated by that use of resources are less than would be generated by using them to produce other, more desired goods and services. In a world of perfectly competitive markets, the resources will be attracted to their most benefit-generating uses and society will obtain answers to the basic resource-allocative questions that are economically efficient.

Such a market is also responsive to change. If the tastes and preferences of consumers change, these changes are reflected in their willingness to buy goods and services at the market price. As the demand for a given good increases, new resources are attracted to its production by the increased profits accruing to its producers. As technology provides new products or lowers the cost of producing existing products, consumers can shift their demand to these alternative forms of consumption.

Under what conditions will the market not work?
It should be clear from the preceding discussion that

the economic results espoused for the market depend on its having all of the characteristics of perfect competition, many of which are not fulfilled in reality in the markets for human services. While that will be discussed below, it is important to note the conditions where even a perfectly competitive market will not yield an efficient allocation of resources. Consider the case where the benefits from the purchase of particular goods and services accrue not only to the buyer of the product, but to others as well. Such would be the case for the purchase of treatment for a communicable disease where the benefits would include the value of reduced risk to others. Another example is the consumption of education, which generates benefits to society beyond these derived by the user. In these cases, left to its own devices, the perfectly competitive market will allocate too few resources to the production of the good relative to the benefits generated since the buyers will only value the benefits *to them.*

Consider also the case where the costs incurred in the production of a good or service do not all fall on the producer and are not, therefore, all reflected in the prices of his products. A current significant example is the cost of pollution. In these cases, the perfectly competitive market will result in devoting too many resources to the production of the good or service relative to the benefits generated, and the costs incurred.

Both of these cases are examples of externalities; the first, external benefits, and the second, external costs. Where externalities are present a perfectly competitive market will not yield an economically efficient use of resources in society. What is needed is an additional source of market influence which can incorporate the external costs and benefits into its workings.

The existence of externalities provides a major argument for public intervention in the workings of the market. The forms of intervention are varied. In the area of human services, in which externalities are generally considered to be present, we find subsidy of producer through grants to offset costs and to enhance the training of manpower, subsidy of consumer through vendor payment programs, the direct production of services through public auspices, and provision and control of markets for services. Funds for such intervention are derived from taxes, justified on the grounds that the benefits derived or the costs avoided by the public from having the services available merit the expenditures.

As was noted earlier, such an allocative strategy, like all command strategies, depends on ascertaining the relative weight of group *vs.* individual preferences and on determining consensus with regard to evaluation of the externalities. The process for establishing the existence of externalities, particularly external benefits, is a reflection of social, ethical, and political forces and the values obtained will change over time. As the notion of "health care as a right" gains credence and commitment it *becomes* important to each of us that others have access to care. That process creates external benefit. Such externalities, referred to as "merit wants" (Musgrave, 1959) are reflected in the process of development of the system of human services described in Chapter 1.

The question of the economic efficiency of allocating resources to human services ends depends on estimates of benefits and costs that are often beyond the realm of economics. However, as resource-using activities, the form, organization, and structure of the human service delivery system can be evaluated in an economic context. As was argued earlier, it is always better to achieve a given end using fewer resources rather than more. The economic principles discussed here can provide a basis for gaining useful insights into the delivery of human services. The next chapter is devoted to an examination of various aspects of the demand, supply, and market structure of the system of human services delivery and its components.

3. Economic Characteristics of the Markets for Human Services

The previous discussion has identified a number of attributes of markets which lead to efficient use of resources in the absence of significant external costs or benefits associated with the use of the good or service being considered. Few, if any, markets in contemporary society possess all of these attributes. However, much public policy is directed at increasing the "competitiveness" of markets or controlling the adverse impacts of "noncompetitiveness" in order to enhance the economic efficiency of these markets. Federal antitrust policy is often aimed at reducing the control of markets by a limited set of suppliers, and "natural monopolies," such as public utilities, are often directly controlled in an effort to stimulate supply and price behavior more like that which a competitive market would generate. In this latter case, the economic costs of competition (such as multiple sets of telephone, sewer, or water lines serving the same area) are deemed to be too high to make the economic advantages of competition obtainable.

The markets for human services also reflect characteristics not consistent with the perfectly competitive economic model. Such markets are often served by few suppliers and impose many restrictions on the choices of both buyers and sellers. Users of services typically have limited and imperfect information as to available options and many transactions incorporate a high degree of involvement of third parties who are neither buyers nor sellers in the pure sense, but whose interests are reflected in each market transaction. Identifying an industry as not being "perfectly competitive" tells little about the degree to which the industry could be more "efficient" if it were more competitive. Rather, the competitive model serves as a measure against which the unique characteristics of the markets for human services can be described and evaluated.

Perhaps a last caveat is in order. No attempt is made in the discussion that follows to present a thorough economic analysis of each of the markets involved in the production and distribution of human services. Such an effort would require far greater resources than those embodied in this exercise. Rather, this study will present a sampling of issues around each major aspect of the economic structure which serves as the unifying theme; it will draw on examples from many of the areas of human service delivery. Ech example is intended to point out the relevancy of the issue, not to resolve all of its implications.

The overall organizing structure of the presentation is based on the model of an economic system presented in Figure 1 (see Chapter 2). Basically, the distribution and production of each component of human services is influenced by the operation of two markets; the product market within which the buyers and sellers of the service consummate their arrangements for exchange and the factor market within which the sellers of the final service and the owners of the resources needed to produce the services make their arrangements for exchange. Examples of activities in the product market include a visit to the community mental health center, a stay in the hospital, and a family counselling session. Examples of activities in the factor market include the hiring of nurses, the construction of a mental health facility, and the provision of inservice training to a social service staff. Each of these general types of markets has its own characteristics. It is clear, however, that the activities of each are interactive and that decisions with respect to the product market depend for their implementation on responsive action within the factor market.

This chapter will examine a number of economic characteristics of the organization and delivery of human services. It is important to remember that there is no single "commodity" called Human Services. Rather, the following discussion is an attempt to organize a coordinated look at a diverse set of services. The organizing theme is market structure and economic organization. The characteristics which are of interest are economic characteristics: resource use, distribution, and allocative strategies. The markets which are to be examined are those in which a whole host of services, generally identified as "human services," are exchanged, produced, and obtained. In part, this discussion is an attempt to identify economic characteristics common to all human services, but it will not be limited only to the shared characteristi;cs. It is equally important that the exercise serve to sensitize the reader to the centrality of economic issues in the development of policies for influencing the supply and use of human services.

In both the product market and the factor market the influences of demand and supply operate to establish the distribution. In the product market, the demand reflects the desire on the part of the users to utilize the services at different market prices. Other influences on the desire of individuals to utilize services are viewed as given. The supply side of the product market reflects individual producers' responses to the opportunity to increase their benefits. The influencing variable on supply is also price. Other things being equal, a higher market price will attract a greater supply than will a lower market price.

In the factor market, the roles are reversed. For here

the product-market producer of the service is the buyer. If factors of production (labor, materials, etc.) are less costly, a supplier is likely to buy more of them since at any given product-market price, lower costs will enable him to reap a greater reward. The suppliers in the product market are those who control the resources, primarily manpower and capital, which are used to produce the services. Much of the elegance and, perhaps, utility of the economic model comes from its reliance on a single market-influencing indicator—the transaction price. For all kinds of goods and services such a unitary perspective is an oversimplification. In the market for human services, the direct influence of price may often be only a small influence on decisions to produce and to utilize.

Perhaps the limitations of the simplification can be ameliorated by thinking of the price as a surrogate for the costs or benefits associated with the transactions. In the simple formulation of demand analysis, the price faced by the potential consumer is a measure of the cost imposed upon that consumer in order for him to avail himself of the good or service. In the real world, there are many costs beyond those represented by the price which has to be paid. Nevertheless, observations about the response to price may be generalizable to the response of potential users of services to differing influences on their costs of utilization.

What is ultimately of interest is a generalized view of the relationship between perceived costs and perceived benefits in influencing decisions to use resources; such a view should then provide the basis for a more meticulous analysis of the actual costs and benefits associated with particular types of resource-using behavior. The next chapter will deal specifically with an attempt to spell out some of the complexities of this type of analysis. However, the theme of relating costs to benefits is central even to the descriptive dimensions of economics, which form the basis for this chapter.

ASPECTS OF THE DEMAND FOR HUMAN SERVICES

Earlier, it was noted that the amount of resources devoted to the production of a particular good or service would be determined in a pure market structure by the interaction of the willingness of the providers to supply such services and the desire of the users to purchase them. The desire of users to purchase service is reflected in the economic concept of demand. In its simplest formulation, the demand for goods or services is expressed as the quantity of goods or services which would be utilized at varying prices. Such a formulation assumes as given all of the other influences on the desire to utilize a particular good or service, and examines the relationship between changes in the price of the service and changes in the quantity of such services which people would wish to avail themselves of. In general, at lower prices more of a particular good or service would be desired than at higher prices.

However, a number of qualifying observations need to be made. First, it is important to note that the degree to which the demand for a particular good or service is responsive to changes in the price can vary significantly. Services which are perceived as generating great benefit to the individual who uses them (e.g., life-saving medical services) tend to be relatively little influenced by differences in the price of such services. For other services, small changes in the price may generate great differences in the quantity that people desire. Clearly the degree to which a particular good or service is seen as desirable will differ from individual to individual. The concept of demand is primarily an aggregate one. Given the mix of tastes and preferences for a particular service within the population being considered, some individuals will avail themselves of the service at very high as well as very low prices while others may only consider the services worthwhile at lower prices. Over the whole market, then, there will be more buyers at lower prices.

NEED VERSUS DEMAND

While the concept of demand is central to economic formulations, when dealing with human services interest is typically focused on the need rather than the demand for services. It is essential to distinguish the economic concept of demand from concepts of need (Boulding, 1966). The concept of need is omitted from explicit discussion in the preceding outline of the economic perspective. To the extent that each individual perceives his own need, it is reflected in his evaluation of benefits associated with various forms of behavior. Very often in discussions of the need for human services, there is a presumption that the existence of need is something that can be identified without regard to the specific circumstances or perceptions of the individual involved. An individual who has certain medical symptoms "needs" medical care or an individual encountering difficulty in social adjustments "needs" counseling and mental health services. Often such needs are defined by technology. For example, the need for kidney dialysis only became real when the technology for providing such services was developed. Much of what is perceived today as "need," particularly for mental health and medical care services, represents forms of service which did not exist a few decades ago. In this sense, even need cannot be seen as a fixed or static concept, but rather one which reflects technological opportunities.

The concept of need is often treated as if it were binary. One either *needs* a particular service (i.e., possesses the characteristics which make it potentially technologically relevant) or one does *not* need the service. Clearly, there may be great differences between identifying need and the likelihood of people to utilize such services even when they are available. This distinction is important in evaluating and examining human services. Most of the planning for human services starts from an estimate of the degree to which such services are *needed* by the appropriate or relevant set of potential users. Often little consideration is given to the degree to which such individuals are likely to utilize the services or under what conditions that utilization would be likely to occur.

That there exists significant difference between the potential need for services in an area and a demand for services is corroborated by the experience of a number of community mental health centers. Such centers are often the suppliers of service to a large area. Their experience indicates that only a small percentage of those in the area who might be expected to "need" services actually utilize the mental health center. This would indicate that demand behavior is not solely a response to the availability or lack of availability of services. To the extent that an objective of human services delivery is to make services available and to encourage the use of such services by those who might benefit most from them, an understanding of the factors that influence the desire on the part of individuals to use services is essential to effective planning and resource allocation. The experience of planning activities suggests that such considerations are often not properly taken into account in the design, organization, and development of the supply of services. In actual fact, the history of underutilized or badly utilized services makes clear the value of additional investigation of the potential demand for such service, as well as relying on a less mechanistic definition of need.

FACTORS INFLUENCING THE DEMAND FOR HUMAN SERVICES

The factors which influence the demand for human services can be categorized roughly into two types: those which reflect expected differences in the benefits associated with utilization of the service and those which reflect expected differences in the costs. In the more limited economic model, only price is considered as the operative influence. This means that only that particular dimension of cost is explicitly considered in the analysis. Clearly, other factors than the specific price charged to the user are significant in a determination of costs. Perhaps more important, the factors which might influence the evaluation of benefits are left out entirely by assuming them to be fixed for the relevant population in the market. What is suggested here is that such a view is unnecessarily limited and is not inherent in the economic perspective. As we begin to know more about the relationships between patterns of utilization of services and the characteristics of the users, it becomes possible to take such factors into account in estimating the demand for human services (Feldstein, 1967; Rosenthal, 1964).

Influences on Benefits to the User

The factors associated with expectations of benefits are of two types: those which relate to the technical "need" for the service and those which influence both the perception of that need and its likelihood of being reflected in the use of services. Examples of the first type are attributes such as age (Anderson, 1963; Graham, 1957) and sex (Blackwell, 1963), both of which are associated with morbidity patterns (Morris, 1967). Such characteristics may reflect "true" differences in "need" which will be reflected in the demand for human services.

While the above characteristics relate to aspects of the population which indicate what might be thought of as "*pure* need," there are other attributes which influence the degree to which such "needs" are likely to be reflected in evaluating the benefits associated with the use of services. Such characteristics would include ethnic and religious differences in response to symptoms (Fink, Schapiro, & Lewis, 1968; Mechanic, 1963; Zbarowski, 1952) and social factors such as education which influence valuation of benefits (Baumann, 1961; Kutner, 1959; Rosenthal, 1964). In addition, the actual relevancy of certain types of service may reflect a social dynamic quite apart from the technology of the service itself. For example, in a society structured on extended families the need for day care services might be quite minimal, whereas a society structured around nuclear family relationships might "require" such services in order to obtain the same degree of potential labor force participation or pursuit of other interests. In these two cases the functional need is identical while its manifestation in the form of desired services is not.

In much of the literature and indeed, much of the behavior of many evaluators of human services, there seems to be a presumptive association between the functional need for a type of service and a need for an identified human service distributed in a particular type of way. Because of the way we define human services, the care delivered in the home by members of the family is not counted as medical service, whereas the incremental days of stay in an institution are. Indeed, much of our evaluation of the need for human services of all types reflects the tendency to identify as appropriate only those services produced by the formally designated system. The above pertains not only to day care and medical care services, but also to income maintenance, counseling, and even educational services.

While the distinction between functional need for a particular set of services and operational needs for an identified class of human service provision is significant, there is a considerable difference between the technical existence of a need *even if perceived by the individual* and the willingness in turn to translate that need into an operational demand for service. In the most general form, this reflects the fact that few needs are perceived as absolute on the part of the individual and the acquisition of service is not seen as being without cost. One can view outreach services in neighborhood health centers and mental health centers as ways of influencing the perceptions of individuals, both as to the benefits to be obtained from services and as to the costs that need to be incurred in order to obtain them (Kent & Smith, 1967). Even in the absence of an identifiable cost associated with utilization of a service generally perceived as being potentially of value, many individuals do not avail themselves of opportunities for utilization. The experience with zero-price physical examinations (such exams are not *cost free* since they utilize the time of the individual receiving them) indicates that the professional technical perception of a need is often not widely shared by the individuals for whom the need is seen as relevant and appropriate.

Influences on the Costs to the User

Having established the difference between technological and social notions of the need for a particular human service, it is still appropriate to ask to what extent economic influences are operational on the decisions of individuals to utilize or not to utilize such services. Clearly, one economic variable which must be considered is that of the price faced by the individual. It is important that the price not be confused with the cost of providing services. Particularly in the area of human services, considerable differences exist between the prices paid by the users and the costs incurred by the system in order to produce the services being utilized. From a demand perspective, it is the costs to the user which are important. The price reflects only one aspect of such costs. There is evidence that, particularly with respect to medical service, there is some price elasticity of demand. That is, increases in the price of services are likely to be associated with a reduction in the amount of such services which people desire to utilize. Conversely, reductions in the price will yield an increase in the use of services. However, the degree to which this occurs varies significantly from service to service. One generalization would suggest that the more essential the service as seen by the user, the less likely it is to be influenced by variations in the price. For certain types of urgent and emergency medical services the price is not viewed by the user as having much significance. The benefits derived from utilization of the service are perceived as greater than those that could be derived from other ways of using the money. However, as the services are seen as being less essential, demand tends to become more elastic; that is, more responsive to changes in the price.

The degree to which this occurs is also influenced by the degree to which the price reflects accurately the user costs associated with utilizing the service. For example, if a potential user of service views his time as having value, a more accessible service will be more likely to be used than one which is farther away or which requires a greater investment of time. There is some evidence that many people served by prepaid medical groups will avail themselves of the services of private physicians even though such services have a positive price as opposed to a zero price for the group. This is likely to occur when the private services can be obtained at significantly lower costs in terms of time and energy. Indeed, we find considerable willingness to pay significantly higher prices for hair cuts at those establishments where it is possible to make an appointment since the cost of waiting is seen as prohibitively high by many potential customers. In many markets for human services, it is difficult to ascertain the price prior to the utilization of the service. This is particularly true in areas such as medical care where the prices of individual services tend to be less relevant than the cost of encounters with the system; the extent of these is often not known in advance. Even more importantly, for many human services there is no direct money price placed on the transaction itself. In those settings, such services cannot be viewed as cost free to the user, but rather the services impose the costs in other ways than direct imposition of a price.

The second economic influence which has been shown to be closely related to the utilization of services is the level of income of the user (Anderson & Feldman, 1956; Roth, 1969). However, there is a certain degree of ambiguity in the interpretation of this relationship. On the one hand, a higher level of income may suggest that a given price imposes a smaller financial burden on the rich than on the poor. However, income levels are also associated with a great number of other social and behavioral characteristics which themselves are positively associated with utilization of services. For example, the actual perception of the need for service is very much influenced by the socioeconomic level (Koos, 1954). It has also been suggested that higher income levels are also associated with participation in social institutions which bring members more closely in contact with the service-providing institutions (Mayhew & Reiss, 1969). This may account for higher utilization of services even when the basic "need" for such services is likely to be less. In many parts of the human service delivery system, certain levels of income preclude the utilization of services, particularly those services distributed to the poor or to low income area residents only. In these cases, a deliberate attempt to offset the influence of income is embodied in the structure of the program.

The existence of insurance coverage is also a major influence on demand. Insurance is of considerable importance in medical care services and of growing importance in the area of legal services, dental services, and mental health services. The insurance mechanism provides a vehicle whereby some part of the money costs associated with the utilization of the service are offset by a third party. Insurance is obtained either by the individual or by becoming eligible through a general program such as medicare, medicaid, or an employment-related group. Many devices are used to influence the degree to which the insurance itself influences utilization. Often insurance coverage is restricted to sharing costs on the grounds that excessive utilization will occur in the absence of a money price imposed upon the individual. There is equally persuasive evidence that the cost-sharing burden tends to defer the use of the services to a point in time when greater amounts of services are required, and therefore, generates higher costs to the system.

Perhaps more important, it is difficult to tell the degree to which the insurance itself accounts for the different utilization patterns observed. For example, those covered by self-chosen insurance are likely to be those for whom the service involved has a higher value in the first instance and who are therefore more likely to utilize such services under any circumstance. In addition, privately purchased insurance is highly correlated with the income level of the individual and therefore may reflect those influences as opposed to any true price offset. On the other hand, the experience with medicaid, a medical "insurance" program for the poor, which resulted in significantly high utilization levels indicates that, in fact, the price-reducing impact of insurance is likely to be of major significance (Feldstein & Allison, 1972; Feldstein, Friedman, & Luft, 1972).

Each of the economic variables noted above reflects directly on the costs to the user of using the service. Other costs are imposed by the way in which the services themselves are structured. For example, accessibility to services and the time costs associated with utilization are likely to be highly influential in determining the degree to which such services will be demanded *at any given price*. Convenience, comfort, perceived quality, and the manner in which the user of service is treated by the provider of service all have significant impact on the degree to which such services are likely to be utilized.

All of the above influences on the demand for services are potentially operational in the markets for human services. Such markets often have in addition peculiar characteristics of their own which lead to direct influence on the demand for services over which users have considerably less influence and control. For example, access to many services is often generated within the system as the result of referral or as a result of utilization of some other service. The demand for such services is restricted to those who filter through the referring mechanism. Clearly, the ease of access or the ease of entry into the system, although a supply-side phenomenon, has considerable influence on the demand for services. For example, fewer than 20% of the blind in this country actually receive services although the need for such services is evident. Nevertheless, the structure of the system of services to the blind and the form in which access to such services is obtained tends to preclude new entrants. As new services are developed, they tend to be made available to those already in the system. Such selection on the part of the supplier of services is probably typical of the market for human services. The next section will examine some aspects of supply.

FACTORS INFLUENCING THE SUPPLY OF HUMAN SERVICES

In the pure economic model, the supply of a good or service reflects a response to the opportunity on the part of the provider of service to receive a reward from production of the service. The simplest relationship is one that expresses an interaction between the willingness of providers to supply services and the price which they are likely to receive. Because the provision of a service requires the incurrence of costs, more services are likely to be forthcoming if the price is higher. Just as the demand model in its simple form suggested that at higher prices fewer services will be demanded, the supply model suggests that at higher prices more services will be offered. However, the distribution of many human services is not responsive either to the potential for profit or constrained by the direct receipt of revenue from the user. Indeed, the supply of human services is most often characterized by influences other than those directly observable in the market. Human services are characterized by heavy reliance on professional judgment rather than the test of the marketplace. The "appropriate" mix of service is often determined by reference to professional and technical norms. The availability of certain medical services reflects a desire on the part of the provider to incorporate new technology in the mix of services which are offered. Development of open heart surgery, renal dialysis units, and coronary care units within the American hospital system is an example of that kind of technological response. Since the demand for such services is likely to be inelastic (not unduly affected by the price) the medical service-providing institutions make decisions about the addition of services based primarily on their own technological preferences and other professional norms not related to the marketplace.

This is particularly true in those settings where the demand on the part of users is restricted to entry into the system of services rather than to individual selection of those components of service which are desired. Very often the decision to develop capacity to provide human services is a response to a technical view that such services are desirable and *willingness on the part of the resource providers who are in many cases not consumers* to make available funds for the development and provision of service. The presumption is often that the demand will be forthcoming if the appropriate services are made available.

Because many of the human service-providing activities are characterized by central funding or cost reimbursement from sources other than the user, the constraints of the marketplace tend to be less influential than the professional and technical norms.

It is probably useful to reiterate the point about the consumer purchasing access or availing himself to the access to a set of services without having specific control over the form in which those services are delivered or the mix of such services which will be made available. Often human services delivery systems are linked — those who avail themselves of welfare services then have access to or often are even required to utilize various counseling services. Often income maintenance services through welfare, Aid to the Blind, or veterans' programs require a certain degree of participation in other human service delivery systems. Since entry or access to the supply of service often is dependent upon referral—in the medical system from the physician and in many counseling services from the social worker, those who provide the services are in a position to exert considerable control over the mix and scale of such services without the constraining influence of demand.

Because the resources for the provision of services are not necessarily dependent directly on the resources of the users of the services it is possible to design and distribute human service activities in ways which might not otherwise stand the market test (Brandwein, 1972; Davidson, 1971). This is particularly significant since many of the human services—counseling, day care, services to the blind, and rehabilitative services—were originally established as philanthropic activities and distributed without charge to the users. Entry to the system was determined by the suppliers of the services themselves. The preferences of the sources of funds and the providers of services were the only relevant preferences in establishing the mix and form of services. In these settings, technological "appropriateness" tends to be more persuasive than the ease of utilization or accessibility to the user. Such systems are left without ready bench marks for evaluation of the economic efficiency with which services are provided.

In service delivery systems characterized by a high level of professional control and structure, significant differences can often occur between that mix of supply most desirable from the point of view of the user and that mix of supply deemed most appropriate by those who control access to the system. However, there may also be some ambiguity as to which set of professional-technical preferences will dominate the system. In the absence of effective markets, however, little ability to resort to the users' preferences as a way of resolving these differences can be identified.

Many of the human services are produced and distributed in such a manner that in order to obtain one of the services, other services must also be utilized. Such a strategy is typical of many human services. Children in school are required to take physical examinations in an attempt to make health services available through the medium of required educational services. Similar joint products are found in the requirements for employment, work counseling, and often job training in the context of income maintenance as part of the welfare services "package." In each case, the joint supply is determined on the basis of required access where a high level of demand exists for only one component of the service.

Of even more significance in the difference between human services delivery and the simple economic competitive model is the absence of competition in itself. In many cases, for a given set of potential users only a single source of supply is available. In these settings, little in the way of tests of user preference are available to the system in order to modify the supply decision even where such tests are desired. The literature of human services delivery reflects a certain degree of ambiguity around this issue. One set of arguments holds that duplication of services is inherently wasteful and inefficient. However, an alternative formulation suggests that the absence of competition precludes any market test of effective use of resources and is itself likely to generate less effective utilization of resources (Task Force on the Organization of Social Services, 1968; Warren, undated). In the competitive model, potential for waste is viewed to be offset by allowing the preferences of users through consumer sovereignty (i.e., the ability to decide whether or not to utilize a particular service) to determine what services will be provided. In the market for human services, however, such consumer sovereignty is typically not operational.

In recent times, the notion of consumer participation has developed as an alternative to the principle of consumer sovereignty for incorporating the preferences of users into the supply-providing decisions of the producers. In the absence of a market where such preferences can be reflected by users in decisions to buy or not to buy, an alternative strategy can be to involve the users of the service directly in production decisions on the supply side. There are many difficulties with this concept, not the least of which is that the distinction between the role of the consumer as user of service and the role of the consumer as participant in provision of service is often unclear. Consumer participation strategies often either serve as a vehicle for diluting the inputs of consumers or, more often, co-opt the consumer to adopt a provider perspective in the course of his own participation in the system (Lipsky & Lounds, 1970; Notkin & Notkin, 1970). Nevertheless, there is considerable question as to whether or not any strategy for incorporating user preferences into the provision of human services can be effective given the fact that the provision of such services lacks the ultimate market test. The willingness of consumers to pay directly for these services in lieu of alternative expenditures of income is usually precluded by the nature of the financing of human services.

In the market formulation, the user puts up the money and the provider produces the goods or service. If the users want the service enough to merit the costs involved, the producer makes a profit. If not, the producer goes out of business, thereby freeing the resources for other uses more in line with the desires of consumers. In the markets for human services, typically neither the producer nor the user puts up the money. Such services are often funded by third parties who may have their own views as to what constitutes an "appropriate" use of resources. The first chapter of this study discussed the development of human services in terms of the shifting sources of financing. It should be emphasized that both professional preferences and user preferences are subject to the additional constraint of adapting to the preferences of the funding source. Such preferences may be expressed formally as requirements for system entry or continued support or informally by the involvement of the source of funds in the operation of the service-providing activity itself.

When a service activity depends on a variety of sources of funds, the exact nature of these constraints is difficult to evaluate. Nevertheless, such influences are central to much of the human service activities which are in existence (Kramer, 1972). Public funds often require certain forms of service provision not necessarily preferred by either the producer or consumer. Restrictions on endowed funds serve to restrict the ability of many service agencies to adapt to new demands from users and new technical opportunities. Few funds are given to service providers "with no strings attached." Such "strings" may reflect a different view of the benefits from service than those held by either provider or user.

The impact of financing does not work only through the direct funding of the provision of services through providers. Public programs which provide services-in-kind or which pay only for certain types of services have the same impact on "the market." Such programs serve to lower the "price" to the user if the services are used in certain ways or to provide certain services "free." If the view of benefits of the user was identical to that of the payer, such activities would only represent a transfer of market purchasing power from the payer to the user. If the views of benefits differ, such activities will yield a market resolution which is different from that which would come about if the money transfers had been made without constraints. Public programs to pay for human services exist because of the view that the use of such services generates external benefits—which accrue to other than the user of the service. However, the existence of externalities means that a simple model of user-provider interaction in the marketplace is inadequate to describe the influences on the production and distribution of human services (Gordon, 1969).

In addition to these direct product market influences on the supply of human services, there also exists a number of factor market influences which tend to shape the structure of human services delivery. The earlier-noted tendency to centralize such services around the professional has led to a number of constraints on the potential supply of such services. Such constraints include licensing and accreditation requirements and often direct legal constraints on opportunities to vary the means whereby such services are provided.

One example of such a constraint has been the restriction in many neighborhood health centers that only services provided by a physician are reimbursable by third parties. This has led to a system whereby nurses, health aides, and paramedical personnel who might technologically be competent to provide those services are prevented from doing so except in conjunction with the services of a physician, thereby restricting the choice of technology to a physician-dependent model. This limits the availability of medical services to that amount which can be supported by the physician. More recently many areas have experimented with the development of nurse practitioners, physician assistants, and others in the effort to offset an increasing demand for services relative to the available supply of physicians' services. The development of paramedical manpower has highlighted the constraints on innovation and technological change placed on the system by legal and regulatory requirements often not directly related to an evaluation of their impact on the services themselves (Biblowit, 1971; Cleckley, 1972).

The centralization of the technology of human services delivery around the highly trained and relatively scarce professional also tends to sustain the centrality of the professional decision-maker in organizing, structuring, and distributing human services. The dependency on the psychiatrist in the community health center, the physician in the medical center, and the trained social worker in the counseling center limits the potential supply of these services to those which can be supported by that particular set of manpower. Such personnel are often limited in number and require considerable investment of time and resources to increase their supply.

The rigidity of the technology of production of human services has precluded in many cases an adaptive technological response to growing demand and has created a circumstance whereby the supply of such services is often well below that which would be demanded. This allows the technological criteria for service provision rather than market criteria to be most influencing. These artificial constraints on response to the demand tend to ensure a less rapid and effective supply response to changes in the desire for services and tend to place significant control on the supply of such services on the producing sources of the skilled manpower, the medical schools and other professional training programs. These institutions are even more insulated from the direct impact of the market for services and are therefore likely to be less responsive to its influence than to their own professional norms, a situation which only compounds the existing constraints in the product market.

This chapter has attempted to use the perspective of economics to describe a number of attributes of the market for human services. Such an effort can only be illustrative. It is hoped, however, that the simplification has not obscured the central theme — that there exist in the market for human services many attributes that can be better understood when evaluated from an economic perspective which lays out the constant interaction in any service delivery system of costs and benefits. The economic perspective is used here primarily to focus and organize the inquiry. It can also serve as a framework for analysis, the subject of the next chapter.

4. *Evaluating Human Service Programs*

It was noted earlier in this study that the economic perspective provided both a descriptive structure around which to observe certain aspects of society and also provided a basis to evaluate and analyze certain aspects of that society. The previous chapter was primarily descriptive. It took the framework of economics—the relationship between supply and demand, users and providers in the context of a marketplace within which distribution takes place—and used it to describe some of the characteristics of the markets for human services. It attempted to point out both the unique attributes of those markets and, in some cases, the characteristics that are more widely shared.

Throughout that exercise, constant reference was made to means whereby the costs and benefits associated with transactions in that market could be evaluated. This is the central analytic theme of economics. The basic economic problem is to get the most out of the resources that are available to society, although what "getting the most" really means is subject to considerable discussion. More formally, the object is to optimize the benefits that can be derived from the use of resources, given the fact that such resources are not in infinite supply and that each use of resources implies that other resource-using activities cannot be undertaken. It is this relationship between costs and benefits which the economic perspective is designed to illuminate. A basic goal of economic

211

analysis is to provide a structure for making specific the dimensions of that general objective.

The market system, particularly the perfectly competitive market structure which was earlier described, is only one device for evaluating the costs and benefits involved in exchange. It yields an optimal result when costs and benefits are only considered relevant when they relate to those individuals directly involved in the transaction. In actual fact there are few transactions of this nature. The use of resources for the production and distribution of human services rarely produces benefits solely to the producer and the user. The essential economic and social nature of human services is that they do not fit into a simple market strategy which leaves producers and consumers to their own devices. It becomes all the more essential to be explicit about identifying the expected benefits and the true burden of costs.

Because human services are often public goods, there are additional difficulties associated with the identification of costs and benefits. While private goods as well as public goods may involve externalities (costs or benefits to those other than the individuals involved in the transaction) it is possible in many cases to ignore the externalities in private transactions as not being central to the allocative decision and we are often willing to do so. For public goods existence of externalities initiates the public involvement in the first place. Therefore, ignoring the externalities is not feasible (Arrow, 1970; Piore, 1968; Steiner, 1970).

Conceptually, relating costs to benefits as a vehicle for determining the appropriate allocation of resources is not a complicated idea. In actual practice, however, it proves to be a difficult task. One major difficulty stems from the problem of measuring and valuing the benefits which may accrue to different individuals, have impact on different sectors of society, or which may take different forms. Without a convenient measurement device which would permit the quantifying of benefits, it is difficult to make comparisons. For goods and services, the market through the vehicle of price provides a yardstick for the measurement of costs and benefits. For all the reasons noted earlier human services and public goods in general are less likely to conform to the market requirements.

Basically the economic strategies for organizing and structuring the analysis of costs and benefits are of two types: cost-benefit analysis and cost-effectiveness analysis. Cost-benefit analysis involves establishing a relationship between the value of benefits generated and the costs which must be incurred to obtain these benefits. Cost-effectiveness analysis, on the other hand, evaluates alternative costs associated with the achievement of a given objective. It should be obvious that the latter is less complex since the issue of valuing benefits is essentially ignored (Rothenberg, 1969).

Within the area of human services, both of these forms of analysis have their place. Often, programs, job retraining and health screening, for example, are argued for on the grounds that the benefits generated from these activities are large relative to the costs which need to be incurred. At the least, it is always argued that the benefits are greater than the costs. This is a cost-benefit argument. An example of cost-effectiveness formulation would be an examination of how the mentally ill *currently receiving care* might be most efficiently served. This type of cost-effectiveness analysis would involve evaluating the use of alternative types of facilities and treatment patterns in order to provide a *given* level of care. Such analysis may ignore differences in the relative efficacy of one treatment modality as against another and ask only the general question "Is there a less costly way to achieve a given level of care?"

While the distinction between the two types of analysis is clear enough, the difficulty with undertaking such analyses lies in the problems of identifying and evaluating the benefits and costs associated with various undertakings. Many of these costs and benefits are not immediately evident in the design and conception of the human services activity itself. The direct costs and benefits, those which fall upon the actual providers and users of the service as part of the activity itself, are usually fairly evident. However, the indirect costs and benefits might be equally significant in evaluating the program. For example, in evaluating job training programs, the additional employment stability and the potential benefits of reduction of various forms of antisocial behavior must also be calculated. On the cost side, the actual cost of providing the training must be supplemented by the costs imposed on the trainees such as alternative job opportunities foregone and the time required to get to and from the job training center.

Often it is not easy to identify whether or not specific indirect impacts are costs or benefits. For example, one of the benefits often attributed to renal dialysis in the home is that it enables the individuals receiving treatment to remain with their families and to be integrated into the home environment. However, there is evidence that sharing a home with the physical equipment required to provide the dialysis to the patient precludes for the family as a whole many dimensions of a normal existence by providing a constant reminder of the illness around which family life is centered and organized. Experience indicates that, for some families, home dialysis yields benefits while for others the costs imposed will far outweigh those benefits. Many human services may generate these kinds of ambiguous costs of benefits, thereby placing even a greater burden on the analyst.

Another significant problem in specifying the costs and benefits associated with a given human service program is identifying the external impact of the service. Hinrichs and Taylor (1972) have attempted to distinguish among such external effects by the causal source and the locus of the impact. They distinguish between external impacts among production activities, where the activity involved in the production of one service imposes additional costs on the production of another, and external impacts among consumers of services, where a consumption of one individual of a service imposes additional costs on other consumers. An example of this latter would be increases in waiting time for service delivery and decreases in the quality of training and education as a result of increases in class size.

In addition they note externalities between production and consumption where production activities lead to increased costs to consumers, such as air, water, and noise pollution as a result of the production process. They also note a fourth direction of external impact where activities by consumers impose additional costs on the production process. Fear of this latter type of externality probably accounts for the "no swimming" signs in most public water supplies.

It is important to distinguish between real externalities and monetary externalities. For example, the development of ambulatory mental health facilities reduces the inpatient population and thereby raises the average cost of producing inpatient services. Such a shift is really a short-run money exchange and does not represent a true externality. Rather, it reflects a transition which occurs as a result of the immobility of capital resources. Over time, the excess inpatient facilities can be closed and the total cost to the system may indeed be reduced or the aggregate benefits produced by the system per dollar of cost involved may be increased.

Another major complexity added to the evaluation of costs and benefits reflects the fact that neither the costs nor benefits are incurred at a single moment of time. Often the benefits from many human services programs accrue most significantly well after the incurrence of the cost. The issue of adjusting the evaluation of costs and benefits for their position in time is one which has merited the attention of many economists (Baumol, 1970). Nevertheless, in each case it is essential to evaluate the present value of a future stream of benefits and often, because human service programs involve a commitment to provide services over time, the incurrence of a future stream of costs. The inherent complexities in a cost-benefit analysis are made more difficult by this time factor.

Identifying the Benefits from Human Service Programs

Identifying the benefits from human service programs is a matter of considerable difficulty. Often the proponents of such a program start with a presumption that such activities are inherently "good" and therefore ought to be undertaken. Because the economic perspective imposes notions of opportunity cost on the decision to undertake a program, it is not sufficient that such activities be good. They should be better than alternative uses of the same resources. While such an analysis requires evaluation of costs as well as benefits, examination of aspects of benefit identification in the area of human services might be useful.

The identification of benefits is, in the first instance, highly sensitive to the efficacy of the service being provided. A useful analysis would require a certain degree of specificity in the objectives of the service. For programs in medical care, it might require a certain reduction in morbidity or mortality from a given disease or a reduction in the degree of disability associated with various types of illnesses. For other types of human services it might imply a reduction in the level of unemployment or in the incidence of various types of antisocial behavior. In any case it is essential to identify specifically the anticipated benefits from the program involved.

Valuing these benefits requires an additional step. Often the benefits from human services programs are valued in terms of the alternative costs foregone as a result of the program. In the case of screening for and treating PKU infants (a disease that usually leads to mental retardation), benefits in some programs were valued as the average yearly cost of services to the mentally retarded times the number of expected years of service that would not be needed as a result of the program. Such a valuation scheme can be deceptive. For example, in the State of California it costs an average of approximately $5,000 per year to provide residential services for a mentally retarded child or adult. Approximately one percent of the inpatient mentally retarded population in the State of California is a result of phenylketonuria (PKU). On average, a mentally retarded individual who requires residential care will utilize 25 years of service. Therefore, the following estimate of benefits was presented: For each child identified as having PKU and treated in such a way as to eliminate or to preclude the mental retardation, $5,000 times 25 years or $125,000 is saved. Therefore, the value of the benefit from such a program is equal to $125,000 per child identified and treated.

There are a number of difficulties in this way of viewing the benefits of the program. If only one percent of the inpatient population is the result of PKU, then the elimination of that source of mental retardation would result at best in a one percent drop in the inpatient population of the state institutions for the mentally retarded. Such a relatively small drop in the inpatient population would not necessarily lead to an equivalent drop in the cost of care. The total cost of service per year in the State of California would be reduced by much less than $5,000 per year per child not admitted. The actual marginal cost of the foregone service is much less than the average. A second difficulty reflects the fact that the incurrence of those benefits takes place over a 25-year time span and that their value at the present time is likely to be considerably less than their total. In any case, such estimates of benefits are likely to be misleading.

This tendency to identify benefits as costs foregone or costs which are now being incurred (usually in other programs) which will not need to be incurred if the proposed program is successful is a standard strategy in arguing for the benefits of many human service programs (United States Department of Health, Education and Welfare, 1967). Job training programs are proposed on the basis that they will lead to a reduction of the costs of unemployment insurance and welfare. Day care centers are proposed on the grounds that they will lead to a reduction in a cost of welfare by enabling mothers with children to enter the job market. Community mental health programs are often proposed on the grounds that they will reduce antisocial and criminal behavior which impose other costs on society. To some extent these arguments are valid but the evaluation of those benefits is often complex. Such estimates of benefits are highly sensitive to the efficacy of the progam in a technical sense and to the actions and activities of other programs often outside of its direct control.

IDENTIFYING THE COSTS OF HUMAN SERVICES

While identifying the benefits from human service programs is difficult, identifying the costs associated with such programs also requires a reasonable amount of caution. Typically, human services occur within the context of other human services and depend on the activities of these other services for some of the inputs to their clients. Often only those costs which are imposed directly on the program being evaluated are acknowledged as having relevance. For example, in estimating the cost of screening children for PKU, part of the costs involved represent the actual testing of the newborn infants. In some states that testing is done by a state laboratory and the costs of operating that laboratory will be reflected in the state's evaluation of the costs of the service. In other states, the tests are required by law but the actual laboratory work is privately done by the hospital or outside labs. These costs are incorporated into the cost of delivery to the parents. In the latter case, such costs do not show up as part of the state cost of service.

The benefits from such a program only accrue as a result of finding and treating an infant with PKU. The costs of screening all of the infants must be matched against the benefits to the few even though for most of those infants no benefits will directly accrue. The potential cost-benefit relationship of such a program is highly dependent on the incidence of the disease which is being screened for. In the case of PKU one case is likely to be found per approximately 15,000 or 16,000 infants screened. In one state which did not provide the laboratory services, the costs of the program were calculated at approximately $5,000 per case identified. Since the average laboratory charge for the screening test in that state was over $2.00 it is clear that the actual cost had to be closer to $40,000 that to $5,000. Many of the evaluations of costs and benefits associated with human services programs fail to identify major components of costs since the source of the evaluation often only identifies those direct costs which would typically show up in the program's budget.

The development of screening programs, of increasing significance in recent years, provides a useful illustration of some of the complexities of cost-benefit analysis. While the purpose here is not to evaluate the desirability or nondesirability of such programs they do provide a way of highlighting various aspects of the process of evaluation. With the development of the technology of metabolic screening of newborns, it became possible to consider requiring that such screening take place. In the mid and late 1960s, there was a surge of state laws passed which required the screening of newborns for PKU, a metabolic disorder which often results in mental retardation of the affected infant. In the first rush to pass legislation, little attention was given to any systematic cost-benefit analysis. The development of such screening programs was widely supported by groups interested in the mentally retarded. The major benefits argued in the political arena, as noted above, were often avoidance of the burden to society and public programs of costs of caring for the mentally retarded. A major set of benefits were those that accrue to the individuals who, by means of early detection and treatment, avoid becoming mentally retarded. For each individual such benefits occur at some future point in time. However, not identifying the value of the future benefits understates the actual benefits that are likely to accrue.

Such a calculation depends on a number of variables. First there is the effectiveness of the screening test itself. That is, will all PKU children be identified as a result of the test? If some percentage of children with PKU are likely to be missed, then the program generates no benefit to those individuals. Not only is the efficacy of the screening test significant but the efficacy of treatment is equally important. For a child identified as having PKU, is there a treatment modality which will ensure that he will not become mentally retarded? To the extent that the treatment is less than perfect the potential benefits are also reduced. Of equal significance is the essential nature of the test itself. For example, do PKU children exhibit other symptoms which might provide the basis for early detection in the absence of the screening test. For example, if the test were not done but an equally strong commitment to treatment were made, would it be possible to identify and find significant numbers of these children without the program and thereby obtain some of the benefits without the costs of screening?

There are equally complex problems in identifying the costs. To be effective all newborns must be screened. This means that the costs of screening are imposed uniformly, either on society as a whole through a public program or on all parents of newborn infants by requiring that such tests be performed. Although the costs are borne by all, the benefits are likely to accrue in large measure only to those who are identified as having the disease.

The actual cost of such a program relative to the benefits will depend to a large degree on the incidence. However, the cost is also affected by the sensitivity of the test. How often does the test have to be done? Are there further tests that are required when an infant is found to be positive from the screening test? In the case of PKU, further tests and individual counseling are also required as well as a general physical evaluation of the infant. These represent additional costs which must be calculated as part of the costs of the system.

While the above-noted costs relate only to the identification of children with PKU, the treatment requires an additional set of costs. Basically the treatment is dietary. In many computations of the costs of treatment, only the costs of the dietary supplement are identified as being appropriate. In actual fact, the maintenance of a child on a strict and rather boring diet requires a significant amount of additional parental and parental-substitute time. The additional costs of babysitters and child supervision may be significant although rarely, if ever, are they considered as part of the costs of such a program. The long period of dietary control imposes certain burdens upon the household which typically show up in a higher need for counseling services and a higher level of expenditures for physical and medical services for the child. These costs will show up as burdens on other human service delivery systems if those services are not found directly within the medical treatment system. Such costs were noted as being equally relevant to the treatment of end-stage kidney failure where the dialysis regimen also imposes burdens on other human services delivery systems if the outcome of such treatments are not to have significant and adverse side effects.

The above observations can only provide the flavor of the considerations that are relevant to undertaking cost-benefit analysis of a PKU screening program. Nevertheless, they provide an opportunity to point out some additional issues of general consequence. Clearly, changes in the technology of screening can have significant impact on the cost-benefit analysis. If a screening device for PKU were developed that halved the cost of testing, then, since those costs are spread over 16,000 infants for each identified case, the cost per case might be significantly reduced. Also, the analysis is highly sensitive to the efficacy of treatment. Every improvement in the treatment process increases the expected benefits although such improvements in treatment might also imply the incurrence of additional cost. Each new option requires another round of analysis and evaluation. Often for human services, each technological change that shows any positive benefits at all is regarded as an appropriate addition to the menu of services. Perhaps on closer inspection, some of these changes might be less desirable than they appear at first glance.

The above example points out another item of particular significance in the evaluation of human service delivery programs. While the service being evaluated in our example is primarily a medical one, it is clear that the costs which are imposed and the benefits which are to be derived are highly dependent on the outputs of other human services delivery systems such as child care, family counseling, and residential services. Each of those human service delivery systems is a setting wherein the costs and benefits of a PKU screening program are likely to occur. This is true of many human service delivery systems.

It is useful to contrast the PKU screening program with two other programs, each of which involves the same technology, that of screening, but which yield a very different estimate of both costs and benefits. One of these involves the screening for Tay-Sachs disease, a metabolic disorder which leads to neurological breakdown and is almost invariably fatal by the fifth or sixth year of life. Tay-Sachs disease is almost entirely restricted to the offspring of Jewish parents of Eastern European extraction. This means that the potential group to be screened is much more readily defined and that many individuals need not be screened at all, thereby reducing the potential cost of such a program. Perhaps more significantly, no treatment exists for Tay-Sachs disease. Only one child in four of a pair of parents who are carriers is likely to have the disease. The purpose of screening is primarily to identify such infants before they are born and provide an opportunity for abortion early in the period of pregnancy. Here the benefits of the program do not accrue to the child. Rather, the benefits are seen as accruing to the parents and to other family members in the avoidance of the economic, social, and emotional costs associated with the birth, care, and inevitable early death of an affected child.

The purpose of such a screening program is to identify Tay-Sachs carriers, to provide an adequate level of genetic counseling for such families, to provide an opportunity for screening in utero and for subsequent abortion if that is what the family desires. Because most of the costs are imposed on the family itself, the decision as to whether or not to have the child is typically left to the family.

To the extent, however, that the medical, economic, and counseling needs of the family fall upon public programs, some of the costs will be external to the family decision-making unit. In this case, benefits will accrue to the state as a result of a family's decision to abort. The existence of public human service programs will often, as in this case, change the locus of impact and, perhaps, even the valuation of both costs and benefits.

A third and even more complex form of screening program is that involving the sickle cell trait. Although there is some uncertainty about the actual incidence, it has been estimated that approximately one in nine Black Americans carry the trait called "sickle cell trait." This is a characteristic of the blood which causes the red cells to have a peculiar half moon shape. It has been established that possessors of the sickle cell trait tend to be particularly resistant to malaria and therefore it is likely that such a trait is more heavily concentrated in those populations genetically developed in areas of high risk of malaria where those with the resistant trait would be more likely to survive and reproduce. For this reason significant numbers of Black Americans of African heritage tend to have the trait. In and of itself, the trait generates no negative effects and individuals who possess it are as likely as not to lead normal healthy lives. However, when two such individuals reproduce there is a probability that some of the children will develop a condition known as sickle cell anemia, a sometimes fatal disease.

There has been in recent years a great increase in both mandatory and voluntary programs of screening for the sickle cell trait. Where do the benefits come from as a result of such programs? Clearly the individual who has the trait is not necessarily made better off by being aware of it. The main argument for such programs is that they provide the basis for genetic counseling. Such counseling makes it possible for those who possess the trait to avoid marrying other carriers, thereby eliminating the likelihood of having children who might develop sickle cell anemia, or to enable those parents who know they both possess the trait either to avoid having children or to watch more closely for signs of the development of the illness. In many ways this is a rather speculative set of anticipated benefits. Even more significantly, it imposes a tremendous burden upon those who submit to screening.

Recently we have begun to question more closely the wisdom of such screening programs and the opinion is clearly divided. Because the trait is racially distributed there are a number of negative side effects resulting from singling out Blacks for identification of a trait which, while harmless in itself, nevertheless provides another vehicle for labeling individuals. Perhaps more important is that the result of the knowledge then requires a significant intrusion of the human service delivery system in the life choices of individuals thereby imposing costs *without necessarily being able to ensure any significant generation of benefits.*

The issues involved in sickle cell screening programs are significantly more complex than those presented here but such programs clearly involve a different set of impacts than the other screening programs. In each of the three cases the technology involved is similar but both the costs incurred and the expected benefits to be achieved are considerably different. In each case they represent a complex set of interactions within the human service delivery system, in this case the medical care system, which proposes to provide the service, and other human service delivery systems on which the program is dependent for many of its benefits and on which it imposes many of its ultimate costs.

A last example from the area of screening may serve to emphasize the point. Multiphasic health testing is a procedure where individuals are given a battery of medical tests in order to identify potential illness. The first experiments in multiphasic screening were carried out under public auspices through free-standing health testing centers often not incorporated within a medical service-providing setting. The early experience with such programs indicated that the identification of illness was often not followed up by proper receipt of service. All of the potential benefits from such a screening program depend on the receipt of treatment from other settings in the human service delivery spectrum. By failing to link those services to the screening process or, conversely, to develop screening processes within the service delivery setting, the achievement of the anticipated benefits proved impossible. More recently we note a resurgence of interest in multiphasic health testing but, almost invariably, within the context of a service-providing setting. We can expect the benefits obtained from such testing services to be significantly greater than those of our earlier experience.

The above examples are all situations which call for the

development of cost-benefit analysis. In each case the benefit from screening is dependent on triggering a whole host of responses in other service delivery settings in an effort to utilize and respond effectively to the knowledge generated in the screening process. Without such responses, the quest for benefits may prove futile. Often, choices to be considered might be most appropriately responded to by means of cost-effectiveness analysis. For example, choices as to the imposition of new technology will often respond to a cost-effectiveness analysis where specification of an identical set of benefits can be made. The costs of alternative means of achieving those benefits can be evaluated in order to find the least-cost alternative. Very often cost-effectiveness analysis can be undertaken in such a way as to avoid some of the complexities of evaluation of benefits. One example can be found in the comparison of alternative treatment modalities for end-stage kidney disease (Klarman, Francis, & Rosenthal, 1968). Two technologies exist, renal dialysis and organ transplantation. In actual fact, these treatment modalities are not equivalent. A successful kidney transplant is a cure, often enabling a return to normal healthy patterns of behavior. A patient on successful dialysis must maintain a fairly restricted life style, remains ill, and is dependent on frequent medical interventions for continued existence. Qualitatively, a vast difference exists between the benefits to the individual generated by each of these life-saving treatments for end-stage kidney disease. Nevertheless, a first approximation to comparing the alternative costs of each can be undertaken by estimating the costs for equivalent numbers of life years saved, ignoring the differing benefits associated with the quality of existence.

Very often in a given practical situation, there is considerable ambiguity regarding which type of analysis (cost-benefit or cost-effectiveness) is appropriately involved. For example, support for developing ambulatory care for mental health services reflects two different arguments. On the one hand there are those who argue that ambulatory services are inherently better and yield higher benefits relative to costs than do inpatient services. On the other hand, many of the arguments made in support of the shift are cost-effectiveness arguments which hold that for a given population the provision of a similar level of service based on ambulatory services is in the long run less costly than one based on inpatient facilities. In actual fact there is merit to both these arguments. Experience in many states has indicated that maintaining a patient for a year under an effective ambulatory care system often proves to be more costly in money terms than maintaining the same patient for a year in an inpatient facility since in the former case higher amounts of actual services are provided to the individuals involved. On the other hand, the move to ambulatory services often represents a shift of the burden of cost from the state to other sources of financing (Rosenthal, 1973). From the state's point of view (regarding its expenditures as the only relevant cost and its obligation to provide service as one which is not adjusted for quality) it is clearly cost-effective to encourage the transfer of the burden of patient care to service delivery systems which it is not responsible to finance. Discussions of development of alternatives to institutionalization emphasize the cost-effectiveness of the alternative care and, in addition, assert a higher level of benefits generated from the particular treatment modality being argued for (Atelsek, Stephenson, Macklin, & Resnick, 1972; Bell, 1971; Caro, 1972). In medical care generally, the move towards ambulatory care services has often been argued as a cost-effective strategy which reduces the cost of providing a given qualitative level of care (Bellin, Geiger, & Gibson, 1969).

Such transfers of locus of service usually involve more complicated dimensions of evaluation. For example, the move to ambulatory care in mental health has made available mental health services to a large number of users who would not have availed themselves of the services of the inpatient facilities currently in existence. Because the ambulatory service itself has potential relevancy for a much larger number of users, it is difficult to identify specifically that amount of the costs and benefits which represents transfers (i.e., cost-effective-strategies for dealing with those already in the system) and that which represents the generation of new benefits to new users who would not have availed themselves of the previously-offered services.

It is important to note one other difficulty in evaluating human services. As was noted in the last chapter, such services are often produced jointly with other human services. Many service delivery settings incorporate a number of different types of services. The development of the multiservice center and the neighborhood health center with medical care, mental health, counseling, day care, and even job training and consumer services are examples of attempts to incorporate within a single setting a whole host of services each of which may generate its own peculiar set of benefits and which may differ considerably from center to center and from one point in time to another (Elinson & Herr, 1970; Feingold, 1970; Foster, 1968; March, 1968). Sorting out the costs and benefits of each individual service may be impossible.

While the above discussion has been only illustrative, it should demonstrate that, although the concept of relating benefits to costs is simple enough, its actual application involves problems of considerable complexity and difficulty. Nevertheless, the perspective is essential to a systematic evaluation of new opportunities for organizing, structuring, producing, and delivering human services. The need for such activity reflects the basic economic assumption of scarcity of resources, an assumption well supported by experience in the area of human services delivery. Given scarcity of resources, it is essential that services be provided in ways which are most likely to generate positive benefits both for the users who avail themselves of those services and for the society as a whole. Many devices for improving the effectiveness of such decision-making have been proposed; formal planning structures, consumer participation, and, often, resort to the marketplace. However, the nature of human services and the large variety of potential benefits and costs involved requires a more disciplined awareness of the nature of cost-effectiveness and cost-benefit analysis. The actual analytical mechanics require stepping back from advocacy and mapping out, in a more systematic way, the specific interdependencies among human services on which each new service delivery strategy is dependent.

5. Final Comments

That the growth of human services is a significant area of both public and private endeavor is clear. Today, human services delivery systems face increased opportunities for meeting human needs and increased demands upon a scarce and limited set of resources. In such a setting, basic economic questions as to *what* resources will be used and *how* they will be used occupy a central place in decision-making. The economic perspective does not serve as a substitute for technology or for human values but represents a context within which both technology and values can be incorporated into the decision-making process. The economic approach provides a way to understand the process of resource allocation and to place the operation of human service delivery systems in a perspective which will enable improvements of their effectiveness. Because of the scarcity of resources, both money and time, it becomes essential that we always consider the efficiency with which human service activities are undertaken. The purpose of this study has been to provide a broad overview of the economic perspective as well as a sampling of some of the directions of analysis which are potentially relevant for understanding and evaluating human service delivery. Such an undertaking can only be initiated here. To the extent that the relevancy of the inquiry is established, the benefits from this endeavor will well exceed its costs.

231

REFERENCES

Advisory Council on Public Welfare. Having the power, we have the duty. *Report to the Secretary of Health, Education and Welfare,* June 1966.

Albee, G. The uncertain future of clinical psychology. *American Psychologist,* 1970, **25,** 1871–1880.

Anderson, O. W. The utilization of health services. In H. E. Freeman, S. Levine, & L. G. Reeder (Eds.), *Handbook of medical sociology.* New Jersey: Prentice-Hall, 1963.

Anderson, O. W., & Feldman, J. J. *Family medical costs and voluntary health insurance: A nationwide survey.* New York: McGraw-Hill, 1956.

Arrow, K. J. The organization of economic activity: Issues pertinent to the choice of market versus non-market allocation. In R. H. Haveman & J. Margolis, (Eds.), *Public expenditures and policy analysis.* Chicago: Markham, 1970, Ch. 2.

Atelsek, F., Stephenson, M. K., Mackin, E., & Resnick, W. *Long-term institutional care and alternative solutions: Final report.* Washington, D.C.: American University Development Education and Training Research Institute, 1972.

Baumann, B. O. Diversities in conceptions of health and physical fitness. *Journal of Health and Human Behavior,* 1961, **2,** 39–46.

Baumol, W. J. On the discount rate for public projects. In R. H. Haveman & J. Margolis, (Eds.), *Public expenditures and policy analysis.* Chicago: Markham, 1970, Ch. 10.

Bell, W. G. *Community care for the elderly: An alternative to institutionalization for functionally impaired low income persons in Florida.* Tallahassee: Florida State Program in Social Policy, 1971.

Bellin, S. S., Geiger, J. & Gibson, C. Impact of ambulatory health-care services on the demand for hospital beds: A study of the Tufts Neighborhood Center at Columbia Point in Boston. *New England Journal of Medicine*, April, 1969, **280**, 808–812.

Biblowit, M. *The physician's assistant.* Unpublished manuscript, Florence Heller Graduate School of Social Welfare, Brandeis University, 1971.

Blackwell, B. The literature of delay in seeking medical care for chronic illness. *Health Education Monographs*, 1963, **16**, 3–31.

Boulding, K. E. The concept of need for human services. *Milbank Memorial Fund Quarterly*, 1966, **44**, Pt. 2.

Brandwein, R. A. *Myths of the marketplace: An analysis and critique of the profit model in the provision of social services.* Unpublished manuscript, Florence Heller Graduate School of Social Welfare, Brandeis University, 1972.

Brown, H. J. Delivery of personal health services and medical services for the poor: Concessions or prerogatives. *Milbank Memorial Fund Quarterly*, 1968 **46**, Suppl., 203–223.

Caplovitz, D. *The poor pay more: Consumer practices of low-income families.* New York: Free Press, 1963.

Caro, F. G. *Organizing and financing personal care services: An alternative to institutionalization for the disabled.* Working paper, Levinson Gerontological Policy Institute, Brandeis University, 1972.

Cleckley, E. *New careers for paramedical personnel.* Unpublished manuscript, Florence Heller Graduate School of Social Welfare, Brandeis University, 1972.

Council of Economic Advisors. *Economic report of the President.* Washington: Government Printing Office, 1964.

Davidson, M. The social services market—A critical

analysis—A proposal for change in the public welfare revision study, Boston Model Cities Administration, May 1971.

Elinson, J., & Herr, C. E. A. A sociomedical view of neighborhood health centers. *Medical Care,* 1970, **VIII**, 2, 97–103.

Feingold, E. A political scientist's view of the neighborhood health center as a new social institution. *Medical Care,* March–April, 1970, **8,** 2, 108–117.

Feldstein, M. S., & Allison, E. Tax subsidies of private health insurance: Distribution, revenue loss and effects. *Health care policy discussion paper No. 2.* Harvard Center for Community Health and Medical Care, Harvard University, 1972.

Feldstein, M. S., Friedman, B., & Luft, H. Distributional aspects of national health insurance benefits and finance. *Health care policy discussion paper No. 3.* Harvard Center for Community Health and Medical Care, Harvard University, 1972.

Feldstein, P. J. Research on demand for health services. In D. Mainland, (Ed.), *Health services research.* New York: Milbank, 1967, 128–165.

Ferman, L. A., Kornbluh, J. L., & Haber, A. (Eds.) *Poverty in America.* Ann Arbor: University of Michigan Press, 1965.

Fink, R., Shapiro, S., & Lewis, J. The reluctant participant in a breast cancer screening program. *Public Health Reports,* 1968, **83**, 479–490.

Foster, J. T. Neighborhood health centers: A new way to extend care. *Modern Hospital,* May, 1968, Vol. 110, No. 5, 95.

Gordon, J. B. The politics of community medicine projects: A conflict analysis. *Medical Care,* 1969, Vol. 7, No. 6, 419–428.

Graham, S. Socio-economic status, illness and the use of

medical services. *Milbank Memorial Fund Quarterly,* 1957, **35**, 58–66.

Harrington, M. *The other America.* New York: Macmillan, 1962.

Hinrichs, H. H., & Taylor, G. M. *Systematic analysis.* Pacific Palisades: Goodyear, 1972.

Johnson, L. Message on poverty to the Congress of the United States, March 16, 1964.

Kelly, J. Towards an ecological conception of preventive intervention. In J. Carter (Ed.), *Research contributions from psychology to community mental health.* New York: Behavioral Publications, 1968, 76 – 99.

Kent, J. A., & Smith, C. H. Involving the urban poor in health services through accommodation — The employment of neighborhood representatives. *American Journal of Public Health,* 1967, **57**, 997–1003.

Kiesler, F. Is this psychology? In S. Goldston (Ed.), *Concepts of community psychiatry.* Washington: U.S. Government Printing Office, 1965, 147–157.

Klarman, H., Francis, J. O'S., & Rosenthal, G. Application of cost effectiveness analysis to chronic kidney disease. *Medical Care,* 1968, Vol. 6, No. 1, 48–54.

Koos, E. L. *The health of regionsville: What the people thought and did about it.* New York: Columbia, 1954.

Kramer, C. Fragmented financing of health care. *Medical Care Review,* 1972, **29**, 8, 878–943.

Kutner, B. *Five hundred over sixty: A community survey on aging.* New York: Russell Sage, 1959.

Lewis, O. The culture of poverty. In P. Moynihan (Ed.), *Perspectives on poverty–I.* New York: Basic Books, 1968, 187 – 200.

Lipsky, M., & Lounds, M. Jr. *On some pathologies in recent social planning involving citizen participation: The case of health services.* Written for the Symposium on

Decision-Making and Control in Health Care, National Center for Health Services Research and Development, Rockville, Maryland, 1970.

Macdonald, D. Our invisible poor. *New Yorker,* January 19, 1965.

March, M. The neighborhood center concept. *Public Welfare,* January 1968, 97–111.

Mayhew, L., & Reiss, A. J. The social organization of legal contracts. *American Sociological Review,* 1969, **34**, 309–318.

Mechanic, D. Religion, religiosity and illness behavior: The special case of the Jews. *Human Organization,* 1963, **22**, 202–208.

Morris, J. N. *Uses of epidemiology.* Edinburgh: Livingstone, 1967.

Musgrave, R. A. *The theory of public finance.* New York: McGraw-Hill, 1959.

Notkin, H., & Notkin, M. S. Community participation in health services: A review article. *Medical Care Review,* 1970, **27**, (11), 1178–1201.

Organization for Social and Technical Innovation (OSTI). *Blindness services in the United States.* Cambridge, Mass.: OSTI Press, 1971.

Peck, H., Roman, M. S., & Kaplan, S. Community action programs and the comprehensive health center. In M. Greenblatt (Ed.), *Poverty and mental health.* Washington, D.C.: American Psychiatric Association, 1967, 103–121.

Piore, M. Jobs. In S. Beer & R. Barringer (Eds.), *The state and the poor.* Boston: Winthrop, 1970.

Piore, N. Rationalizing the mix of public and private expenditure in health. *Milbank Memorial Fund Quarterly,* 1968, **46**, Suppl., 167–170.

Rosenthal, G. *The demand for general hospital facilities.* Chicago: American Hospital Association, 1964.

Rosenthal, G. *Toward income adequacy.* New York: United Community Funds and Councils of America, 1968.

Rosenthal, G. Health care. In S. Beer & R. Barringer (Eds.), *The state and the poor.* Boston: Winthrop, 1970.

Rosenthal, G. Manpower policy: The role of the federal government. *American Behavorial Scientist,* May – June 1972, 697–711.

Rosenthal, G. *State financing of mental health services.* Prepared for Task Force on Financing of Mental Health Services, National Institute of Mental Health, 1973.

Roth, J. The treatment of the sick. In A. Antonovsky, J. Kosa, & I. Zola (Eds.), *Poverty and health: A sociological analysis.* Cambridge, Mass.: Harvard University Press, 1969, 214–243.

Rothenberg, J. *Cost-benefit analysis: A methodological exposition.* Prepared for Evaluation of Social Action Programs Conference; American Academy of Arts and Sciences, 1969.

Rothman, S. M. Other people's children: The day care experience in America. *The Public Interest,* 1973, No. 30, 11–27.

Schulberg, H. C. State planning for community mental health programs: Implications for psychologists. *Community Mental Health Journal,* 1965, **1**, 37–42.

Schulberg, H. C. The challenge of human service programs for psychologists. Published in *American Psychologist,* 1972, **27,** 566–573.

Scott, R. A. *The making of blind men.* New York: Russell Sage, 1969.

Silver, G. A. Role and function of federal health policy. *Journal of the American Podiatry Association,* 1969, **59**, 1–8.

Steiner, P. O. The public sector and the public interest. In R. H. Haveman & J. Margolis (Eds.), *Public Expenditures and policy analysis.* Chicago: Markham, 1970, Ch. 1.

Task Force on the Organization of Social Services.

Services for people. Final report. Washington: United States Department of Health, Education and Welfare, 1968.

Teele, J., & Levine, S. The acceptance of emotionally disturbed children by psychiatric agencies. In S. Wheeler (Ed.), *Controlling delinquents.* New York: Wiley, 1967.

United States Department of Health, Education and Welfare. *Delivery of health services for the poor: Program analysis, human investment programs,* 1967.

Warren, L. The decartelization of the human services. Unpublished manuscript, Florence Heller Graduate School of Social Welfare, Brandeis University. Undated.

Wilensky, J. L., & Lebeaux, C. M. *Industrial society and social welfare.* New York: Free Press, 1966.

Zbarowski, M. Cultural components in responses to pain. *Journal of Social Issues,* 1952, **8**, 16–30.

DEVELOPING HUMAN SERVICES IN NEW COMMUNITIES

by

Donald C. Klein, Ph.D.

Part 3 of *Developments in Human Services,* Volume II
Edited by
Herbert C. Schulberg, Ph.D.
and Frank Baker, Ph.D.

Library of Congress Catalog Number 74-9693
ISBN: 0-87705-172-0
Copyright © 1975 by Behavioral Publications, Inc.

BEHAVIORAL PUBLICATIONS, Inc.
72 Fifth Avenue
New York, New York 10011

Printed in the United States of America
56789   987654321

Library of Congress Cataloging in Publication Data

Klein, Donald C
    Developing human services in new communities.

    (Developments in human services, v. 2, pt. 3)
    Includes bibliographical references.
    1. Social service.   2. New towns.   3. Social
policy.   4. Community development.   I. Title.
II. Series. [DNLM: 1. Social planning—Social
service. HV40 K64d 1974]
[HV40.K48]   361   74-9693

Contents

Part III: DEVELOPING HUMAN SERVICES IN NEW COMMUNITIES

DONALD C. KLEIN

Acknowledgments

Many people in Columbia, Maryland and other new communities have served as the faculty for the crash course which resulted in this publication. Among them were my colleagues in the NTL Community Research and Action Laboratory; Tom Wilson, the former manager of the Columbia Parks and Recreation Association, and his senior administrative staff; Leo Molinaro, President of the American City Corporation, and several of his associates; Claude McKinney, former Director of the Urban Life Center, and its member organizations; Wallace Hamilton, John Levering, Peter King, and Peter Wastie, all of whom played key roles in the institutional development process of Columbia; Morton Hoppenfeld, the chief planner responsible for giving form and substance to the dream of a comprehensive new city to be built on the rolling farm land and forests of central Maryland; Shirley Weiss and other staff members of the Center for Urban and Regional Studies of the University of North Carolina at Chapel Hill; Floyd McKissick and members of his Soul City development team; Stanley Murrell and the other NewCom Planners of the University of Louisville Urban Studies Center; the President and other staff members of the Irvine Corporation; Royce Hanson, New Communities Study Center, Reston, Virginia; and members of the Twin Oaks community in Louisa, Virginia.

I am especially grateful to the following friends whose detailed criticisms of an earlier draft were incisive and helpful: Morton Hoppenfeld, John Levering, Stanley Murrell, Charles Simpkinson, and Shirley Weiss.

This study draws heavily on the experiences of developer James Rouse and the Rouse Company staff in what they call "the Columbia process." Without Jim Rouse's creative optimism the new town movement in the United States today would be greatly diminished; without his emphasis on human services as essential components of new communities, the social input in new town planning would be much less visible. I acknowledge with special appreciation his personal cordiality towards me and the work of the NTL project in Columbia.

Preface

Widespread inadequacies in the human condition and concern for the difficulties and complexities of existing social arrangements have resulted in urgent pressures on professionals to revise present care giving mechanisms. Human service programs such as multi-service centers, which incorporate a wide variety of relevant services, are emerging as an alternative framework to the existing pattern of rigid, categorical services for meeting the bio-psycho-social needs of individuals and populations.

The editors of this series are developing materials which can serve as guideposts for those newly entering or already engaged in the field of human services. A flexible approach to the production and distribution of these materials has been devised. The series periodically publishes indepth discussions and reviews on the following human service topics:

> Emerging conceptual frameworks of human services such as systems and ecological principles.
>
> Administrative and planning tools such as information systems, economic strategies, and legal mechanisms.
>
> Innovative service programs within new organizational models and new communities.
>
> Educational programs for changing professional roles and new manpower requirements.

After several years, those who are standing-order subscribers will possess an encyclopedic library of human

services in either hardbound volumes or softcover separates.

Volumes I and II contain an introductory overview by the editors, substantive sections on different human service topics, and a comprehensive index. Each of the substantive sections, without introductory overview and index, is available as a separate.

Volume I

Teaching Health and Human Services Administration by the Case Method—Linda G. Sprague, Alan Sheldon, M.D., and Curtis P. McLaughlin, D.B.A.

The Planning and Administration of Human Services—Harold W. Demone, Jr., Ph.D. and Dwight Harshbarger, Ph.D.

Strategies in Innovative Human Service Programs —Harry Gottesfeld, Ph.D., Florence Lieberman, D.S.W., Sheldon R. Roen, Ph.D., and Sol Gordon, Ph.D.

Developments in Human Services Education and Manpower—Robert M. Vidaver, M.D.

Volume II

Developing Program Models for the Human Services —Mark Lawrence, M.D.

Economics of Human Services—Gerald Rosenthal, Ph.D.

Developing Human Services in New Communities —Donald Klein, Ph.D.

The Editors

1. Introduction

The planning and development of new communities is an undertaking designed for inverse paranoiacs . . . those blessed individuals who see the promise in every possibility, the opportunity in every crisis, and the inevitability of every desired outcome. During the past few years I have hobnobbed with a number of such individuals, including developers, institutional designers, social planners, and managers engaged in the complex process of new town design and implementation. Invariably they have impressed me with their optimism, pragmatism, and practical wisdom.

This study is not written for my new friends and colleagues in new town development, though some of them may find something new and useful in a behavioral scientist's view of their field. Rather, it is addressed primarily to psychologists, sociologists, and other students of human behavior who are asking themselves what contributions their knowledge and approaches can make to environmental design generally and new community development specifically.

I write this study in the hopes that increasing numbers of applied behavioral scientists will be drawn to the exciting field of social planning. Since the latter draws on individuals from varied backgrounds and disciplines, it is important for me to define the field as I see it — not because my definition should be considered definitive but rather to make explicit, insofar as possible, the bias which shapes my selection of material and emphasis.

Social planning for me involves the deliberate allocation of resources (including territorial, fiscal, and human) within the community so that the needs and aspirations of individuals, families, and other groupings for a high quality of life will be realized. It embraces the design of social institutions and of those processes that will enable citizens to achieve significance within the community. It includes provision of preventive, remedial, and rehabilitative resources that are readily accessible to all residents at all stages of the life cycle, and it encompasses a concern for the social values to be realized by designing communities that are safe, supportive, and dignifying for people of diverse backgrounds and lifestyles. It includes attention both to the design and implementation of institutions and the delivery of resources in the context of a comprehensive view of the entire community, its geographic region, and its linkages to resources at other levels (e.g., state and national). Social planning is a means whereby providers of resources, potential users and existing clientele, administrators, and policy-makers can integrate their separate perspectives in the design of human service delivery systems for the community.

Like many another concerned with developing environments that would nurture the best in human beings, I was attracted to the new towns movement because of its potential for creating aesthetically stunning, technologically sophisticated, humane communities for large numbers of people, rich and poor alike. A few years later I view the movement more realistically and with greatly lowered expectations. It is not the salvation for urban ills; it is one of several thrusts towards a long overdue confrontation of our grievous deficits in housing, physical safety, and social-psychological supports for most citizens in our affluent society.

Between June 1971 and July 1972 my wife and I undertook during a self-designed sabbatical to visit a variety of individuals and groups involved in one way or another with community development. We had just spent a year intimately involved with the new town of Columbia, Maryland where I had established an in-community consulting, training, and research center under the aegis of NTL Institute for Applied Behavioral Science. The year in Columbia had been an exciting one for us, full of learning and new experiences; it had left us almost totally drained, in need of rest and a chance to get perspective on all that had occurred.

IMAGES OF COMMUNITY

One of our first stops during the wanderyear was at Twin Oaks in Louisa, Virginia, an intentional community based on the principles laid down by B. F. Skinner in his famous utopian volume *Walden Two* (1948). Consider the contrast between Columbia, Maryland and Twin Oaks, Virginia! Both are preplanned ventures in community development, both were launched at approximately the same time, and both are considered by their developers to be some kind of response to the troubles of today's society. Columbia boggles the mind of a behavioral scientist accustomed to thinking in units of two-person relationships, small group interaction, or even complex industrial and other organizations. It sits on 14,000 acres or 21 square miles of land (more than Manhattan Island); in six years it has grown from woods and farmland to a budding city occupied by 30,000 people living in four villages; and it is expected to reach a capacity population of 110,000 by 1980. It is an incipient city which struggles to develop a sense of community among its residents despite their diversities of race, class, and age.

Twin Oaks in late 1971 numbered 34 people living in a few communal structures on about 120 acres of farmland. It began with eight settlers five years ago; it looks towards a capacity population of perhaps 1,000 — someday. It is a commune struggling to develop the economic base, diversity of activity, and constancy of population which would indicate that it had indeed become a viable community. It already has a sense of community reflected in the cohesiveness of its members (Kinkade, 1973).

As 15 of us sat in an Iroquois sweat house built by Twin Oaks residents I thought briefly of the many task forces, work groups, advisory bodies, and village boards which gather in Columbia during any typical week. Our sweat, our common nakedness, the ritual of each in turn splashing water on the hot stones to create steam brought us close together in our humanness. How much feeling of fellowship and empathy were embodied in the busier rituals and work structures of Columbia, structures which, in their own way, were supposed to create a kind of consensus out of diversity?

I was faced with the inexorable juxtaposition of two prevalent images of community: on the one hand, the primary social affinity grouping bonded together by commonalities of background, values, commitments, experiences, and life styles, not to mention a very real physical and psychological interdependence; on the other hand, the highly complex macrosystem that is the geographic community of today, which performs prodigious feats of providing—however imperfectly—food, clothing, shelter, physical protection against marauders of various sorts, education, normative guidance, health care, and recreation as well as opportunities for self-enhancement and personal significance in the eyes of others.

It was self-evident that Columbia could not possibly develop a technologically sophisticated macrosystem and also be capable of the primary affinity bonds of Twin Oaks. I was not even sure, for that matter, that Skinner's dream of a utopian community could be realized if Twin Oaks succeeded in its aspiration of growing to 1,000. I felt equally convinced that Columbia would fail in its aspiration of providing a high quality of life for its residents if it did not strive to adapt every bit of modern social and behavioral technology for that purpose. However successful Columbia and other new cities might be in solving the economic and physical problems involved in large-scale city building, they would fall short of my goal for them if they did not also create human-scale opportunities for achieving the intimacy, security, and growth-producing potentials afforded by the primary community.

We left Twin Oaks convinced that the task of new city developers was immense. For in Twin Oaks itself we discovered virtually all the basic cleavages which, if not attended to in any human settlement, become the basis for polarization and conflict. By adopting Skinner's labor credits system, the Twin Oaks planners had installed a structure which prevented many of the occupational inequities which plague our society. They had also eliminated virtually all manifestations of sexism in work assignments, allocation of power, and community recognition. Nevertheless, in spite of the most favorable assets of small size, simple physical environment, and beneficent social inventions, there were worms of loneliness, alienation, suspicion, and mistrust of authority gnawing at the Eden's apples. If Twin Oaks faced such problems, what could be expected in Columbia and the dozens of other new cities to be developed in the United States by the year 2000?

2. *What Is Meant by Human Services?*

It should be emphasized at the outset that I am defining human services in such a way as to go well beyond the traditional limits of health, education, and welfare. The more involved I became in thinking about new towns, the more convinced I was that *planning for human services must take into account all those physical and social arrangements which affect significantly the physical safety, personal security, problem-solving capabilities, and social significance of the community's residents.* By this definition, an effectively functioning, humane police force and law enforcement system is a crucial human service. I agree entirely with the underlying philosophy which led one group of planners to propose that in their new town public safety be merged with and responsible to public health authorities! (Urban Studies Center, 1971).

PHYSICAL ASPECTS OF HUMAN SERVICES

There are innumerable aspects of the physical environment which have direct relevance for human services. Most obvious is the need for well-designed specialized structures that do the job they are supposed to do. Failures of design can have serious detrimental effects on the functioning of human service institutions. For example, I recently was told by a teacher about the exciting new open-school design elementary building in

251

a Massachusetts town which could not function as intended because the architects had failed to introduce adequate sound control.

Also obvious, but often strangely overlooked, is the need to locate a service facility so that it is readily accessible to those whom it is supposed to serve. As Columbia grows, for example, I believe it will be important to augment the downtown hospital and clinics center with satellite health stations of some sort located in at least some of the villages so as to reduce the need for families with children as well as handicapped individuals to make the trip downtown to the combined hospital-clinic facility. Availability of public transportation, the amount of time required, and the cost of a trip to various facilities directly influence utilization patterns.

A physical environment which provides well-designed tot lots readily accessible to small children and their parents, which designs foot paths enabling pedestrians to avoid busy thoroughfares, and which facilitates joyous gatherings of people in protected malls, plazas, or cul-de-sacs is an essential part of its community's human services.

There are also requirements of specific groups for a *barrier-free environment* which responds to their special needs. For example, a community which builds houses, office buildings, shops, and other structures with long, steep staircases and other obstacles to easy pedestrian movement is failing to provide an essential human service for elderly, feeble, and otherwise physically handicapped people. One of the arguments for enclaves of houses, shops, and other facilities for elderly, retired people is that such environments can be designed with ramps, elevators, handrails, and other features specifically tailored to their special needs. It is possible to design entire barrier-free communities which will make unnecessary the segregation of elderly and handicapped persons.

Easily overlooked in the physical design of new communities is the provision of *low-cost space* for use by informal, noncommercial, or small entrepreneurial groups intent on doing their thing in the interests of arts and crafts, music or other entertainment, learning activities, flea markets, and the great variety of activities which in existing communities can readily find inexpensive quarters in deserted stores, lofts, rundown homes, and the like. Such space is essential if individuals and groups are to have genuine opportunities to express themselves, learn, and use their talents in growth-promoting ways outside the framework of nine to five employment. Youth activities especially lend themselves to do-it-yourself space which either is available for free or at a fee well below the six dollars a square foot which is usual in Columbia's office buildings.

Then there are the *unexpected demands on space* as leisure time and other activity patterns change with the times. A current example is the rapidly growing need in new towns for storage space for boats, trailers, campers, and motor homes which cannot be left in front of homes or parked in cul-de-sacs.

There is also growing recognition of the value of creating a do-it-yourself approach to the use of space. Neighborhood play areas for school-age children, for example, can be designed so as to provide opportunities for users and their parents to dig, build, and create play structures of their own rather then depending totally on prebuilt and fully installed facilities.

Temporary structures also play a part in new town designs for human services. It is important wherever possible to build not for the ages but for the short-term future, especially in the case of new towns whose full development requires from 10 to 20 years or more. Whereas at one time it is enough for a village to have a single community room, five years later it may require a complex of community facilities for meetings of various kinds, teenage activities, and a branch library. I foresee increasing experimentation with temporary structures of various kinds (such as prebuilt structures, modular units, mobile buildings that can be installed or removed in a day by a trained crew, and inflatable structures). Whatever the technology, it is necessary to have space that can be modified, enlarged, and moved in order to accommodate to the shifting human service needs in virtually any area. In this way valuable land can maintain its productivity in human as well as economic terms.

Finally, there are physical resources having to do with *establishing meaningful communication* among residents and between citizens and authorities. Cable TV has the potentiality for two-way communication and special public affairs programming; it is not unusual now for the cable to be put in place routinely as part of the utilities of the new town. Bulletin boards in strategic spots in neighborhoods, village centers, and gathering places of all kinds can be a useful aid for informing and involving residents. In Columbia group mail boxes were installed on each residential block so that neighbors would have at least one occasion each day to be in contact with one another without special invitation or prearrangement.

THE SCOPE OF HUMAN SERVICES

Human services embrace physical and institutional resources for:

1. meeting individuals' needs and aspirations in such a way as to promote optimal growth and development;

2. enabling people to live together in families and other primary groupings so that they enjoy mutual support, economic stability, sexual fulfillment, and pleasure and companionship in the use of leisure time; and so that

they can respond appropriately to the needs of children for whom they accept responsibility;

3. facilitating the efforts of individuals and groups to cope with the many problems and challenges faced during the average lifetime; and

4. dealing with community problems and forestalling them when possible; fostering leadership; making it possible for residents to participate effectively in community decisions; facilitating understanding across barriers of race, culture, age, and class; and providing suitable ways for the community to marshall resources as needed to develop additional human services.

It becomes clear that the matrix of human services must include institutional efforts to provide high-quality resources in such areas as education, health, and safety (including mental health), spiritual institutions, and leisure time facilities. Additional specialized resources also should be required in such areas as: a broad spectrum of full- and part-time child care services, such as day-care centers, family day-care homes, nursery schools, and hourly day-care services; resources for vocational training, job counseling, and job placement; and facilities for disposal of the dead.

Another sort of human service, described more fully in later sections, provides the array of resources which are intended to facilitate problem solving, development of new services, and conflict resolution within the community. Cable television, computer systems, techniques for easy data collection about residents' needs and attitudes, as well as the services of skilled community development specialists and action-researchers might become the components of such a resource center.

Finally, there are the opportunities provided within the governance system of the community as well as within the policy boards and working groups associated with the human service institutions for meaningful participation in the community's affairs. These, too, fall within the broader scope of human services. For without the excitement of participation and challenge, including controversy and even conflict, there is for some people no joie-de-vivre and little to life but dusty existence.

3. What Is a New Community?

SCALE AND COMPREHENSIVENESS

The term new community (or new town) as used in this study refers to a large-scale development that is comprehensively planned as a unified whole so as to provide, in addition to housing, all or most of the services and amenities required to sustain life and provide for the needs of its inhabitants. Attention is paid to providing opportunities for employment, education, the creative use of leisure time, and health maintenance. The scale of new town development makes it possible to use modern construction technologies in imaginative new ways while, at the same time, being efficient enough to provide housing at a cost most people can afford. The fact that most new community developments are carried out in a preplanned, comprehensive fashion also makes it possible to think of facilities and services as a totality rather than in isolated, fragmented ways.

LOGIC OF TECHNOLOGY

The development of new towns follows logically and inexorably from the fact that technology now makes it possible to erect thousands of housing units rapidly while, at the same time, chewing up thousands of acres of precious land. Left to the forces of the marketplace alone, the new housing technologies can only continue to cover the landscape with suburban tracts exacerbating even further the already acute problems of urban sprawl. Some means must be found to harness the technologies more creatively. New town development is one such means. In a *Saturday Review* special supplement on new towns Myron Lieberman (1971) put it this way:

> Erecting thousands of housing units within a relatively compact area leads to chaos when construction is not integrated with industry, education, transportation, health services, and other life-support systems. Such coordination is part of the logic of new-community development [p. 20].

TYPES OF NEW TOWNS

New community developments already underway or on the drawing board in the United States vary in size, comprehensiveness, and relationship to existing urban areas. Some, like Columbia and nearby Reston in Virginia, are *satellite developments*. They are within commuting distance of a metropolitan center while remaining separate from it. They are not primarily dependent on it for employment, health care, or other goods and services. Nevertheless, they benefit from what the metropolitan center has to offer, not the least of which is a supply of prospective home buyers seeking the varied amenities of city life without the disadvantages of dirt, noise, and crime.

Peripheral new towns, by contrast, resemble much more closely the suburban communities whose housing tracts are familiar to most people. They lie within a metropolitan region and their residents are more apt than those of the satellite new town to commute to the city for employment, entertainment, shopping, and the like. Foster City, located alongside the Bay near San Francisco, is an example of a peripheral new town.

New towns in-town represent an attempt to apply the

concepts of scale and comprehensiveness to substantial substandard or unused tracts of land within the city. For example, the abandoned site of the former training school for boys in Washington, D. C. has been earmarked to become Ft. Lincoln new town. There is also the possibility of experimenting with *paired new town development,* that is, a peripheral or satellite community on the fringe of the metropolitan area linked by rapid transit, shared use of facilities, and even common governance to a twin development in-town. The nonprofit Metropolitan Fund of Detroit recently gathered a team of economists, ecologists, architects, and social scientists to relate new community building and the inner city (Lawson, 1971). They developed plans to pair up as many as ten new towns in undeveloped suburban areas with counterpart sections downtown. Twenty to forty miles apart from one another, they would be paired up politically, socially, and economically, linked by rapid transit systems, and governed by the same officials. Their children would be sent to the same school system and they would share recreational and other human services.

The purest example of new town—and also the rarest in the United States for reasons which will become apparent later — is the so-called *freestanding, self-contained,* or *autonomous community* which lies well beyond the commuting radius of any other city and whose citizens must depend on its own resources for employment and all other provisions. One such freestanding new city in the United States, currently being developed, is Lake Havasu City in Arizona. It received considerable national publicity recently when its developer imported one of London's bridges stone by stone and erected it as a kind of promotional Eiffel Tower designed to attract the curious, some of whom might remain to reside or even establish businesses. Another freestanding new city has been designed for a poor section of rural northern

North Carolina by former director of CORE Floyd McKissick. Located in a largely black county, Soul City is intended to become a multiracial city which reflects the needs and lifestyles of urban black families attracted to it from Harlem and other established black settlements as well as rural blacks who, it is expected, will find the new city a more congenial urban environment than Detroit, New York, Chicago, or other end points in their move towards urbanization. Whereas Lake Havasu City began with an ideal area for water-based recreation and a climate suitable for retirement couples, Soul City has little to offer besides the relatively flat, worn out farmland and scrub growth of a large plantation that for years has been economically marginal. Lake Havasu City already has one major industry, which turns out the McCulloch chain saws of its developer. Soul City has no industry and must find ways to attract, more or less simultaneously, both the shops and the people to man them.

Freestanding new communities, especially those designed to meet the needs of unskilled laborers, blacks and other minority groups, and rural poor, have an uncertain future in the marketplace economy of the United States. In other countries it has been possible for governmental authorities to combine comprehensive planning with the power to bring together major industrial and commercial facilities and their employees within new communities designed to relieve overcrowding of nearby cities. It is unlikely that government in this country will have such power to implement far-reaching social designs within the next decade or so. It is hoped that government loan guarantees and partial subsidization of planning and development costs will make it possible for Soul City and other such socially relevant and daring projects to be implemented successfully.

COSTS OF DEVELOPMENT

The costs of new town development are prodigious. There is, first of all, the matter of land acquisition — it cost about 25 million dollars to secure the initial land for Columbia. Once the land has been purchased it must be made ready to receive houses and other structures. This means sewers, electrical and gas connections, roads, provision for drainage, water supply — all of the basic physical improvements without which even the smallest settlement remains uninhabitable. Only a few individual entrepreneurs, corporate developers, and investment groups are in a position to bring together the capital required to finance purchase of land and to develop and pay taxes on it while it lies idle during the years required to move from land acquisition to settlement. The jargon of new town development refers to "front-end" costs, which in the case of Columbia so far amount to something like 85 million dollars. No wonder that a leading urban economist stated in *Saturday Review* (Downs, 1971) that creating new cities is an extraordinarily risky form of private investment, probably the riskiest of all.

NEW TOWNS AND URBAN POLICY

And yet, despite the costs and limitations inherent in our political and social ideology, the United States has inexorably inched its way towards a national urban policy that appears to be counting heavily on new town construction. Between 1970 and the year 2000, it is generally estimated, we must somehow accommodate an additional hundred million people in the United States. This is the equivalent of a new city of 250,000 every month!

Simultaneously we face the task of rebuilding inner cities, making it possible for disadvantaged groups to enjoy decent housing, including helping large numbers of them move out of impacted central city areas.

It seems obvious that private enterprise alone cannot even begin to do the job. In 1970, for example, the Department of Housing and Urban Development surveyed the field and found that only 63 large developments, few of them genuine new towns, had been completed or undertaken in the United States since 1947 (Department of HUD, 1970). There was good reason to believe that, without massive governmental involvement of some kind, we would fall far short of even the most modest objectives predicated on actual need.

In England, where the new town movement began, the government has broad powers to act under the New Towns Act of 1946. The British have also passed laws prohibiting expansion of older cities beyond certain boundaries. Moreover, industry is subsidized to locate away from major urban areas. British new towns have two major objectives: first, to provide places for the growing population to live and work; second, to relieve the pressure on major cities, principally London and Glasgow. Thirty new towns have been built in Great Britain since 1946, on the average more comprehensively organized and on a far larger scale than their U.S. counterparts.

FEDERAL NEW TOWNS LEGISLATION

Efforts to involve the Federal government in new town development bore first fruit in 1968 when Congress included Title IV in that year's Housing and Urban Development Act enabling a limited number of private developers to secure Federal guarantees for their loans and obligations. By 1970 support for new community development as a major feature of national urban policy had grown considerably. Earlier fears that new towns would constitute only cosmetically superior versions of suburbia had been allayed. Large-scale new town development could also be applied to inner cities, thus causing mayors of major cities to throw their support in favor of Federal legislation. The result was the Urban Growth and New Community Development Act of 1970 which undertakes to assist new large-scale developments by both public and private developers in several ways:

1. Federal guarantees backing debt obligations for land acquisition, initial development, and the installation of utilities; up to 50 million dollars per development.

2. loans to cover interest payments on money borrowed to finance front-end costs;

3. public service grants to local governments to help pay for essential public services which must be in place before a large-scale new development is fully settled and able to provide an adequate tax base;

4. planning grants to public developers to fund up to two-thirds of their planning costs, together with a provision enabling Federal payment of two-thirds of any special costs for private developers planning comprehensive new developments rather than the usual housing tracts;

5. special supplemental funds added onto 13 existing Federal programs when used in connection with new cities approved by the Department of Housing and Urban Development (among the programs eligible for supplementary grants are: the Hill-Burton formula grants to state and local agencies and private nonprofit organizations for construction, expansion, and modernization of health facilities; grants to state library extension agencies for construction of public libraries; grants for construction of facilities for community colleges, technical institutes, private colleges, and public institu-

tions for higher education; and neighborhood facilities grants for the development of multiservice neighborhood centers);

6. provisions for technical assistance to developers and for carrying out large-scale new community development demonstration projects as models for such development on Federal surplus land, if so authorized by the President and funded specifically by Congress.

The 1970 Act, which supersedes Title IV of 1968, also makes some progress in setting forth a set of social goals for new communities receiving loan guarantees (Dept. of HUD, 1971). The Act specifies that a new community development program is eligible for assistance only if:

1. it provides an alternative to disorderly urban growth or improves conditions in established communities so as to help reverse migration from existing cities or rural areas;

2. it will be served by adequate public, community, and commercial facilities, including facilities needed for educational, health, and social services, recreation, and transportation;

3. it makes substantial provision for housing within the means of persons of low and moderate income, such housing to constitute "an appropriate proportion" of the community's housing supply.

As of January 1974 sixteen projects in ten states had received Federal commitments for loan guarantees totalling 325 million dollars. At least twenty-four other new community projects were at some stage of the process of seeking Federal backing.

4. Who Develops New Communities?

A unique combination of talents, imagination, energy, and resources is required for the successful development of large-scale comprehensive new cities. The history of the new towns movement is marked throughout by a fascinating combination of lofty social purpose, magnificent dreams, comprehensive concern for the welfare of man, and followthrough that is frequently flawed. It is not surprising to find it so. To conceive of the development of a total city designed to provide a high quality of life for its citizens, numbering from 50,000 to one million, is indeed to dream the magnificent dream. To carry that dream through the detailed stages of design, land acquisition, development, marketing, and termination of the developer's role requires a kind of practical wisdom and breadth of competence that few dreamers possess. Profit and loss sheets, especially the latter, have a way of modifying humane social goals, as the developer of Reston discovered when financial reverses coupled with inadequate capitalization and insufficient organizational depth made it necessary for him to relinquish control to Gulf Oil Company, which had supplied much of the front-end money. Moreover, few large-scale developments can be autonomously erected in completely isolated areas where there are no hostages to fortune in the way of constraints imposed by local governments, planning bodies, and boards, whose cooperation is essential, or in the way of pressures created by the fears or pre-judices of those already living in the area to be "new-towned."

THE ORIGINAL DREAMER

The originator of the new town movement, Ebenezer Howard, who wrote his first treatise on the subject in 1898, found that his influence was markedly reduced when it came time to build Letchworth, the new town near London stimulated by him (Buder, 1969). Howard himself was the prototype of a long and honored list of urban reformers, in whose ranks James Rouse, the developer of Columbia, should be included. In a recent interview (Rosenthal, 1971) Rouse speaks of "the generating power of solutions." He means that if people understand what a city can be, that is, if they have a believable vision backed by the necessary financial and technical sinews, then genuine urban solutions, not band aids, will be forthcoming. Howard, too, combined a basically optimistic view of human nature with the excitement over the potentials for human betterment held out by science and technology shared by many of his enlightened contemporaries. He saw urban growth as no longer essential for industrial development because of recent developments in rapid intercity transportation. Therefore, he proposed a cluster of eight garden cities of about 30,000 population apiece, thus combining the human scale and social contact of the small town with the diversity and other economic and cultural advantages of the large city. Most of the new communities developed in Great Britain and the United States since Howard's time have, in one form or another, followed his basic model. Typical in this country were the Greenbelt communities sponsored by the Federal government which unfortunately after World War II were allowed to become little more than suburban developments.

THE ROLE OF PRIVATE ENTERPRISE

Whereas in Europe modern new town development is largely in the hands of public corporations and other governmental bodies, in the United States it has so far largely been the domain of far-sighted private enterprise. These latter have consisted primarily of three types: *private developers*, such as Rouse and Simon, assisted by large-scale financing from banks, insurance companies, or other corporate bodies; *holders of large land tracts*, such as the Irvine Company, which is currently well into the development of a new city of 400,000 people in Orange County between Los Angeles and San Diego on the site of the gigantic Spanish landgrant Irvine Ranch; and *large industrial corporations* interested in translating their engineering and complex systems knowhow into the potentially profitable urban development field.

If new towns are to meet the social goals of economic and racial mix, it appears unlikely that private enterprise by itself will be able to do the job. As already noted, the financial risks are enormous even in the case of those developers engaged in expansion of existing towns or in establishing peripheral and satellite communities within metropolitan areas where the demand for housing can be expected to be great. There are exceptions, notably that of Irvine, which is being built on land already owned by the Irvine Ranch and is in such an affluent area of rapid population expansion and industrialization that it can finance most of its extensive development on the basis of current income. But Irvine exemplifies the kind of new town derided by those who are concerned about the social and housing needs of low income and minority groups. It is, for the most part, a lovely community of middle income, affluent whites, spotted only occasionally by an Asian or black face, or a Spanish surname.

THE ROLE OF GOVERNMENT

I believe that certain of the necessary services of new communities, most notably transportation and the human services with which this study is concerned, cannot be developed and maintained on a pay-as-you-go basis, not, that is, if they are to be readily available to the least affluent within the new city. I will go further into this matter later on. At this point the matter of financing is being raised in order to offer another argument in favor of the European model of more direct involvement of governmental bodies in new town development.

Some progress is being made in this regard. Several states have passed new town enabling legislation and a few have authorized creation of *public development corporations* for the purpose of managing and planning community development programs of various kinds. The New York State Urban Development Corporation is already engaged in creating at least three new communities and reportedly has two more under consideration. Established in 1968, the Corporation is headed by one of the most able and energetic urban planners in government today, Edward Logue. The mission of the Corporation (Logue, 1971, p. 28) is "to bring a comprehensive approach to the problems of urban deterioration, economic stagnation, unemployment, shortage of housing, and lack of civic facilities." The Corporation has broad powers as well as responsibilities, including the ability to issue its own bonds as a means of raising funds.

There are those who believe that the Federal government should itself become directly involved in new town projects, because, it is argued, only the Government would be in a position to mount massive projects on the order of the Tennessee Valley Authority by commanding the financial resources and manpower on the scale necessary to meet the growing need. If the Government were to engage in city building, it would not be the first time—witness Los Alamos, Oak Ridge, some TVA communities, and, of course, Washington, D. C. itself. But there is a vast difference between creating so-called single-purpose communities as a means of achieving some objective for which there is general consensus and moving the Federal government into the large-scale social planning required for locating, designing, and building multipurpose new towns anywhere in the country. In this day and age, marked by a movement to return governmental initiative to the States, direct Federal intervention in new town development is unlikely. We must wait to see whether current revenue-sharing programs lead to adequate state involvement in new towns. I am not optimistic. However desirable it may be to stimulate local initiative in dealing with local concerns, the needs of existing localities will probably take precedence over the use of such funds for building new communities.

THE NEW TOWN DEVELOPMENT TEAM

Whether under government or private aegis, new town planning and implementation requires the coordinated effort of teams of people to carry out the project over many years—from its original conception, through land acquisition, design, negotiation with public authorities in regard to zoning and other matters, creation of the infrastructure, social and institutional planning, land sales, building, marketing, and management of the community during a long period of settlement. Engineers, architects, physical and social planners, specialists in finance, systems analysts, economists, investment bankers, lawyers, housing technologists, experts in transportation, institutional developers, city management specialists, recreation workers, child care experts, educators, and health workers—all these and more have played a part, for example, in the development of Columbia. What makes it possible for such a diverse set of groups to work together successfully? My observations and discussions with members of the Rouse Company staff suggest at least three major factors: (1) a set of clearly articulated objectives having to do with what a new city could be; (2) disciplined use of a carefully developed and repeatedly updated economic model; and (3) the leadership of the principal developer himself.

The first factor, possibly the most important of all, requires a set of *social goals* for the community and a simple conviction that, if the goals are worthwhile, it is only logical to suppose that reasonable people will see to it that they are attained. As one member of the Rouse group put it, the goals need to be simply stated and concrete; the consequences of their attainment must be clearly spelled out in advance (Molinaro, 1971). That is, it is important to make clear not only where the community building effort is going but what difference it will make if it gets there. "We must try to detail in advance what their achievement will mean in terms of how we live, play, work, rest, communicate, raise our families, worship, organize, politic, and dissent [Molinaro, 1971, p. 31]."

To monitor such a complex and far-flung enterprise through its successive phases over a period of a decade or more it is necessary to have a detailed model which enables the planner and his staff to track progress, anticipate the consequences of alterations in one aspect on all other aspects of the project, and determine at any phase whether or not changes must be made in any facet of the overall design. Columbia's development has been monitored by an *economic model* which indicates how things are going at any moment in time in profit and loss terms. The economic model indicates at what rate land sales to builders must occur, how much money is to be spent on roads and other basic physical improvements in a given time period, what funds are available to the manager of Columbia for recreation programs; it enables the developer to determine whether he is on schedule in debt retirement, whether the cash flow is adequate to balance over time the enormous initial investment by dint of income ultimately received from appreciation of land values. The model is updated on the basis of actual performance and revised projections every three months. It enables the coordinators of each aspect of the project to have a clear idea of the financial resources at their disposal, the obligations they can incur, and the results they must come up with in order to keep the entire development on target.

As we shall discuss more fully later on, Columbia, along with all other new town developments, to my knowledge, suffers from having to rely solely on an economic model for tracking both its physical and social development. There is urgent need for an equally detailed evocative model of development for social institutions and services, which takes into account both the immediate and long-term human as well as economic costs and benefits of such social development.

Finally, there is the developer himself who, in certain important respects, embodies the new community. He is, of course, the carrier of the ultimate authority for the project and, like all corporate presidents and institutional heads, it is in his hands to make decisions and to delegate responsibilities to various of his subordinates. In the case of the new city he is also the *carrier of the dream.*

He presides over the creation of the community much as a composer weaving the melodies of his mind into a fully orchestrated composition.

From their memoirs I have observed that heads of state and foreign ministers place much reliance on assessment of their counterparts' mentality, sincerity, and skill, as much as or even more than on their analysis of the larger geopolitical matters with which they grapple. This personalization of international (and also national and local) politics is often noticeable as the new city develops. Columbia to many of the old residents of Howard County, in which it is being built, is James Rouse. If one can believe in his sincerity and competence, one can rest easier about the ultimate impact of this massive invasion of one's rural turf. It is the same with many of the early settlers of Columbia itself. It is my impression that not only did they buy the concept of "building a new America" (Columbia's slogan), they also vested their trust in Rouse himself as the carrier of their joint dreams.

As the new community moves beyond the early settlement phase, however, I suspect that management and authority both must shift from the father-developer to a more mundane and possibly bureaucratic leadership system. Informal contacts with the developer no longer occur so readily. Managers of various structures within the community become interposed between residents and the developer. If the developer intervenes in day-to-day affairs, there occurs an increasing sense of strain between the carrier of the dream (the developer) and the implementers of the reality (the managers). Thus, part of the genius of new community development is knowing when and how to withdraw the personal aspects of the developer's leadership.

5. Do Opportunities Exist for Social Innovation?

DREAMS AND REALITIES

On first blush, the new town appears to be an ideal proving ground for social as well as physical innovation. It should be a veritable world of tomorrow, bringing into being the cities of the future which catch the imagination of visitors to international expositions. The fact is that there is no Habitat in Columbia or, so far as I know, in any other new town. There are no moving sidewalks . . . yet; no covered, climate-controlled downtowns . . . yet; no housing areas served by catered food services . . . yet; no two-way cable television systems capable of putting each citizen in direct touch with the governing bodies of his community . . . yet; no comprehensive, computerized, health-maintaining, multiservice human resource center available in each neighborhood . . . yet.

There are no moving sidewalks but there is in Columbia a system of rights of way (still undeveloped for lack of funds) for a transit system connecting villages to downtown. There is no covered downtown but there is an in-town covered shopping mall which, with its massive asphalt parking area, dominates a large part of Columbia's downtown; there is no catered food service but there were Seven-Eleven type food stores in each of Columbia's neighborhoods,* which consist of about

*not all of which have succeeded financially.

4,000 people; there is no two-way cable TV system but there are plans for cable television (postponed temporarily because of requirements established by Howard County government) to provide several channels for local public service use; there is no ultimate human resource center but there is a prepaid medical plan and hospital available to all residents who can afford to subscribe and wish to do so.

COLUMBIA: THE COMMUNITY AS INNOVATION

The major innovation of the new town is the new town itself, that is, the comprehensive development of a community in such a way as to relate physical and social planning to one another and on a sufficiently large scale to make available the array of basic services needed to sustain life and meet other basic needs. There are few aesthetic, technological, or social revolutions forthcoming from the new communities now being developed. Instead, new town developers are more apt to select and adapt on a community-wide scale physical and social technologies already demonstrated elsewhere.

The result is that, with few exceptions, today's new towns appear on the surface to be little more than well manicured, tastefully laid out examples of the best from existing suburban areas and medium-sized communities. It was only after I learned to look beyond superficial considerations of house design and architectural style that I came to appreciate and sometimes even savor the social innovations which, from the developer's viewpoint, are embodied in Columbia.

Columbia is laid out on the basis of so-called *overlapping communities* widely used in European new towns. The basic unit for purposes of physical and social planning is the *neighborhood*, which is organized around a service center containing a small food store open from early morning to late at night, an elementary school, a playground, a community meeting room, a pool, and often a facility for child day-care. The service center is in walking distance from home for elementary-school-age children and for mothers pushing baby carriages. Through automobile traffic is routed around the neighborhood and pedestrian paths make it unnecessary for pedestrians to cross busy automobile roads.

Changes in county zoning regulations negotiated by the developer with county officials make it possible to cluster residences in various ways, to increase population density within residence areas and, as a result to open up a considerable part of each neighborhood for use as play area and parkland. Housing styles and values are varied, ranging from the typical detached house on the half acre lot of suburbia to small apartment units of varying sizes. Many of the units are variations of the row or town houses which are becoming increasingly popular in many parts of the country as a result of soaring land costs. The range of housing costs in each neighborhood is designed to attract an economic mix from somewhere above the poverty level to somewhere just below the most affluent. In addition to some detached subsidized housing scattered through the community, there are subsidized clusters of 50 townhouse-style residences per neighborhood. The economic mix within such neighborhoods is by no means revolutionary and, in fact, seems retrogressive to those radical social activists who are engaged in battling for tens of thousands of housing units needed for ghettoized blacks and other minorities. However, within the current social framework (of government housing policy, available mechanisms for building housing for poor people within existing middle-income communities, the exigencies of the market place, and the deeply held convictions of builders and mortgage bankers) the economic mix within Columbia's neighborhoods represents an innovation in its own right. I understand that it was necessary for the developer to be both persuasive and adamant in order to convince builders that they would not lose their shirts erecting homes in economically and racially mixed neighborhoods.

The next largest unit within Columbia is the *village*, which consists of about four neighborhoods organized around a larger service center; this center includes secondary schools; a shopping center with supermarket, restaurant, drug store, professional office space, and a number of small specialty shops; at least one city-wide facility (such as a covered year-round swimming pool, arts and crafts center, tennis club, ice skating rink, health club, or public library); a community center which provides a recreation program for children, teenagers, and adults; and open recreation areas and playing fields. The village also serves as an intermediate unit within the management and resident participation system of the community. Representatives are elected to a village board and to the Columbia Council, which is part of the quasi-governmental system that oversees many of the community's services. The village boards are important links between Columbia's developers and the residents. Though they have no powers to govern or direct, they have been able to advise, lobby, and fight for their points of view, mobilize public opinion on various issues, and have a significant voice in annual budgetary decisions. Each village has at least one of the low-to-moderate-income subsidized housing projects mentioned earlier. It also is the locus for such services as gas stations, automobile repair shops, banks, and short-order food shops.

In the first of Columbia's villages is an ecumenical religious center, one of the new town's most innovative social institutions. Planned in conjunction with most of the major national religious bodies, the center provides worship and organizational space for most of the town's Protestant, Catholic, and Jewish groups and serves as administrative center for the community's religious affairs. Over time the center also has come to be used for counselling purposes and for meetings, workshops, and other gatherings having to do with man's search for purpose, such as yoga groups, interfaith and interracial sessions, sensitivity training laboratories, encounter groups, and the like.

When finally completed in 1980 Columbia will consist of seven villages plus the downtown, several industrial areas, and at least one set of high-rise apartments associated more with downtown than with any of the villages. Downtown is designed to serve as a magnet shopping and recreational center for a region which includes not only the 50,000 people in Howard County outside of Columbia but also extends into and overlaps with parts of the Baltimore and Washington metropolitan areas. It will include restaurants, office buildings, at least one inn, nightclubs, movie theaters, a large plaza facing onto a man-made lake suitable for boating, and—if the dreams of some of its institutional developers are realized—a garden-park-entertainment area similar in ambience to Copenhagen's famous Tivoli gardens. Close to the center section of downtown there are three institutions of higher education, including the Howard Community College, an experimental field center of Antioch College and Dag Hammarskjold College, a new internationally-oriented institution which has been on the drawing boards for several years. Located in a nearby parkland and picnic area are a dinner theater and 5,000-seat summer music pavilion. The hospital and clinic facilities of the Columbia Medical Plan also are adjacent to downtown.

Responsible over-all for the creation and management of certain essential services not provided by the County is the *Columbia Parks and Recreation Association,* the nearest thing to city government for Columbia, which is an unincorporated area of the County. The Association's budget comes from a fixed assessment of 75c for each $100 assessed valuation. It is responsible for parkland, picnic areas, internal bus transportation, playgrounds, the community's recreation program, day-care centers, neighborhood and village centers for youth, and other programs.

It is in the interplay among Columbia's overlapping communities that one finds expressed the dominant social philosophy of its developer—namely, to provide the richness of choice afforded by the best of our modern cities with the intimacy of support to individual growth and family well-being that is afforded by the most caring of small human settlements. Rouse himself expressed it this way:

> Institutions which degrade man and barriers which separate men from one another are under relentless assault. Thus, the cold, grim oppressiveness of the scaleless, inhuman cities is under attack on many fronts ... This new city will look different because it will be broken up by parks, open spaces, schools, playgrounds, transportation systems, etc., into definable communities in which people are important [Rouse, 1967, pp. 10 – 11].

EXPERIMENTAL CITIES

Although a number of recent new towns appear to be following "the Columbia model," there is hope that some developments will adapt and experiment with other approaches. Not that Columbia is a bad or unsuccessful community. Quite the opposite! Its very success in both the eyes of its residents and the marketplace will predispose other developers, especially the private corporations, to turn out Columbias in a cookie-cutter fashion. I cannot help but feel that something will be lost in the imitation. European new towns, which also began as an extension of the garden city concept, have tried strikingly different approaches, most notably Cumbernauld near Glasgow, which marches housing units up a hillside to a fortress-like city center, and Tapiola near Helsinki, a small (17,000 population) jewel of a town which relates to its natural surroundings in aesthetically breathtaking ways. In this country there are growing indications that we will some day have in being one or more of the experimental cities recommended by Athelstan Spillhaus in *Daedalus* in 1967. He suggested that such cities become the proving grounds for evaluation of technological and social innovation. The first one may well be courtesy of Mickey Mouse via EPCOT (Experimental Prototype Community of Tomorrow) which the Disney organization intends to develop as part of Disney World in Florida. Commenting on the exciting possibilities of such an urban testtube associated with the sophisticated family-oriented recreation area created there, Peter Blake commented in a recent issue of *New York* entitled "Mickey Mouse for Mayor": "All the extraordinary technical innovations introduced in Disney World as a matter of course have been known to every U.S. urban designer for decades . . . [Blake, 1972, pp. 41–42]." Perhaps the American public will someday be challenged successfully to use its tax money to foot the bill for urban progress. In the meanwhile, urban innovation may occur most surely under the heading of fun and games!

THE REFORMIST NATURE OF NEW TOWNS

The new town movement generally falls within a reform rather than radical social change perspective. New towns do not, in fact, restructure society. Building a new town does not put muscle into the enforcement of air pollution standards so as to control smoke emanating from factories elsewhere. There is little reason to believe that most new towns will be less dependent on the automobile than are existing cities. And, unless there is a serious national commitment to providing meaningful employment and an adequate basic income for all, it is doubtful that new towns can do much better than existing ones in building satisfactory housing for poor people or in creating optimal integration of class and economic levels (Eichler, 1971).

New towns can, in my opinion, create viable mechanisms for a modicum of meaningful citizen involvement in the affairs of their locale even during the development period when, in virtually all cases, the significant control remains in the developer's hands. So long as citizens' welfare, in their own minds, is congruent with the welfare of the developer, it is possible to have authentic participation of citizens in the affairs of the community, always assuming, of course, that the developer seeks residents' inputs and makes use of them. When residents' confidence is shaken—as reportedly happened in Reston when control passed from the hands of the original developer to Gulf Oil—then citizen input tends to shift to a conflict model, issues of mistrust arise, and communication is confused with control.

New towns can do something about the physically dreary, conformist atmosphere of the typical suburb. Columbia and other current new towns in this country do something about this problem. They are far outstripped, it is reported (Underhill, 1970), by the lovely new city of Tapiola. Underhill writes:

> Tapiola seems to have had the greatest social planning input of all the communities discussed. It was designed by a multidisciplinary team effort composed of housewives and social scientists in a position to review and approve all of the proposed plans. *Tapiola's beauty, convenience and diversity appear to be a result of this socially oriented planning process* (p. 23; italics added).

New towns can conserve the land and maintain open space. They can make some strides towards reintegrating the work setting and the residence, thus reducing the necessity for long commutes and family fragmentation typical of the bedroom community.

Finally, they can provide the physical setting and human services needed to maintain a higher level of physical and emotional well-being than that found in most of the older cities of this country.

BARRIERS TO RADICAL NEW TOWN DESIGN

I would like at this point to review briefly the forces which tend to mitigate against major experimentation within new towns as things stand today, not with an idea of saying "it can't be done" but rather to make explicit barriers which must be reduced or circumvented if radical change is to occur. Most basic and least in the control of new town developers is the lack of a coherent national social philosophy and plan in this country which would hold as a high-priority goal the elimination of poverty (both in economic and social terms) and the creation of a high quality of life for all. As things stand today, most people without adequate income cannot buy their way into new towns; those that do are less able to purchase the goods and services which in some societies they would have as a matter of right, not privilege. Rent subsidization is of some benefit. But while those with rent subsidies may live in the same neighborhood or block as more affluent families, their standard of living, their access to health and educational opportunities, and most important, their sense of significance probably will be less complete than in the case of their wealthier neighbors. Low rents through nonprofit mechanisms are of some help also. But if people live in enclaves of nonprofit housing, however good a job the architect has done in creating an aesthetic and livable environment, they are set apart from those living in nearby enclaves and, under such circumstances, it is not hard for stigmatization to occur.

Within a marketplace economy, as has already been suggested, the developer must be in the position of optimizing profit, meaning that he must walk a middle path between the extreme of repeating well-established and obviously inadequate patterns for providing human services, among other things, and the opposite extreme of risking his costly investment by venturing major social innovation which prospective buyers of homes and establishers of industry may eschew. Architects and planners may think in terms of what people will find pleasing and useful; developers must think in terms of what they will *buy*. And people buy homes for many reasons, not the least of which is careful consideration of whether or not it will be possible to *resell* the home when it is time to move again. Center-stair, two-story colonial homes may be neither as aesthetic nor as functional as post-and-beam modern or prefabricated modular constructions; they are, however, presumed by most realtors, bankers, and buyers to be more salable. The possible economic rewards for participating in a major innovation in housing are so far not sufficient to motivate large numbers of people to take the risks involved. No wonder that so many sections of Columbia and other new towns take their cue from *Better Homes and Gardens*; the wonder is that so much innovation in housing types and architectural styles does occur.

An obvious reason, of course, is that most of us find it hard to break out of accustomed patterns and ways of thinking, especially when such patterns are supported by and fixed in social custom or law. No matter, for example, that we have a plethora of critics of the public school system, some of whom make best-seller lists calling for a deschooling of society. Planners *and the patrons* of new towns will continue to associate education with school systems, and why not, seeing that schooling is required of all children by law until age 16. We are all accustomed to thinking of human services in terms of one or more institutions operating to respond to each human need: schools for learning; hospitals and clinics for health; recreation departments for leisure time. And one of the reasons we do this is that, to some extent and for many people, the system works: it delivers services, it localizes responsibility for performance of each service, it embodies a clear management arrangement for administering the services, and so on. If we are intent on deschooling our new communities, then we must determine how it will be possible for children from such communities to make it to Harvard if such is their desire. It does no good to assure parents that it is no longer necessary to attend an Ivy League school or that college educations are highly overrated. Their life experience tells them otherwise and even if they are halfway convinced why should they give up half a crust if there is the risk of receiving less than that in return?

It would be easier to break out of status quo approaches if there were generally acceptable social criteria for assessing the potential worth or actual impact of social innovations. Models of social and institutional development are urgently needed. Without them, planners and developers are forced to rely on woefully inadequate yardsticks, most of which are based on little more than common sense.

The problem of yardsticks is highlighted by the fact that builders, developers, and others involved in community building can find little apparent impact on land values resulting from the presence or absence of many of the services and amenities which social planners may suggest. No doubt land values increase when prospective purchasers are assured of high-quality schools; values also rise when there are exciting recreational opportunities afforded by ponds, picnic places, and playgrounds; they may rise somewhat when comprehensive health services are added though I am not aware that this latter has been demonstrated. However, beyond such obvious basic human services land values appear not to be affected. Will people really pay more for their housing if by so doing they are able to buy memberships in a prepaid medical plan? Will there be greater demand for housing in a community that boasts of a comprehensive human resources center? And what about other human services, such as day-care centers, community development specialists prepared to facilitate resident involvement in community planning and decision-making, programs of continuing education, youth employment projects, preventive family counselling, and the like? It is hard to demonstrate the long-range costs of not having such services and long-range costs are often paid for out of other pockets than those which would pay for preventive programs. Such facilities are deemed desirable by human service specialists, psychologists and other behavioral scientists, social planners, and many architects and developers. By the yardstick of economics, however, as reflected in the prices which can be charged for homes built on land, it is doubtful that prospective home buyers attach equally high value to such desirable social innovations.

There is another set of barriers to social experimentation inherent in the relationship between the developer and residents of a new community. The developer knows that many people fear that their lives will be unnecessarily controlled in a planned community, that they will be subject to the scrutiny of "big brother" in the form of the developer and his staff. The history of U. S. company-built towns is full of examples of abject apathy or fierce hostility resulting from attempts to arrange residents' lives, however well-meaning the intent. Today's private developers especially will be loath to launch inquiries into peoples' lifestyles, living patterns, or reactions to life in the new town even though information gained from carefully conducted studies in an existing village might help immensely in planning a subsequent one. Most people do not wish to be guinea pigs in anyone's experimental community; few developers will wish to make them so, if only because it is good business not to drive away prospective settlers.

And finally, though it might seem a foregone conclusion that the results of planning and building one village would be fed into the mix of information used in designing subsequent ones, in practice it is difficult to install and maintain the internal feedback system required to do so. In some cases the problem is simply that the team of people responsible for managing the community (e.g., in Columbia the manager and staff of the Columbia Parks and Recreation Association) is not the same as the team of people responsible for its planning and development (e.g., in Columbia the Howard Research and Development Corporation, a subsidiary of the Rouse

Company). Students of organizational behavior know that it is difficult to maintain effective communication even among subsystems of a single organization responsible together for the several functions pertaining to the organization's ultimate product. When, as in Columbia, the systems are organizationally separate and responsible to different policy bodies and constituencies, it is extremely difficult to build the communication channels and accountability systems required to assure a constant flow of feedback from those responsible for areas of the community already in place to those planning subsequent sections.

The possibilities for data-based development of subsequent sections also are reduced by the fact that it is difficult to gauge how well a neighborhood or section is "working" for its residents until the early settlement period is over and life in the area has settled down beyond the initial transition period. It takes several years to complete construction of a major area, such as one of Columbia's villages; beyond that point it probably requires another one to three years for living patterns to become stabilized. Given the timetable of completing the entire city over a 10- to 15-year period, the planning and initiation of most areas must begin long before the "results" of earlier designs can become apparent.

6. What Is Unique About Institutional Development in New Communities?

Despite constraints, the potential for imaginative social design is great in new communities, especially in their presettlement and early settlement phases. In the former, there are few problems and resistances to change to be worked through with existing residents or institutions. Decisions can be made by a group of experts assembled by the developer. The best of expertise and experience from outside the community can be drawn upon. And, as was emphasized earlier, a piecemeal approach can be avoided. During the early settlement period, there are still few traditions or vested interests to serve as barriers to social innovations. Early settlers often are interested in becoming involved in the process of innovation itself. The Columbia experience indicates that such early settlers include a number of people who bring with them a kind of pioneer spirit, a desire to become involved in the community's affairs, and an enthusiasm for social innovations which promise a better way of life.

RESOURCES FOR SOCIAL INNOVATION IN THE PRESETTLEMENT PERIOD

One important resource for social innovation during presettlement is the *major nearby human service institution* whose leadership may perceive in the new community an opportunity either for enlargement or enhancement of that institution's mission. An example for Columbia was The Johns Hopkins Medical Institutions whose leadership early on became interested in becoming involved in providing an innovative pattern for health services delivery that would enhance the school's community service and teaching missions. It took several years of planning and negotiation for key faculty members and others in the university to resolve major objections and the numerous concerns expressed by a number of people within the school. The result was a prepaid health plan developed in partnership with a major insurance company. In place about two years after first residents were arriving in Columbia, the plan after five years moved into its own clinic and inpatient center, which ultimately may become a facility for the entire county. Development of the Columbia Medical Plan was also facilitated by the fact that few health facilities exist in Howard County; there is no public hospital and there were few other medical resources to lay claim to Columbia as part of their territory.

A different situation is faced when a service delivery system already exists for the area in which a new community is being developed. In Columbia, for example, the county school system is required to provide public education for all children. The developer who wishes to introduce educational innovation is obviously dependent on existing authorities in such a situation; it is also true that he can offer resources to school officials which may benefit all children in the system, not just those in the new city. Timing of neighborhood and village construction can be set out well in advance and coordinated with the ability of school authorities to construct and finance new schools. Sites for new schools can be made available by the developer. Developers' staff members and outside consultants can be made available to assist school authorities. Trips by school officials to educational programs elsewhere can be encouraged and financed. In a variety of ways, the need to provide for the education of the new town's children can become an opportunity for the school system to update itself, by adapting the best of practices from elsewhere, instituting its own innovations, and providing new stimulation and inservice training for its personnel.

The result of collaboration between Columbia's institutional development staff and the Howard County public schools is a modestly innovative system of so-called open schools, the physical layout of which encourages teachers to be flexible and experimental in the educational opportunities afforded children. The internal open space of each building can be readily divided by sight and sound barriers into a variety of configurations depending on the nature of activity, size of groups, etc. Experiences gained by the system in Columbia's open schools are being disseminated throughout the system as new schools are built elsewhere in the County and as existing school staffs indicate interest in experiments going on in the new town.

Still another resource for institutional development is the public or private national organization. The interfaith center and entire ecumenical approach developed for Columbia, for example, was the result of a process of institutional innovation wherein the new town's institutional development staff worked closely with representatives of national religious bodies. It is doubtful whether local clergymen and their congregations would have been as amenable to a completely ecumenical approach as was possible in the collaboration among national church leaders. Because the plan emerged during the presettlement phase there were, in fact, no local congregations to be taken into account in Columbia itself.

The major finding from the Columbia experience with

presettlement institutional development is that representatives of large institutions, whether nearby or national, public or private, responsible for some area of service within the new town or not, are frequently excited by the prospects for social innovation afforded by the new community. The latter can be used as an institutional clean slate on which their new designs can be written. The task for the institutional developer appears to be one of discovering how the new town can become a means of realizing such designs. Those responsible for administering major social institutions rarely have much time for dreaming; what dreams they do have are usually quickly fogged over by daily operating demands and financial constraints. The advent of the new town with its resources of opportunity, access to possible funding sources, availability of land, provision of technical assistance, and the heady challenges of large-scale development and major social relevance makes dreaming more exciting because it becomes more capable of influencing the waking life of the institution.

Planning for a Nonexistent Population

Presettlement institutional development involves the design of services for a population whose characteristics are not fully known. It can be a risky business for white middle-class planners, most of them adult males, to design health delivery, educational, recreational, and other human service systems for a community whose residents, in the case of Columbia anyway, are only 80 to 85 percent white, about 50 percent male, and possibly 40 percent adult. Despite Harry Stack Sullivan's famous dictum, "We are all more human than otherwise," there are many aspects to that humanity. It is difficult for even the most sociologically sophisticated planning group to design an optimal environment for people markedly different from the planners in sex, class, race, or generation. Time lag may also be a factor in rendering plans obsolescent in only a few years because of rapid changes in cultural norms and expectations.

There are several ways in which the developer can alleviate the difficulty. One, of course, is to ensure that the composition of the planning and development staff reflects as nearly as possible major constituencies among prospective residents. Another approach is to involve consumers who resemble prospective residents in the planning. Already alluded to was Tapiola's development in Finland, where housewives served on the panel of experts that was consulted as plans were formulated.

Population projections can be made with some degree of accuracy on the basis of experiences elsewhere. Most multipurpose new towns have a disproportionately high number of young families with preschool and early school-age children. Communities like Columbia can confidently expect that their neighborhood-village-city design, oriented towards neighborhood schools and easy access to service facilities by mothers and children, will attract many young families. One can be reasonably sure also that the racial mix of the new town will be a function both of the racial mix of the nearby metropolitan area(s) and the capability of the new town for providing low-income housing, assuming always that the developer maintains a truly open community in the face of the many subtle pressures against it which can be exerted by racist realtors, bankers, and members of the developer's marketing staff. (Columbia has been maintained as a racially open community despite the fact that the city was created and marketed by an almost totally white staff.)

Once the probable nature of the prospective population has been forecast it is possible to survey comparable groups by means of field interviews with stratified samples, the involvement in planning of continuing panels of people (such as the housewives group used in Tapiola), group interviews, or a combination of approaches. Of the approaches, I favor the panel method which involves respondents *over time* in a responsible fashion. One-shot cross-sectional surveys of prospective consumer reactions are notoriously fallible and potentially disastrous. Well-known examples were the failure of such polls to forecast eventual consumer resistance to the Edsel and a small car developed by Nash when they were finally introduced on the market.

INVOLVEMENT OF ADJACENT RESIDENTS

During the presettlement phase there are others having a stake in the new community whom the developer may choose to involve or who may involve themselves in the planning. Among them are existing residents of surrounding areas, such as, in the case of Columbia, the 40,000 people already living in Howard County. Some of them may choose to become residents of the new town. All of them will be affected by its presence. Their initial and continuing support or opposition can make the difference between success and failure. There are a host of controls which local residents can impose on the new town through various governmental mechanisms at their disposal. For example, the timing of major county road construction may make the difference between completion or noncompletion of an entire village on schedule. Changes in zoning can affect the nature of house construction, what types of homes can be built, the cost of dwelling units, density of population, and the various uses to which land may be put. It is important, therefore, for the developer to ensure that surrounding residents do not become opposed to his plans out of unwarranted fear or misinformation. They should be kept fully informed; their concerns should be understood and responded to; their officials should be involved in decisions which will affect their constituents.

Under certain circumstances the need to involve nearby residents poses a host of serious problems. They are illustrated by what occurred when citizens were involved by planners of the Fort Lincoln Project, the new town in-town initiated by the District of Columbia Government on public land in the midst of a middle-class, largely black residential area of Washington.

The citizens' planning council, organized by the planners only after the project was underway, was so wracked by political and factional disputes that it had within one year "lost its mandate of confidence both in the District building and among many of the citizens [Peachy, 1970, p. 2]." D. C.'s mayor disbanded the council and in its place appointed a new citywide committee with advisory powers only. Peachey's analysis of what took place highlights some generic problems that may arise in situations where local citizens, nonresidents of the projected community, are involved in its development. Peachey himself was a member of the planning council. As a social scientist he was able to treat his experience both as participant and conceptualizer. Certain factors stood out for him:

1. neighboring residents serving on the council did not — and could not in the nature of things — feel the same immediate stake in Fort Lincoln per se that they might have had if they were scheduled to become residents of the new town area itself;

2. middle-class neighbors were primarily concerned with the possible unfavorable impact of prospective low-

income Fort Lincoln residents on the surrounding area, in terms of increased crime, downgrading of educational standards, and other feared consequences;

3. there were sometimes heated disagreements over the extent of the surrounding neighborhood that should be considered to fall within Fort Lincoln's so-called "affected area";

4. there were unresolved disagreements about who should represent the affected area and how they should be chosen, issues which are familiar ones in both Model Cities and antipoverty programs;

5. within the pervasive atmosphere of mistrust of elective and appointed officials, it was not surprising to find the council demanding both community control of the Fort Lincoln project and veto power over specific plans, neither of which would local planning agencies give over to a nongovernmental body;

6. feuds among citizens' groups associated with the council presented serious dilemmas to the planning director, who was charged with implementing policy behind which there was no clear resident consensus.

Peachey puts the problem into the perspective of a political scientist by pointing out that formerly "the exercise of the franchise was more adequate as a link between citizen and government than at a time when public agencies create and shape the human environment. Until new definitions are found, government planners may find it hard to go beyond extending empathy to the beleaguered citizens which, as the planning of Fort Lincoln demonstrates once more, is not enough [Peachey, 1970, p. 34]."

The Fort Lincoln experience underscores the importance of defining clearly both the *scope* and *nature* of citizen responsibility in the new town planning process as well as the *timing* of citizen involvement. It also points to an inherent fallacy in expecting a relatively small group of citizens selected on some quasi-representative basis to serve as spokespersons for major elements of a community. Many methods, both formal and informal, must be used simultaneously and throughout the project to involve various groups, organizations, and individuals. The ways used must ensure that citizens have the information they need, will be heard, and will have both legitimacy and influence. Every opportunity should be given for residents to express their concerns and discuss alternative approaches with planning staff. And whenever possible residents should be enabled to visit other new community developments.

The complexity of the community organization task inherent in involving adjacent residents cannot be overemphasized. In my experience it is the person with *development experience* who is usually better able to tune into the psychological and political dynamics in ways which citizens find supportive and helpful. However, technical planners without community organization training or experience are often insufficiently aware of the dynamics. They come to the task without the needed skills. It would be highly desirable for planners to receive training in sensing and relating to the interpersonal, group, and organizational processes involved. Such training would equip them more adequately for coping with the kinds of problems that are generic to new town development. Though it would be helpful for at least one member of a city-building team to be a specialist in community development processes, it is preferable for the entire team to have some awareness of and skill in dealing with them.

An example of a highly process-oriented approach to community devlopment is the Hartford Process, a three-year project involving the design for both the rehabilitation of existing sections of the city and for the development of new-town areas within Metropolitan

Hartford (Berkeley, 1971). Carried out by the American City Corporation, a subsidiary of the Rouse Company, the Hartford Process has made extensive use of social scientists, planners, and others skilled in community development work. After exploring the idea of a citizens' forum to consider proposals developed by the planning groups—an approach analogous in some respects to what was actually attempted in Fort Lincoln—they embarked on a different tack which they believe has been successful. Their development body (Greater Hartford Process, Inc.) established a joint-venture arrangement with an already existing neighborhood development corporation which had previously been encouraged and funded by the State Department of Community Affairs. More similar to the Tapiola model was the Hartford Process' innovative Community Think Tank, which brought together a dozen or more local people from the mostly black inner-city area for a two-day session on the development process itself, using as a resource leader-consultant an outside black specialist in group process and community development.

7. How Is Social Science Affecting New Town Development?

THE COLUMBIA WORK GROUP

Few new town developments in either Europe or the United States have involved social and behavioral scientists in the early planning. As noted earlier, Tapiola was an outstanding exception. In this country Columbia remains an atypical example of a new community in which social scientists were heavily involved at the outset generating bright ideas and exploring alternative approaches to human services without remaining permanent members of the development team. The Columbia Work Group (Hoppenfeld, 1967; Lemkau, 1969) consisted of consultants from education, health, recreation, family life, psychology, government, sociology, economics, housing, transportation, and communication. The chairman was the well-known psychologist and social planner Donald Michael of the University of Michigan. The group met twice a month for two-day sessions over a six-month period. Its task was to make a "social analysis" of the interactions of people and a city's institutions. The analysis was then taken into consideration by the development staff along with the more traditional considerations of land use, engineering, finance, aesthetics, and the marketplace. The Work Group addressed the community function by function, ranging through a consideration of health, recreation, education, libraries, and other services as well as the needs of special groups such as mothers of young children. Papers were prepared in each area by one member of the Group for

297

consideration of the entire body. Emphasis was placed on possible interrelationships among institutions, as, for example, the potential counseling function of the ecumenical religious center or the possibility of having restaurants cater meals for the public schools. There was no attempt to arrive at consensus among the varied views and perspectives of the members. The principal planners and developers remained in charge of putting together courses of action and devising specific pieces of the overall plan. While certain specific ideas emanating from the Work Group were picked up and have come into being, most notably the Columbia Association and related processes, the comprehensive medical plan, the cooperative religious center, and a multipurpose community center for each of the seven villages, other apparently attractive suggestions were not implemented, most notably a strong emphasis on a physical design that would keep automobile traffic at a minimum; an innovative plan for an institute designed to foster family life in a variety of educational, preventive, and therapeutic ways; and a program of job training and human resource development designed to reduce underemployment and increase the employability of economically marginal individuals. However, in 1972 a small group of psychologists and counselors in Columbia formed the nonprofit Family Life Center to provide educational and counseling services that rely heavily on volunteered services of professionals.

By not having responsibility for followthrough, financing human services, and other aspects of implementation, Work Group members from elsewhere could take the best of what was available in their respective disciplines and bring them together in creative new ways. They were not bound by economic or other constraints.

On the negative side, however, none of them remained with Columbia's development long enough to have a part in influencing the implementation of specific designs or devising the means whereby social planning would continue over time as an intrinsic part of the community's growth. There were many aspects of design which outside members could not get into since the full Group was restricted to social analysis rather than to the total and continuing task of institutional development. The social scientists could not become sufficiently enmeshed in the management of social institutions, the process of resident involvement, the development of information and feedback systems, the creation of monitoring and accountability mechanisms, nor the institution of specific phases whereby the several institutions might be developed and interrelated with each other. Such matters remained in the hands of the developer's management team and institutional development staff.

Nevertheless, the Work Group's output of ideas, design intimations, and recommendations was remarkable. A single paper prepared by sociologist Herbert Gans, a Work Group member (Gans, 1968), encompassed a wealth of sociological information and developed criteria for physical design, population mix, and institutional resources that remain relevant almost a decade later. Gans predicted, for example, most of the areas of individual, family, and social tension which have since become manifest. Among other suggestions, he recommended the establishment of a position based on the Scandinavian ombudsman, to help surface and channel incipient community issues and tensions which might otherwise fester underground. Several years later one of the first settlers of Columbia, employed by the Rouse Company, became the developer's representative.

NewCom, Kentucky

In contrast to the more general social analysis of the Columbia Work Group is the detailed planning carried out by a community psychologist and a team of physical planners at the Urban Studies Center of the University of Louisville in Kentucky (Murrell, 1973; Urban Studies Center, 1971). The Louisville project was unique both because of the detailed fashion in which it applied behavioral science research to new town design and because the planners began with a psychological analysis of the psychosocial needs of residents. Psychosocial considerations were articulated first and then dovetailed with physical and economic analysis. For example, the psychological specifications stated: "NewCom must be as responsive to sociofugal tendencies (preferring not to interact with others) as to more sociopetal tendencies." The physical planners translated the requirement into physical design by specifying: "In addition to paths leading *through* areas of high social interaction, there should also be an alternate path *around* the area for those who prefer not to interact [Urban Studies Center, 1971, A-17].

The NewCom project, supported by an OEO grant, undertook to establish the preliminary specifications for a community which could be developed within the Louisville metropolitan area. Though no private or public developer stands ready as yet to implement the design, the study group was interested in more than a planning exercise. Legislation was initiated in the State legislature to clear the way for new town construction and several suitable sites were identified. The NewCom planners also had the specific social goal of designing a community that would serve as a transition and training ground for Appalachian white and urban black families, in addition to providing a social mix that would include at least 50 percent middle-class whites.

The community psychologist on the planning team reviewed relevant research findings with regard to three areas: (1) affiliation needs; (2) locus of control, power, and authority; and (3) the psychology of achievement. These findings were related to specific institutions deemed to have the most psychosocial relevance; governance, education, social service, leisure time, and the areas of health and safety, the latter two combined in a highly innovative way. The planners did not hesitate either to extrapolate from their findings or to make educated guesses as they arrived at the following underlying principles of psychosocial design:

1. The good design should *optimize individual choice,* not restrict it.

2. It should provide *comprehensive and definite guidelines* that should seek to anticipate as many contingencies as possible.

3. The design process should *provide for corrective mechanisms* that will facilitate changes in both the design and the subsequent community on the basis of empirical experiences.

4. The design should reflect its creators' realization that a *community functions as a system*; interrelationships among units should be taken into account.

CHOICE POINTS IN NEWCOM DESIGN

As they struggled with choice points in both psychosocial areas and institutional recommendations, they were guided by the usual planning yardstick of seeking optimal tradeoffs among all possible costs and benefits. The choice points which the community psychologist considered crucial from a psychosocial viewpoint serve as a highly useful orienting framework in our further consideration of implementing human services in new towns (Murrell, 1973).

Power Distribution

One such choice point involved the question of how widely power should be distributed among NewCom residents. Analysis of the literature led them to conclude that a too narrow distribution would result in inadequate flow of information to decision-makers, resident frustrations and dissatisfaction as a result of insufficient participation and poor decisions, and subsequent dysfunctional anger or resident apathy. A too broad distribution, on the other hand, would result in inability to arrive at decisions, unclear allocation of authority and responsibility, and resulting citizen frustration, inability of the community to govern itself, and even anarchy.

The proposed governance system is based on the linking-pin concept proposed for organizations by Rensis Likert (1961). It begins with voting districts consisting of approximately 200 families, each represented on a village council that serves from 1,000 to 1,400 families. Each village council in turn elects a spokesperson to the NewCom Assembly, which with an at-large mayor is the overall governing body of the community. Neighborhood governing groups are required to meet at least monthly. The system ensures that a member of each group (the linking pin) is placed in another group at the next higher level of the community. Though not a radical departure from traditional governance based on the representative principle, the system has the distinct advantage of structuring in a means for facilitating communication and coordination among several groups.

Homogeneity vs. Heterogeneity

Another choice point was concerned with optimal heterogeneity of NewCom's population within both neighborhoods and villages. The literature indicated that homogeneity would facilitate social interaction within the homogeneous area while, at the same time, predisposing the community as a whole toward conflict between such areas. Extreme heterogeneity within an area would not, on the other hand, facilitate social interaction but would reduce interarea conflicts and the potential for stigmatization of less favored areas by those more affluent. The option which the planners exercised was a design very similar to that carried out in Columbia; housing clusters of about 25 families would be homogeneous in terms of housing costs while neighborhoods themselves would be as heterogeneous as possible. Because educational settings and the smallest governance units were at the neighborhood level, it is likely that there would tend to be cooperative interaction among people from different social and economic groups as they worked on common interests and concerns.

Optimal Size of Service Units

In their consideration of optimal sizes for psychosocial units the team was greatly influenced by the psycho-ecological work done by R. G. Barker and his colleagues who studied social interaction and participation in Kansas communities (Barker, 1968; Barker and Gump, 1964). Their findings are clear: smaller units offer far more intimacy, involvement, and opportunities for influence than do larger ones, with the result that people take more responsibility for their community's social institutions than is the case in larger settings. Larger units, on the other hand, offer more variety, specialized equipment, and resources. Given today's learning and communication technologies, however, it should be possible to design smaller psychosocial units without surrendering the advantages heretofore reserved to larger ones. NewCom planners, therefore, opted for smaller sizes, "trying to maximize psychosocial benefits within economic convenience, and educational considerations [Urban Studies Center, 1971, p. A-24]." There is no doubt that such a decision is crucial. It shapes the nature of human services in a new town, ease of accessibility of such services, prospective users' sense of ownership of their service institutions, and residents' participation in policy development.

Extent of Services

Equally important for human services development was the question of how much service should be provided to residents. On the one extreme, they sought to avoid a coercive program, one which would create dependence on helping institutions, or make it possible for officials to meddle in residents' affairs. On the other extreme were obvious disadvantages of providing inadequate resources in such critical areas as health, education, recreation, and family support. Their decision was to create a multifaceted social services program at the village level. In addition to providing direct services, both by itself and in conjunction with other groups (e.g., the educational system), the unit would be responsible for assessing new problems, identifying opportunities for providing new services, initiating new programs to be operated by others, as well as coordinating and evaluating service delivery programs of all other social agencies. The social service agency also would be responsible for "taking the psychosocial pulse" of the village at regular intervals in

order to determine resident needs, preferences, and
concerns; to disseminate its findings to the village board
and other officials; and to make recommendations regarding needed programs to appropriate governance
bodies.

Monitoring Mechanisms

Considerable thought was given by the NewCom team
to building in corrective mechanisms that would ensure
optimal response to resident needs, coordination among
disparate service institutions, and flexibility of services in
response to changing conditions and new technologies.
They invented two devices: Monitoring Boards and
Habitability Surveys.

The Monitoring Boards, one for each institutional
area, would be composed of representatives from each of
the villages. Each board is to study and evaluate the
performance of the service area for which it is responsible; it is intended to facilitate the flow of information
between the users and providers of services. The Board
collects information and submits reports and budgetary
recommendations to the governance bodies responsible
for the agencies concerned. Each monitoring board
would have one vote in the NewCom Assembly. However, it would have neither policy-making nor direct
budgetary powers over its agency.

The Monitoring Board's chief instrument would be
the *habitability survey,* a biannual inquiry into user satisfaction and the strong and weak points of each service
delivery system. The boards would be required to
specify, in advance, the criterial levels below which an
agency could not fall without being considered unsatis-
factory. NewCom regulations would require the removal
of the administrator of any agency deemed unsatisfac-
tory as a result of the habitability survey.

The NewCom design points the way towards a useful

differentiation of policy, management, and monitoring functions and their location within the community in such a way as to foster a continuous attention to the quality of service and the need for change. It emphasizes the importance of installing some kind of visible, sanctioned, and institutionalized corrective mechanism. If such a mechanism functions as it should, change does not have to be preceded by long-standing frustrations, the snow-balling of dissatisfaction, crisis, or conflict. It also does not have to await action on the part of delivery personnel and governing bodies; instead it places the users of services into the feedback and monitoring process in what appears to be (on the drawing board at least) an effective fashion.

Other exciting features of the NewCom design reflect the kind of social analysis and design of mechanisms which behavioral experts presumably would bring to new town design if given the opportunity. A community-wide Human Services Resource Unit is intended to provide computer back-up, research staff, and technical assistance to the community's service delivery groups. Certain delivery groups (i.e., social services, leisure time, village health, and religious institutions) are housed together at the village level and share secretarial staff. Key staff members from health and social services are jointly appointed within education and other areas at the neighborhood level.

COMPARING COLUMBIA AND NEWCOM

Practical considerations—legal, economic, and attitudinal—would no doubt impose certain modifications on NewCom's psychosocial features. However, such alterations would have to be done carefully and with full attention both to the direct consequences within a specific area and to possible indirect ramifications throughout the entire spectrum of NewCom services. For the planning team has succeeded in designing a comprehensive, interrelated set of resources and functions in which each part is affected by all others. It is an elegant plan, finely tuned and responsive to residents' needs and changing concerns. In some respects it is the very antithesis of the free-swinging "bright idea" approach used by the Columbia Work Group and the Rouse Company institutional development team. Compared with Columbia there is relatively little room for ad hoc inspiration or serendipity in NewCom's approach to institutional development, whereas such factors were given free play in Columbia. There is relatively little attention given to inputs by major outside institutions in the NewCom design; such inputs were frequently pivotal in Columbia. The NewCom design is just that—a totality which puts its pieces together like a jig-saw puzzle; the Columbia approach to human services, on the other hand, though sophisticated in many respects was comparatively piecemeal, with the result that it is possible to have a highly sophisticated human service in one category coupled with no service at all in a related area (e.g., a prepaid medical plan in a county which provides the barest minimum of school health services). I am not trying to judge either approach. It may well be that the NewCom design is a major advance over the approach to human services used in Columbia, which itself represented a major step ahead of approaches used in most other new town efforts. On the other hand, NewCom in practice might turn out to be overly refined in some ways and subject to some malfunction as a result of the extent to which it rests on a system-wide grand design in which all parts are interdependent. Some indication of difficulties which might be faced in modifying the NewCom design to meet certain political and economic exigencies is given by the designers' insistence that NewCom not be located in any county which refuses to allow it to operate an educational system "permanently independent of that county's extant school system [Urban Studies Center, 1971, p. B-90]."

SOCIAL SCIENCE IN BRITISH NEW TOWNS

After initially overlooking the potential contribution of social scientists to earlier new town developments, British authorities began in the middle 1960's to incorporate sociologists as part of some planning and development teams (Willmott, 1967). Willmott describes his involvement in a two-year planning project for a major expansion of the community of Ipswich. Perhaps it is the fact that the sociologist is involved in an on-going way in an actual development project or perhaps it is simply the difference in perspective between the United States and Great Britain; in any case, it seems to me that the social scientist's contribution in Great Britain as described by Willmott is, at one and the same time, both more pedestrian and more practically rooted in real problems than the more elegant conceptual and systems-oriented approaches used both in Columbia and by the NewCom team.

Initially Willmott prepared papers setting out some sociological criteria and suggesting appropriate policies which the team might follow. He included simply written hypothetical "profiles" (case histories or scenarios) of three families before and after they made the move to the new community. He also was involved in the planning team's daily decisions, more often than not basing his opinions on hunches without firm sociological data in hand. He was limited by time and funds to carrying out small scale surveys of prospective residents. He also conducted interviews with opinion leaders, key officials, and employers whose industries were moving to the new area. Finally, he made it a point to visit other similar projects to see what could be gleaned from their experiences. He also selected critical issues from his review of studies of earlier new developments, among them the importance of (1) working towards a more balanced population by age and occupation structure, (2) facilitating the settling in of new residents, and (3) promoting harmonious relationships between existing residents of an area and the newcomers. In regard to the latter concern, he surveyed Ipswich to determine how the residents felt about the proposed expansion with an eye to identifying possible areas of mutual interest to be used in fostering intergroup harmony.

Willmott reports that the sociologist often finds himself in a *spokesman role* speaking for what he sees as the needs and preferences of the people being planned for — whose case otherwise often goes by default. He also emphasizes the importance of including in social planning a concern both for the policies which will affect the kind of community and the nature of its population and for management approaches which will ensure that social needs are attended to. He found that, while it was relatively easy to generate hypothetical concerns and general inquiries, it was far more valuable to the planning process to formulate specific questions designed to help resolve a specific planning or management issue.

8. What Human Services Are Required for Early Settlers?

PRESERVICING

A very real consideration which cannot be overlooked in the presettlement phase of social design is the relatively costly nature of human and other services in the early period of settlement. The so-called *"preservicing"* of a new community entails the high costs of institutional design and development. If taken seriously, preservicing requires major outlays of cash for the construction of facilities and the hiring of a disproportionately large number of people to manage and staff those facilities which, it has been determined, are to be in place by the time the first resident or family arrives. Any model for the development of human services must take into account the extent of the preservicing deficit which must be incurred in order to provide relatively costly per-capita services for a small number of people. It must also determine whether and how the initial costs are to be recouped over the subsequent years. Somehow in the calculus must be included the immediate and ultimate monetary costs and other untoward consequences of not providing adequate human services from the outset.

FIRST FAMILIES

Extensive preservicing is strongly advocated by a study group commissioned by the British Ministry of Housing and Local Government. Among other reasons, the group maintained that provision of adequate services to first arrivals would have a favorable effect on all succeeding groups of newcomers. The group recommended that government policy provide for an *Arrivals Officer* whose job would be to advise and assist new residents. In its report entitled *The First Hundred Families*, the group stated:

> The relatively high cost per family of the initial amenities and the salary of the arrivals officer should be regarded as an investment which is likely to pay high dividends through the avoidance of discontent and friction while the community is settling down in its new environment [Ministry of Housing, 1965, p. 7].

In addition to calling for an arrivals officer, the group recommended the following resources to aid the settling-in process and to begin the development of resident initiative:

1. an official on the scene who would be visible and responsible for general coordination of all services;

2. up-to-date information, including a map; the development plans for the town; information on social services, churches, and other facilities, including hospital and emergency services and physicians; general information on such matters as bus service and trash collection;

3. office space for the arrivals officer and social service personnel which would also include space for residents' meetings;

4. basic services, such as bus transportation, a small shop for food and other necessities, postal and telephone services, and the like;

5. educational arrangements for children;

6. basic medical facilities;

7. essential footpaths from dwelling units to shops, community buildings, and bus stops.

INVOLVEMENT OF EARLY SETTLERS

During the early settlement period, the developer enters into a markedly new phase of design and development. He is now in a position where he must be responsive to resident needs and concerns. He has the opportunity to enlist their interest and participation in the development process. He must walk a fine line between being insufficiently responsive and involving, on the one hand, thus running the risk of generating frustration, anger, mistrust, and unnecessary opposition, and, on the other hand, being overly involved and responsive, thus running the risk of generating overdependence and mobilizing latent resentment of his domination of the community.

In addition to informal curbstone contacts between development staff and new residents, there are also advantages to arranging more organized opportunities for interaction. Informal gatherings over coffee in someone's living room, periodic neighborhood meetings to discuss the concerns of both developer and residents, as well as picnics, cookouts, and other forms of celebration whenever a suitable occasion arises are all useful means for building relationships and seeing to it that new arrivals belong and have a part in the community. The process is enhanced, of course, when development staff are also residents of the community.

A simple telephone information service and, where possible, an information desk at the neighborhood center are additional resources for easing the adjustment task of newcomers.

It is easy for development and management staff of a

new community to become defensive in the face of resident criticism. It is hardly possible to overestimate the investment which development team members build up in the community they have designed and are busily putting into place. Residents, on the other hand, if they are at all interested in becoming active participants in the new town, are apt to express concerns, suggest changes, challenge basic design concepts, and pose problems which they believe require solutions. Even a simple request for information may be experienced as a challenge or criticism.

PROBLEMS OF TRANSITION TO THE NEW TOWN

Behind some of the early complaints may be hidden agenda, including the desire to count for something, perhaps even to play a significant part in the community's further development. Other complaints may well manifest increased emotional tensions and anxieties associated with leaving an established residence and making one's home in a new town that is in its early stages of development. Making the transition from one community to another in any case is accompanied for almost all of us by increased tensions, occasionally acute emotional crisis, associated with leaving old friends, neighbors, and family. Making such a move often means giving up an old job and taking on new work responsibilities. There is the loss of old settings, old relationships, and old roles . . . together with the strains occasioned by the search for new friends, the adjustment to an unfamiliar situation, and the taking on of new roles and responsibilities.

Moving to the new town, especially in its early stages, has for some people the added element of unrealistic expectations. Physical planners are not alone in the conviction that a well-designed, beautiful physical environment may be the answer to psychological problems and emotional ills. People moving to new towns sometimes expect their personal lives and family relationships to be magically improved. Instead they may find that the new environment has fewer built-in institutional and informal supports. There is often the barest minimum of services of all kinds, ranging from shopping facilities to family counseling agencies. The accustomed personal supports afforded by relatives and former friends are no longer available. The homogeneous nature of the population sometimes means that few, if any, teenagers or retired people are available to provide baby-sitting services in order to give parents evenings or weekends away from their children. Then, too, for some people the move to the new town requires a marked change in lifestyle. There is little opportunity in the typical new community for the informal neighboring or the hanging around on street corners, the easy access to the tavern or pool hall, or the stimulating night life and excitement of the more crowded inner city neighborhood. Small wonder then that observers almost always note a marked sense of temporary let-down and disappointment, often sharp depression and despair, which have come to be termed "the new town blues."

The transitional problems of early residents can be ameliorated somewhat by the provision of the basic minimum of services and staff members whose job it is to be helpful (such as the British arrivals officer mentioned earlier). I believe that the job is too important to be delegated to one individual or a small staff alone. As others have suggested, notably sociologist Herbert Gans (1968, p. 200), all members of the development and community management team should be helped to understand and relate to the social and emotional dynamics of community life, including those associated with the new town blues. As the British study group asserted in its report on the first hundred families, how new arrivals are helped to understand and cope with their early adjustment problems is apt to make a fundamental difference both in terms of their own later participation in the community and also in terms of the kind of community it turns out to be in the long run.

9. How Can Community Development Approaches Be Adapted to New Towns?

The new town, however beautifully designed and laid out, cannot become a caring community if it does not from the outset provide the simple human supports necessary for all its residents. This means that people cannot be left alone simply to fend for themselves. Everything that is written and said about the community must indicate to new arrivals that they are valued, that their needs are important, and that the developer and his staff are readily available to them. Although personal and family counselling agencies, professionally staffed, are important in the long run, they are no substitute for an atmosphere which makes it obvious that people in this town care about one another and stand ready to help.

COMMUNITY SELF-HELP

Every encouragement should be given to initiatives from within the community to provide resources on a self-help basis. In Columbia and other new communities which we have visited or heard about such initiatives have often represented significant supplements to the best laid plans of the communities' designers. They have included recreational programs such as little league teams, swimming and boating instruction for children, and

317

neighborhood-designed playgrounds; coffee houses, crisis counseling, and self-help employment programs for teenagers; user-managed commuter bus services to nearby urban centers; flea markets, crafts fairs, and a farmers' market featuring produce grown in the surrounding county; and in Columbia a totally nonprofessional helping agency known as Friendship Exchange. The latter sprang up early in the development of Columbia and provided invaluable services to early settlers during the first few years. It was built on the principle of people sharing their resources and helping one another. Assistance was provided at times of crisis, including not only a sympathetic listener but also direct assistance (e.g., finding shelter and clothing for a family burnt out of their new home). Friendship Exchange was supported by the developer and by resident members who provided their own helping resources and funds to make available a combined office and gathering place where residents could come when they were lonely for coffee and sympathetic companionship. A similar but more goal-oriented self-helping resource in Columbia is the Women's Center, a facility also staffed by volunteers to help the community's wives and mothers find increased meaning in their lives and develop increased consciousness of themselves as women in today's society. Initiated by the cooperative ministry, the Women's Center has used seminars, speakers, sensitivity training programs, and consciousness-raising groups as part of its program.

No one knows how much help new arrivals need from agencies specifically designed to offer assistance during the transitional period. I suspect that surprisingly little specialized help is called for if the overall atmosphere of the community is welcoming, stimulating, and supportive. Human services professionals can play an important part in helping voluntary groups develop an atmosphere which enables residents to care about and help one another.

COMMUNITY DEVELOPMENT RESOURCES

There is much that can be included within the design of a new community to facilitate the sense of caring and self-help. The provision of meeting places has already been mentioned. They should be readily accessible within both the neighborhood and the wider community, include provisions for both large and small gatherings, and be designed so as to accommodate themselves to a variety of uses. It helps to have facilities for providing simple refreshments.

The attitude of the developer and his staff is also an important factor. Many developers hesitate to "interfere" in the social life of the community; they expect residents to be independent and self-generating, perhaps even resentful of the developer's assistance. Some developers believe that it is outside their responsibility to be concerned about basic human services beyond those necessary for recreation, education, and perhaps health. I think the developer and his staff can play a part in creating the context for caring and self-help. This does not mean that they should become the jolly green giants of the community, shaking money from the trees whenever a need is identified by residents. Provisions can be established for making community development funds available to responsible groups of residents. Such funds can be used in the planning and development of the kind of self-helping human services already described. They could be clearly earmarked for this purpose within the new town's economic model. And it would be desirable for such development monies not to be administered by the developer or his staff but rather by residents themselves, through such mechanisms as a foundation or a nonprofit development or human services corporation.[1]

[1]A nonprofit Columbia Foundation has been created to provide seed money for new projects and to support resident initiative in Columbia.

Finally, there is the possibility of building into the fabric of the community from the outset a *human resources agency* which is intended not only to provide direct helping services and to stimulate or monitor the creation of others (as suggested in the NewCom plan) but also to become engaged in the process of leadership enhancement, using teaching, consulting, and community organization techniques developed over the years under the aegis of community development specialists, usually in underdeveloped areas of the world.

THE COMMUNITY DEVELOPMENT PROCESS

Community development in international usage refers to "the process by which the efforts of the people themselves are united with those of authorities to improve the social and cultural conditions of communities [White, 1964]." Applied by a human resources agency in a new town, the community development process might consist of several aspects: (1) it could provide a consulting staff to encourage local community organization and to offer advice and technical assistance regarding organizational procedures, approaches which have worked elsewhere, writing proposals for funds to foundations and government agencies, and the like; (2) it could help organize surveys, demographic research, and community studies on a self-help basis wherever possible, providing training for community volunteers in study techniques where needed; (3) through informal contacts with residents and by more formal means, such as workshops, seminars, and skill training programs, it could encourage citizens to assume positions of leadership and help them develop the competencies needed; (4) it probably would need to work closely with the neighborhood associations, village boards, and overall community governing bodies to enable such groups to establish effective processes for communication, problem solving, and cooperation among them.

NTL COMMUNITY RESEARCH AND ACTION LABORATORY (CoRAL)

In September, 1970 NTL Institute opened an experimental community development resource in Columbia. Known as the Community Research and Action Laboratory (or CoRAL), one of its missions was to explore the nature of consulting, training, and research services which could be provided. Our entry was made with the full knowledge and sanction of the developer, who assigned his Director of Institutional Development to maintain liaison with us. We were, however, on a pay-as-you-go basis, subsidized neither by NTL nor the Rouse Company. We had in mind to provide such services as:

1. human relations training oriented towards enhancing the personal lives of community residents;

2. training in group, organizational, and community development for community leaders, development staff, and governing bodies;

3. consultation and technical assistance to organizations and institutions within the community;

4. preventive counseling and training for parents on family life and child-rearing, together with consultation to schools and other agencies concerned with families and their children;

5. development of "early warning" mechanisms for monitoring resident needs and attitudes, noting incipient problem areas, and developing ways of feeding back our information to development staff and residents.

The community then was barely three years old; three villages were under construction and there were about 12,000 persons in its rapidly growing population. We had already contracted to provide consulting and training services to the staff of the Columbia Parks and Recreation Association, which managed those community services and facilities not provided by the County. And we were involved in two other client systems: (1) an undergraduate behavioral science program under the aegis of the experimental campus which Antioch College had established in the new city; and (2) an effort by the Johns Hopkins Medical School Department of Psychiatry to develop a human resources center which, if funds could be secured, would be located in Columbia to facilitate health delivery programs there and elsewhere in the State.

I do not wish to detail all of CoRAL's activities either with its initial clients or in its subsequent projects. A summary should suffice to indicate the nature of the work, the ways in which our resources were used, and what we found in the community that bears on this discussion of human services and needs.

Our work with the Columbia Association began, at the request of its Manager, with internal organizational development efforts. Members of the management team were interviewed individually about their work and their satisfactions or dissatisfactions with the Association's operations. Results were fed back in the context of an extended workshop to all those who had provided data for the inquiry. Meanwhile, I was meeting weekly with top management staff of the Association both to acquaint myself with the scope of work and to serve as an informal consultant to the management team on its own working relationships and on community concerns with which they were dealing. Repeated attention was paid to defining the extent of the Association's responsibilities for responding to citizens' requests for information or for taking direct action on neighborhood or village crises.

At one point I was able to be of direct help to Association staff and village boards by presiding at their mutual request over extended budget deliberations which involved CA staff and budget committees from the three villages. It was apparent that the budgeting process required a most careful consideration of the structures and procedures needed to handle the intergroup dynamics involved, not to mention a high level of group process and interpersonal skills to manage them. Subsequent efforts to organize skill training for village boards were shelved when the composition of the boards changed as a result of annual elections.

We soon became aware that resources for youth in Columbia were not adequate to their needs. The situation was complicated by the fact that Columbia was already becoming a magnet for hundreds of young people from the County and beyond. It was not uncommon for 400 to 500 teenagers to gather on a summer weekend evening at the lakefront plaza in downtown Columbia to talk, play guitars, smoke, and — at times — cause acute discomfort on the part of adults wishing to stroll there. Adult distress had led to the closing temporarily of one village teen center and a coffee shop for young people operated in another village. Antioch College students, concerned about drug problems among high school youth and disaffection between young people and their parents, had opened Grass Roots, a "counter culture counseling center" which secured funds from state health authorities and considerable community interest and support. We helped train counselors at Grass Roots and provided regular consultation to their staff. We discussed with Columbia Association staff what could be done to ease both adult-youth tensions and apparent cleavages which were developing between black and white teenagers. We also involved representatives of most of the youth-serving organizations in Howard County in a series of self-training sessions designed to build more effective collaboration among them, to increase their concern for the youth crisis which we thought was imminent, and to explore possibilities for developing training and other programs which might ease tensions between groups of youth and between adults and young people. Finally, we consulted with a group of citizens seeking to establish Awareness, Inc., a detached youth worker program, providing technical assistance as the group successfully formulated a proposal and secured government funds, helping recruit a staff director, and providing consulting resources to staff and board as the program got underway. Our activities even extended to participating in the design for recruiting and training young people as a new kind of "security guard" for the massive covered shopping mall which was opened as a major attraction in Columbia's downtown and which was expected to attract large numbers of young people. Mall planners did not wish to have the problems with young people which have plagued shopping centers elsewhere. They did not want merchants or customers hassled by teenagers; neither did they wish the teenagers to be hassled by store owners or security police. We used the approach of redefining the role of security officers, emphasizing their potential for helping customers, and of providing the young people selected with human relations training and practice in dealing with varied situations which might face them on the job. At the same time, the Youth Awareness group arranged to develop a youth shop and center in the Mall, with the cooperation of the management, which young people could consider to be their place and which would make some income by selling items created by them.

Our efforts in regard to youth and those of the groups with whom we worked met with only limited success. Awareness, Inc., was abandoned at the end of its first year of operation as the result of policy disagreements and withdrawal of financial support. Youth-serving agencies have not come up with a coordinated program for young people in the County. Intergenerational and racial tensions among young people persist, though they have not reached the crisis proportions which were anticipated at one time.

No doubt some of these problems are insoluble in any ultimate sense, arising as they do out of the tensions in our society. There are no physical or institutional "solutions" which can insulate a new city from its surroundings. Nevertheless, we can probably draw some helpful lessons from our experience. First of all, it would have been helpful to have had mechanisms in the community from the outset which would involve young people themselves in responsible positions for both planning and implementing designs for youth. Second, there is a need to develop better ways for enabling young people to play a constructive part in the work, educational, and social-institutional life of the town. The developer can take some leadership in such an effort. Young men and women can be hired as part of the developer's own design and management staff. Businessmen and industries can be encouraged to do likewise. Some of the community development funds proposed earlier might be used to subsidize hiring of teenagers on staff of schools, libraries, hospitals, and other agencies. Schools can be especially helpful in monitoring such activities and working out arrangements for course credits and released time. No matter what the specific approaches, the important point is that youth needs can be approached in such a way as to foster healthy growth and creative community involvement, rather than, as is so often the case, from a problem perspective. It is also clear that a baby-sitting approach is of little value. The needs of today's youth are not met only by the comparatively simple provision of teenage centers for an evening's ping-pong or rock-and-roll session at the coffee house. The detached worker approach seems to have more value if it is backed up by an informed and interested group of adults and if there are sufficient funds to permit rapid response to new needs and situations as they arise. One of the major efforts of the detached worker staff might well be to identify and train young people themselves as paraprofessionals working with other teenagers. Another major effort might well involve recruitment of nonpaid adults whose special skills could be placed at the disposal of younger citizens. To be avoided like the plague is a problem emphasis, whether on drugs, delinquency, or any other specific adult concern about youth. Though these symptoms of malaise cannot be ignored in any comprehensive program of human services for young people, they cannot become the primary emphasis without slighting more fundamental considerations of how well the community values and engages young people in its undertakings.

We found a number of individuals and groups interested in creating a network of helping services which would foster indigenous resources, avoid undue dependence on professional agencies and individuals, while providing urgently needed services not yet available to residents. As part of the effort to design a human resource development center in conjunction with The Johns Hopkins Department of Psychiatry, we had conducted a survey of formal and informal helping resources either located in Columbia and Howard County or available to residents. We discovered scores of agencies whose available services were not being used. We found that many agencies did not know of one another's existence. And we discovered no fewer than three organizations whose ostensible purpose was to coordinate helping services and institutions in the County!

A HUMAN SERVICES PROJECT

Prior to the survey described above, our primary goal had been to identify new human services needed in Columbia; subsequently, our focus changed to a consideration of how best to engage all those concerned in paying attention to how existing as well as additional resources might best be used and allocated to meet the needs of Columbians and the 50,000 other residents of the County. There were any number of exciting plans for developing comprehensive family life institutes, human resource centers, and radical new individual and social group work programs in conjunction with the nearby U. of Maryland School of Social Work. The problem was how to draw together residents, agency people, and planners —all those with a stake in what was ultimately decided— in a way which would open up communication, make good use of their resources, and end up with decisions about priority areas to be pursued and mechanisms for pursuing them.

We played a consulting role as other key agencies, most notably the community college located in Columbia and the county's association of community services, took the leadership in organizing and implementing a three-phase planning effort: (1) during the first phase background information was assembled bearing on available resources and community needs in the County; (2) the second phase brought together scores of agency people and users of services in an intensive weekend planning workshop out of which emerged task forces in 12 areas (Advocacy of Citizen Needs, Aging, County-Columbia Relations, Community Mental Health, Day Care, Delivery Systems, Education, Employment and Poverty, Health and Handicapped, Housing, Transportation, and Youth); (3) during the third phase it was the responsibility of each task force to develop proposals and to report back to the coordinative body. Some task forces made considerable progress, even to the point of launching specific action projects; others failed to get off the ground or found that, in fact, they were duplicating work already being done in the County. The planning group received task force reports and attached highest priority to the proposal of the Delivery Systems group, which called for creation of a nonprofit county corporation that would (1) continue the work of the project; (2) serve as a human services "think tank" for the County; and (3) promote the development of needed delivery systems (temporarily under its own aegis if needed). Composed of representatives from all segments of the County and its organizations, the corporation's task would be to plan and promote changes, improvements, and innovations in social services and structures across the County.

The project adapted many aspects of the community development process to the new community setting. As the editor (Dewey, 1972) of the final report put it, the seminar and what followed are examples of "citizen participation in the structuring of society" worth chronicling because:

> A grass roots ad hoc citizen's group . . . set out to make a change in human services delivery in Howard County. Along the way they were able to appropriate authority and authenticity to what they were doing, raise funds, attract a multitude to their plan, and accomplish what they set out to do. In

addition, they have given the County a permanent
. . . mechanism for change.
and
All of this took place in an environment that today is
unique, but tomorrow may be quite common: the
environment of a large "new town" developing
rapidly within a formerly rural region. The kinds of
tensions between rural/urban, between old/new,
between status quo/growth that environment provides make community organization and human
service delivery especially difficult and challenging
[p. 1]."

Partly as a result of CoRAL's influence, the original
citizens group and the Board which subsequently took
charge of the project once funding was assured brought
a strong process orientation to their work. The officers of
the Board, for example, spent considerable time forming
themselves into a leadership team, sometimes sharing
authority and responsibility collectively rather than restricting themselves to the separate roles and functions of
president, vice president, treasurer, and secretary. Time
was spent with the entire Board working to build the
relationships needed to ensure the ability of the diverse
group to deal with subsequent tasks and problems. The
group also made use of a psychologist as process consultant to facilitate its work, to ensure participant involvement, and to help in designing meetings and in setting
agenda. Board decisions were worked out on a consensus
basis rather than using parliamentary procedures of mo-
tions and votes.

The role of staff assistance in making the project a
success should be emphasized. Though there was effective volunteer leadership, considerable clarity as to purpose, and a strong sense of group solidarity, full-time
paid staff made it possible to attend to the innumerable
mechanical and organizational details inherent in such a

complex effort. Staff ensured that follow-up would take place from one phase to the next. It took care of minutes, created a newsletter to keep everyone informed, secured meeting space and other facilities, consulted with the leadership group on agenda, and in various other ways helped to coordinate the many facets of the project.

The project's experience highlights many of the complexities of human services development. Just the examination of the task forces which emerged from the second phase reflects some of the intricacies. Certain task forces were organized around function (e.g., Education, Community Mental Health); others focussed on a segment of the population (e.g., Aging, Youth); others on some problem area (e.g., County-Columbia relations); still others on aspects of the entire delivery system (e.g., Advocacy, Delivery Systems). It is clear that the human services pie can be sliced along at least four simultaneous dimensions. The carefully conceived, comprehensive, systems-oriented approach designed by the NewCom team, as the Louisville group itself anticipated, presumably would get somewhat mussed-up once residents themselves got their hands on what would be involved in the general category of NewCom's "social services." But that's what grand designs are for. I suspect that the Howard County Human Services Project would have met with even greater success if it had emanated from the kind of continuing planning, stimulating, and designing body provided for by the NewCom plan.

EVALUATION OF CoRAL EXPERIENCE

The CoRAL experiment in its original form lasted only one year. It was then subsumed within a Human Resources Development Center under the aegis of an independent board of directors drawn both from The

Johns Hopkins Department of Psychiatry and NTL. Funded at its inception only by a training contract with the Maryland State Department of Health and Mental Hygiene, Drug Abuse Administration, the new center was nonetheless intended to serve statewide human resources training and consulting needs while simultaneously serving as a human resources agency for Columbia and Howard County. It soon became clear that it was not possible to develop such a comprehensive program on the basis of a single narrowly defined contract. When the year's contract ended, the Center itself—and with it the original CoRAL—passed out of existence.

My full-time involvement in the experiment ended after the first year. Both exhilarated and exhausted from the intense demands of responding to day-by-day community needs and trying to build a basis for long-range funding, I took a year's leave of absence which also enabled me to do the work required to produce this study.

The CoRAL experience is not easy for me to evaluate. From the standpoint of economic viabiity there is no question that we failed. Like the original developer of Reston, we embarked with inadequate capitalization and an insufficient in-depth supply of experienced trained staff. We responded to too many needs and challenges all at once, partly because we could not resist the challenge, partly because we were motivated by the search for clients and income. Though we had long-range goals and a fairly detailed plan for development over five years, we developed neither the criteria nor the management procedures that would hold us on course or enable us to revise the plan as needed.

We were incorrect in assuming that CoRAL could support itself largely by activities within Columbia alone. We were, without realizing it, engaged in a preservicing venture whose per capita cost could be born neither by NTL nor 12,000 Columbians and their emerging organizations.

We demonstrated to our satisfaction that a need exists for the kind of facilitative agency that CoRAL was designed to be. Interest in our resources was high among many with whom we were in contact, including members of the developer's staff, management of the Columbia Association, and leaders of village boards and other organizations. We became involved in virtually all activities having to do with human services' development as well as in both official and unofficial efforts to forestall crises in intergenerational, racial, and other areas. Despite some frustrations and reversals, we rapidly built up an acceptable record for quality of work.

A most satisfying aspect of the year for me was the eagerness and capacity for growth demonstrated by increasing numbers of colleagues who joined CoRAL once it was established. Coming as interns, unpaid staff members, part-time project personnel, and graduate student fellows, the CoRAL team soon included—in addition to behavioral scientists—students of public administration and planning, women seeking new careers, and even a high school student. Nevertheless, it was a mistake to place major emphasis on CoRAL as a learning community for ourselves. The collegium model is not an effective management approach for securing general support grants, government contracts, and consulting relationships with business firms or local agencies. And yet there was a yeasty quality to Columbia as a new town—including our eager desire to relate to it on the basis of our commitment to a self-helping community orientation—which predisposed us to experiment with the model.

What do I conclude from the year's effort and what followed?

1. The functions set forth in the original CoRAL design can indeed be performed in a new community during its developmental period.

2. If Columbia is at all representative, there is a high level of readiness among new town residents to make use of the resources of such a facility.

3. Applied behavioral science inputs are relevant to the process of fostering the emergence of a well-functioning new community. They can be used successfully to support emerging leadership, build additional skills among individuals and groups involved in community problem solving and crisis prevention, bring together in effective ways resources from different parts of the city, serve as helpful third-party consultants when intergenerational problems, special needs of single-par-evaluation of new services as needs arise, and assist in formulating proposals as part of the search for outside funds.

4. To establish a firm base of operations, a human resources agency such as CoRAL will probably require three to five years' partial subsidization in order to carry it through the period when the new city's population is inadequate to support it. On the basis of past experience with a nonprofit community mental health agency, I believe that subsidization could be terminated by the time the population reached no less than 30,000 and no more than 50,000. Though subsidization might be secured through an outside grant, I think it would be financially feasible to include it within the preservicing costs built into a developer's original economic model. I have no doubt that such costs could be matched or exceeded by subsequent savings in terms of: more rapid mobilization of human resources, diminution of community tensions, and the development of an adequate continuing data base for more efficient planning and problem solving. By forestalling more costly remedial efforts, pre-crisis work alone with respect to such areas as ational problems, special needs of single-parent families, resident-developer disagreements, or interracial and in-

terracial and interclass tensions should more than off-set the initial deficits involved in the subsidization of a facilitative agency like CoRAL.

Following abandonment of the Human Resources Development Center, several of the behavioral scientists involved incorporated a continuing non-profit organization that could carry forward research, consulting, and training activities in Columbia and the surrounding county. Known as CoRAL II, the organization has embarked on a study of youth behavior in the new town under a grant from the National Institute of Mental Health. The size and scope of CoRAL II seem more consistent with the present phase of the new town's development. It may well be a more realistic phoenix rising from the ashes of the demise of the overly ambitious NTL experiment.

10. *Are There Blueprints for Human Services?*

There are many constraints of law and custom on the nature of human services, especially as to the institutional form which they will assume. For example, as suggested earlier, it is unlikely that education in new communities will be unhooked completely from formal school settings. However, there should be room for modest experiments, such as the one proposed by the NewCom planners, who suggested that at least 20 percent of student learning time, by regulation, be allocated to activities away from school buildings and grounds.

MULTISERVICE CENTERS

There is considerable room for experimentation in relation to the location of services. Two trends are apparent. The first is towards multiservice centers in one form or another where health, social services, job counseling, and other resources are brought together under one roof, if not under a coordinated administration. Obviously such centers are intended to make the utilization of services easier for the consumer, to enable the pooling of resources in the interest of the client, to minimize the fragmentation of individuals and families into small, discrete problem areas, and to provide administrative convenience and economics.

335

DECENTRALIZATION

The trend towards coordination is balanced, as it should be, by movement towards decentralization of service centers, making resources part of the everyday scene of the neighborhood, thus reducing the threshold between potential users and providers of service. There are ample possibilities, it seems to me, for experimenting with the use of neighborhood people chosen for their interest in being helpers, their wisdom, and their interpersonal skills as first-stop resources for those wishing to make use of them. Trained in being good listeners, knowledgeable about the variety of helping services in the new community and its environs, and naturally sympathetic people, such first-stop helpers could provide direct services, follow-through on referrals to agencies, and remain in touch with individuals and their families, as needed, throughout the duration of the concern for which assistance is sought.

There are inherent tensions involved in enlarging caregiving teams by adding nonprofessionals. However, I am confident that sympathetic professional staffs, skilled management, and the use of modern team building approaches can combine to bring about successful professional-nonprofessional collaboration.

USER PARTICIPATION

There is also need for ways to facilitate resident participation and user control of services designed for their benefit. The NewCom plan for Monitoring Boards and Habitability Surveys represents one such proposed experiment. Any of the several schemes which have been devised to enable poor people to purchase their own services from available purveyors also represent efforts to shift the balance of power more in the users' direction. As things stand now, in most public institutions—such as education, welfare, and community hospitals or clinics—neither the providers nor the users of service have much direct power over one another in the sense of being able to choose or refuse to enter into a professional-client relationship. Nevertheless, in such settings the balance of power is in the hands of the providers. It is the rare group of professionals who look with favor on involving their clients in regular appraisal of the services offered them. Except at far-out institutions like Harvard, college students rarely make public their ratings of professors for all to see — and the professors would like to keep it that way. Similarly, physicians, public school teachers, and social case workers do not often make efforts to secure information about user satisfaction. It probably will be necessary for the users of services or the designers of service institutions in new communities to insist on and make provision for such appraisals. Ideally perhaps, surveys of user satisfaction could be made through the collaboration of providers and their clients; realistically speaking, however, the monitoring function may need to be separated both from the purveyors of services and the policy boards to whom they are responsible — in the manner proposed by the NewCom group.

SHARED FACILITIES

The design for human services in new towns can take the opportunity to pool physical resources and create facilities that can be used for a variety of purposes. An example might be schools (or learning centers) designed to serve their neighborhoods and villages as recreation areas, meeting facilities, and service delivery resources in areas other than the learning of children. It has been proposed that instead of planning for schools that can be made available to other groups in the community, "new communities plan community facilities that will meet the needs of students [Lieberman, 1972, p. 409]." Community auditoriums, tennis courts, libraries, and other resources all can be designed and located so that they can accommodate children of various ages during learning hours. Such a plan would mean that facilities used by students no longer would be under the direct control of school authorities. They would be planned, budgeted, and administered by nonschool agencies with, as Lieberman put it, "due regard for the entire spectrum of community needs and resources (p. 409)." Lieberman, himself a noted educational planner for new communities, suggests that by shifting responsibilities from schools to other agencies the typical political vulnerabilities of the schools would be lessened. He points out that in the past the community school approach has added educational "frills" as a way of gaining public involvement and support. Later on school budgets become highly vulnerable to attack because they have become too large, too visible, and too involved with items that are not central to their educational mission. He points out that a swimming pool may seem to be a fad or a frill in a school budget while having an entirely different appearance in the budget of the recreation department. If Lieberman's advice is followed, educational budgets will become smaller and therefore less vulnerable. At the same time, the educators may have gained useful allies among other municipal agencies.

Other examples are provisions for child care facilities in large townhouse or apartment clusters, study rooms for public school and other pupils in new apartment buildings or neighborhood centers, a neighborhood multiservice facility connected with the local elementary school, a youth center and shop in the downtown shopping mall, and a youth opportunity center in the industrial park associated with the school system's extended education program. Once the concept of multiple use is grasped and there is a commitment to designing each facility so that it can be related to other purposes as desired, the options become virtually unlimited. Needless to say, the opportunities for creative deployment of human services also become multiplied.

Carried to its logical extreme, the concept of multiple use leads some new town social planners to propose common community ownership and management of public structures. Under consideration for the new town of Gananda (near Syracuse, N. Y.) is a Facilities Corporation, a nonprofit body that would create and manage multiuse facilities, including space for educational programs. Facilities would be leased on a time/space basis. Though certain highly specialized facilities and office space would be leased on a sole use basis, other areas, such as meeting rooms, auditoriums, and some recreational facilities, would be leased to more than one human services agency and would be available for use by citizens.

The model appears somewhat similar to that taken for granted in the case of space allocation in most colleges and universities. The Gananda plan, however, introduces more user control of space allocation by virtue of the leasing mechanism. The Facilities Corporation would not have the power to arbitrarily assign space to certain agencies. The latter would have the prerogative of refusing to lease unsuitable facilities and, in some cases, might even decide to rent commercial space or build their own structures.

The approach has the potential of reducing the costly "down time" of public buildings, such as schools, which are unused so much of the time. It also does away with the need for costly public bidding techniques customarily used in the construction of municipal buildings. It appears to provide a flexible, highly responsive means for the allocation of human services' space that can adapt readily to changes in population needs and incorporate new technologies as they become available.

DIRECT SERVICE VS. PREVENTION

A knotty problem in the provision of health services, especially in regard to mental health, involves the relative allocation of resources for health promotion and prevention as distinct from treatment and rehabilitation of those already emotionally disturbed or psychologically handicapped. The comprehensive community mental health center movement sponsored by Federal legislation in recent years has represented an effort to combine all functions within a single administrative unit or set of coordinated facilities. In most cases, however, the primary focus of concern has been on the care and rehabilitation of those presenting problems. Community consultation, education, and training, technical assistance to health-promoting institutions of the community, direct services in the area of prevention (e.g., preschool checkup programs), and involvement in community efforts to develop other badly needed human service facilities (e.g., day-care programs for children of working mothers) usually take a poor second place in the activities of so-called comprehensive programs, with, it should be emphasized, a few outstanding exceptions.

In part, the problem appears to involve what I have come to call the "suction effect" of direct service delivery to existing clientele. It is difficult, if not impossible, for the professional staffs of any agency to avoid being sucked into becoming ever more concerned about the service needs of those presenting themselves for help as opposed to using their limited energies toward maintaining well-being on the part of those who do not ask for help. Moreover, as users of services become increasingly represented on the boards of agencies, they, too, are sucked into devoting their attention mainly to treatment and rehabilitation. They become increasingly focussed on whether the agency is growing to keep pace with new levels of demand and on how well it is performing its services for existing clients rather than on how well it might be carrying out preventive functions with others not already ill.

There is room for experimentation, I believe, with configurations that will introduce some degree of policy, administrative, and staff separation between those health people concerned with treatment and those whose mission would be health promotion and prevention of illness. It is not likely, for example, that Columbia's health plan, geared as it is to comprehensive medical care for its members, will ever devote a major part of its resources to school health, health education on a community-wide level, accident prevention, the development of a rescue squad service, etc. Ideally there would be a separate health facility appropriately staffed with health planners, educators, and community organizers responsible for maintaining and improving the overall health (physical and emotional) of the entire population.

Other areas for innovation and experimentation suggest themselves, including ways in which local services could be more effectively articulated with metropolitan, regional, and national institutions; the use of computerized means for tracking community use of various resources for all kinds of human service needs; and the imaginative use of nonprofessionals and new careers staff within the several human service systems of the new town.

Few such experiments will be introduced fully in any

single new community. Nevertheless, I believe that many of them will be adapted and improved upon as the hundreds of new towns of all sizes and kinds, now being developed or under consideration, take shape in the years ahead. All that is required is motivation for human improvement (which lies behind the commitment of many of those entering new town development work), a system of rewards for successful innovation (which might include, in addition to economic success, recognition by HUD and the several planning and architectural groups), and a willingness to maintain innovations at a reasonable scale where the penalties for failure will not be extreme.

11. *How Can Human Services Be Financed?*

I have already pointed out that (1) there are enormous front-end costs involved in the high-risk enterprise of building new towns; (2) preservicing the community in areas of human services must be counted among such costs; and (3) it is doubtful that all such services can (or should) be developed and maintained on a pay-as-you-go basis.

RELUCTANCE TO SUBSIDIZE

The major financing problem revolves around an apparent reluctance in this country to subsidize poor people with as much abandon as we subsidize the more affluent. Take public transportation as an instance. By heavily subsidizing roads and the petroleum industry we have helped to place two or more cars in the hands of more affluent families able to purchase them. At the same time, we have found it hard to invest the funds — whether in existing or new towns—for the deficit operations that seem inevitable if other forms of public transportation are to be readily available to all. Columbia has experimented, for example, with an ingenious dial-a-ride plan which at low cost to the patron was for a short period able to make a minibus available to any resident within 10 minutes during all but peak periods. But the plan, which was highly successful from the viewpoint of riders and its originators, was severely cut back when it became apparent that, like most other bus companies in the United States, the dial-a-ride bus system was a major loss item financially.

A common means of financing human services within new towns involves some form of tax-like assessment, which in Columbia was set from the beginning at a maximum of 75c per $100 valuation. By making such monies directly available to the Columbia Parks and Recreation Association, it was possible to establish a comprehensive economic plan which could cost out the development and maintenance of projected resources with reference to an income level tied to population and industrial growth. The plan has the added advantage of not burdening county residents outside the new town with additional taxes to pay for many of the amenities in Columbia itself.

Human Services and Land Value

Some of the initial planning and development funds for human services must come from whatever funds are available for the town's development in the first place. Certain human services are related in everyone's minds —financier, developer, builder, and buyer alike—to the value of property. Return from new town investment comes primarily from the tremendous appreciation in the value of land which occurs when infrastructures are put in place, certain human services are established, homes are built, and population density grows. Schools, churches, health facilities, and recreation areas all represent a good investment both in terms of quality of life and, to some extent, economics. It is not at all clear, however, just where the appropriate limit is. In Columbia, for example, the neighborhood pools are part of the Columbia Association's quasi-public facilities and are available at a moderate additional charge. The covered village swimming pool, however, is more costly. Similarly, the indoor tennis club, certain other tennis facilities, skating rink, and some other facilities are open only to those able and willing to pay extra fees. The Columbia Association looks forward to making money from such enterprises, thus having additional income to use in economically nonviable undertakings.

INSURANCE MECHANISMS

The situation becomes even more serious in regard to the insurance mechanism for funding human services, which is being used more and more widely by new town developers. The idea has much to commend it.

The Columbia Medical Plan

Let us take a look at the Columbia Medical Plan as an example. In concept the Plan resembles other prepaid group practice enterprises, such as Kaiser Foundation Health Plan in California, the Health Insurance Plan of greater New York, and Group Health Association in Washington, D. C. It differs in certain respects in its structure, sponsorship, organization, and finance (Towle, 1972).

The Columbia plan involves a contractual agreement among three entities, the Columbia Hospital and Clinics Foundation which owns facilities, manages the enterprise, and employs all nonphysicians; The Johns Hopkins Medical Partnership, which is the mechanism used to provide physicians; and insurance companies, notably Connecticut General Life Insurance Company, which underwrites the risks and is responsible for enrolling members in the Plan.

The plan is open to Columbia residents and any others in the County affiliated with an insurable group. Its benefits are extensive. They include:

1. unlimited ambulatory visits for physicians' services, as well as periodic health reviews, emergency care, laboratory and radiology services, immunizations and injections, and referrals to specialists at The Johns Hopkins hospitals for consultations;

2. prescription drugs;

3. full hospitalization for acute illness with no limit on stay and no additional cost;

4. pre- and postnatal maternity services, including delivery;

5. psychiatric services at a nominal fee for 15 outpatient visits per year with increased fees per visit thereafter and hospitalization limited to 30 days annually;

6. home visits if ordered by the physician;

7. ambulance service;

8. reimbursement for emergency services required outside the plan's service area.

At present writing the cost per family for belonging to the plan is $65.55 per month (a lower benefit option costs $57.60 per month). There is an additional per visit fee of $2 for outpatient care, $2 for prescription drugs and medicines, $100 for the maternity package, $2 per visit for the first 15 psychiatric outpatient hours and $10 per visit thereafter; $5 for the first home visit and $2 for each additional visit for the same illness. The added charges are about twice as much for the low-option plan.

There is no doubt that middle-income families can enjoy under this plan the very best outpatient, inpatient, and comprehensive health-maintaining care at an acceptable cost within our current economy. There is equally no doubt that some less affluent families are further penalized by being unable to participate in the major health facility of their community. The fees are reasonable for midde-class families but they are by no means nominal and they are out of the reach of others. It is clear that unsupplemented, insurance-based medical care plans are not an adequate solution to truly comprehensive medical care for all classes in the new community.

There is also the problem of enlisting residents' participation in this form of medical service. Some children as well as adults themselves no doubt will suffer from the latters' decision to gamble on good health. Forty-five percent of Columbia's residents had signed up for the Plan by early 1972. It is not clear how others' health needs are being met. Presumably many of them are covered under industrial plans, Blue Cross-Blue Shield, or other packages.

Meanwhile, the Plan can devote its resources only to its own members, with few forays into community medicine. Neither the insurance carriers nor plan members presumably would be prepared to see their funds used for more extensive approaches to health maintenance in the community.

Prepaid Legal Services

It is important to assess both the advantages and disadvantages of the insurance mechanism for it is being proposed for use in a variety of human services outside the health field (Ylvisaker, 1970). For example, plans for prepaid legal services were inaugurated in the late 1950's and there has been an explosion of interest in them since then. By 1972, it is estimated, there were about 2,000 such plans. The American Bar Association has established a special committee on Prepaid Legal Services. As in health insurance schemes, prepaid legal services plans involve payment by individuals and families of a fixed rate per year in return for services as needed. The plans are sponsored largely by unions and minority group organizations. In 1970 approximately 32 million family units with incomes from five to 15 thousand dollars per year were covered.

A recent plan was launched in 1971 by the Construction and General Laborers Union of Shreveport, Louisiana, numbering 1,900 people (Group Legal Services News, 1972). Plan members contribute two cents per hour from their wages; the plan is supplemented by grants from the American Bar Association, American Bar Endowment, and Ford Foundation. It pays the cost of legal services by any attorney in Louisiana. Members may choose an attorney from a preselected panel provided by the plan. Benefits include:

1. legal advice up to $25 per visit and $100 per year or case up to a maximum of $250 per family;

2. up to $325 for preparation and filing of briefs and for attendance of the lawyer at hearings or trials;

3. $40 for court costs and witness fees;

4. $150 for out-of-pocket costs.

Member contributions and benefit schedules are based on the expectation that about 30 percent of the members will require benefits during the course of a single year.

Adversity Insurance

Imaginative adaptations of the fixed payment and insurance approach have been suggested (Levin, 1969; Warmington, 1972) to cover the costs of social work and other human services. One plan, described as "prepaid adversity insurance," involves preventively-oriented insurance for coping with a variety of family crises. It would embrace legal assistance, family counseling, psychological services, budget counseling, vocational assistance, and homemaker service. There are many advantages to such a plan:

1. by bringing family counseling and related services under the umbrella of insurance, now widely accepted in the case of life and health insurance, it reduces the stigma attached to the use of social and family services;

2. it provides subscribers with a choice of services from among available agencies and practitioners;

3. it will enable more people to make use of such services, thus providing existing agencies with a more adequate base of support;

4. it ties support of helping services to extent of patronage, thus enabling the consumer of services to have an effect both on availability and quality;

5. it makes possible more efficient marketing of human services by means of the participation of employers, public agencies, neighborhood associations, united funds, and other groups in the plan.

The originator of the plan proposes that providers of service include a wide range of helping agencies, including family service, child guidance, and mental health agencies; pastoral counseling centers; encounter and sensitivity training programs; and adoption agencies, as well as practitioners in manpower and employment counseling, social work, psychology, and the law.

Unless subsidized to a considerable extent, I suspect, no such plans will meet the needs of poverty-level people and their families. This problem would be mitigated considerably, of course, if the nation were to become committed to a guaranteed annual income plan. Until such time all insurance or prepaid schemes have the disadvantage, already noted, of providing comparatively high levels of service for their members without attending to the general distribution of human services within the wider community.

A CASE FOR TAX-SUPPORTED SERVICES

There appear to be at least two rationales for pushing privately-funded prepaid plans and similar mechanisms over governmentally-administered, tax-supported systems. One is the widespread belief on the part of social planners that United States taxpayers will not accept the level of taxation required to provide the extent of human services taken for granted in many European countries and, in the case of health services, in Canada. Another is the unfortunate experiences disadvantaged people have had with publicly-administered health and welfare services. The problem so far has been that publicly-supported services have been primarily available for those unable to care for themselves in other ways. If the array of human services were available in tax-supported agencies as a matter of right for all persons, regardless of income, presumably the level of services would rise.

The problem of funding is a serious one. How it gets resolved will have important consequences both for the quality of available services and who can make use of them. If people from different income levels have access to different types and qualities of service, we are committing ourselves to a maintenance of the present system which rewards privilege with additional privilege and punishes deprivation with additional deprivation. The result will be a deepening of the cleavages between those who are relatively more and less affluent, thus reducing further the possibilities for the sense of community and high quality of life towards which new towns are aiming.

The straight unmodified entrepreneurial model for funding human services has serious drawbacks. Private profit-making enterprises—whether in health, day-care, legal services, or recreation—will be able to skim the more affluent cream off the top of the market, leaving the less rich segments of the population to rely on other means or go without. However commendable in terms of services provided, private insurance schemes will be unable to lower costs to the point where poor people can participate. Such people will continue to be stigmatized both by being unable to afford "luxury" items such as certain recreational opportunities and by having to rely on public services which are little more than charity.

I see no adequate substitute, therefore, for an ultimate reliance on a tax-supported system of human services for all levels of the population in which such services are a matter of right, not privilege. In the meanwhile, all available approaches to funding can be drawn upon, including direct assessment of renters and owners of property within the new town following the Columbia Association model; reliance on available Federal mechanisms within the several agencies of HEW, Labor, and HUD; and grants from local and national foundations. There is also the possibility that, in certain localities, State, county, and local governments will use Federal revenue-sharing as a means of supporting broad-based human services in new communities.

12. What Conclusions Can Be Drawn, If Any?

There are no blueprints for human services which can be applied as templates by new town designers. Each community's array of resources must in the final analysis depend on market considerations, the nature of the town's social objectives, the dreams of its developers, the characteristics of the population, the nature of existing resources in the surrounding region, funding possibilities, and the convictions of the experts and policymakers who are responsible for producing and passing on the approaches used.

Anthony DeVito, an administrator in the Office of Technical Analysis for HUD's New Communities Administration, at a conference on new town social planning underscored the importance of building a detailed development model based on an orchestration of the above considerations. His approach begins with a detailed projected profile of the population, both initially and at five- or 10-year intervals. By dividing the population into 10 age categories (newborns to age two, two to six, six to 10, 10 to 14, 14 to 18, 18 to 25, 25 to 40, 40 to 55, 55 to 70, and those above 70), taking into account different needs of males and females, and dividing the population into four income quartiles, DeVito arrives at no fewer than 80 groups which, in his opinion, need to be examined by new town social planners in order to arrive at an adequate assessment of shelter and human services needs. Given market considerations and developers' objectives, it is unlikely that anywhere near 80 such subgroups will populate any new community. It is far more likely that the great majority of new residents will be middle-income couples with a relatively large number of preschool and school-age children. Nevertheless, DeVito's approach has the merit of ensuring that social planners will not overlook significant differences in lifestyles among subgroups in the projected population.

Population analysis will have to go further, in certain cases, than those groupings called for by DeVito. Differential needs, attitudes, and lifestyles of ethnic and racial groups will need to be anticipated in localities where large numbers of black, Spanish-speaking, Appalachian white, or American Indian residents are expected. In some cases, specialized human service delivery programs will be essential to meet the needs of a particular subgroup, either during a transitional period or permanently. An example would be providing bilingual education for children of Puerto Rican parents.

Having described a presumed lifestyle for each subgroup within the population profile, DeVito suggests that the attempt be made to anticipate the rate at which each group can be expected to populate the community. Settlement can be expected to vary according to the distribution of subgroups within the surrounding region and also will be markedly affected by the developer's decisions about the different market values of residential units to be constructed each year.

Once having arrived at an expectation of what the community's population will look like over a 10- to 20-year period, it is possible to enter into contact with existing social delivery systems in the surrounding area and to determine with them the extent to which they can be expected to respond to the needs of the various subgroups. In Columbia, as in other new communities, a great number of proprietary, private nonprofit, and public agencies already were in place and potentially, if not presently, geared to the needs of the newcomers. In some cases, however, existing agencies are not prepared to expand their scope to include a new geographic area and large numbers of additional clientele. Similarly, health, education, day-care, employment counseling, or other resources simply may not exist or may be inadequate to meet the needs of existing residents of a region. In either case it will be necessary to determine which deficits must be met by the development of new delivery systems, how these new agencies are to be provided, and how they are to be funded.

It is clear that the new town social planners are inevitably faced with difficult judgments of social priority. They must take into account not only the anticipated needs of population subgroups and the ability of existing agencies to respond to those needs, but also must determine how best to allocate the limited amounts of money available for human services each year from income to the developer and all other sources.

It is small wonder that new town social planners generally experience themselves as being low man on the totem pole in the developer's team. Those in physical planning and design are instrumental in making the city habitable in the first place. They contribute directly to the ability of the developer to realize income from his original land investment. So, too, the economist and marketing expert make an essential contribution to the profitability of the undertaking. The social planner, on the other hand, is more apt to be the developer's "hair shirt," who points out the needs of prospective residents for costly services only some of which add to the marketability of the community. It is the rare human services institution which can be expected to make money or even break even on the basis of fees for services from the population at large. Similarly, it is the rare social planner who can be expected to wield equal influence on the developer's team with the hard-headed physical and economic experts who are in a position to pass judgment on the deleterious effects of social facilities on profitability.

Probably the best that can be expected of social planners under such circumstances is for them to provide the developer with alternative schemes for the provision of recommended human services, beginning with a bed-rock plan that provides the minimum resources deemed essential and including a delivery plan that promises to meet the broadest possible spectrum of human needs within the developer's social objectives. Each plan must be geared into the developer's economic projections and overall decisions regarding population density, types of residences, and land use patterns. Provided with workable alternatives and clear indications of what each will provide, the developer is in a position to make the final crucial decisions about land use and settlement against which detailed plans for human services development can be made.

POSTULATES FOR HUMAN SERVICES DEVELOPMENT

Within such a complex and often open-ended situation, there are some conclusions that suggest themselves and recommendations which are worth making. I will express them as postulates because they are matters about which I have strong convictions with hardly any proof.

Postulate #1: Human services development in any new community will of necessity reflect the social philosophy and commitments of the developer and his staff. I think this point is discussed sufficiently in the foregoing material.

Postulate #2: Human services development must be tied to a relatively detailed and finely tuned economic model. Services cost money. They cannot all be related to land values, private funding mechanisms, or tax support in the present scheme of things. Priorities must be established so that limited available funds will be used to the greatest advantage.

Postulate #3: Social scientists and social planners generally are best included in the development team throughout the development process so as to share fully in the responsibilities for human service design and implementation. Neither physical, economic, nor social planners alone are in a position to derive a workable design. Human services require careful estimates of space needs and financial requirements. They are dependent for how well they work on elements of the infrastructure, including transportation and parking facilities. Available physical technologies for construction of facilities also will affect what options are available to the social designer.

Postulate #4: To be avoided above all is the assumption that human services can be treated as discrete modules in the design of a city. All aspects of the city's design are part of its services for its residents. The new town is a carefully contrived "people container" whose every aspect affects whether and how its residents are able to find ways to meet their physical, psychological, and social needs. *All* aspects of the environment are part of the community's educational system, not the school alone; all aspects influence its leisure-time activities, not the recreation program alone; all aspects determine its citizen's safety and physical well-being, not the prepaid health program alone.

Postulate #5: The developer—whether private entrepreneur or public corporation—cannot devise and install all components of the city's human services system. Some elements are basic and must be in place, including essential educational, health, recreational, and day-care facilities. Others are equally essential as means of easing the transition of new arrivals and facilitating the process of resident involvement in further planning and design of services. Needed from the outset are meeting places, a community development staff, and limited seed money for funding developer-resident partnership in further creation of service facilities.

Postulate #6: Development of human services must take into account the dimension of shifts in population size and characteristics over time. Not only will population increase until the new town has reached its ultimate size over a 10- to 20- year period, it will also change in regard to such factors as the number of school-age children, the proportion of elderly, retired individuals, and the numbers of people requiring geriatric services. A human services plan, therefore, must specify the sequence of both the nature and extent of resources needed over time in order to anticipate shifting population needs over the original settlement period and beyond.

Postulate #7: An open-ended planning design process should be built into the new town. Such evolutionary planning (Godschalk, 1967) means that provision is made for both physical and social modification in the light of actual experience and shifting needs or technologies. Social science techniques for data collection and feedback of information to planners and residents alike are essential components of such a process.

Postulate #8: Means must be designed for data gathering, feedback, and monitoring of human services. Social institutions are resistant to self-appraisal and change in terms of information gathered from users and the community-at-large. Monitoring and change mechanisms represent one of the most promising innovations possible within new town design.

Postulate #9: The responsibility for human services coordination, resource mobilization, and development should be clearly located within the matrix of individuals and institutions within the community. In the presettlement phases such responsibility falls within the scope of the development staff. Subsequently it is probably useful to designate some other resource, such as the city government, community association, or separate human resource development corporation, as the body responsible for seeing to it that human needs are met.

CRITERIA FOR HUMAN SERVICES

The criteria for human services should be clearly spelled out as a guide for subsequent development. Certain criteria already suggest themselves and several were touched on in earlier sections of this study.

User Participation in Devising and Monitoring Service Delivery. It is generally acknowledged that adequate service delivery involves both the provision of services, on the one hand, and their utilization by those for whom they were intended, on the other hand. Gaps in service delivery sometimes result from the fact that actual and prospective users are involved neither in planning nor in monitoring how services are to be made available to them. In a marketplace economy—at least as ideally conceived—customers' patronage from among competitive goods and services serves as a roughly effective means of ensuring that people get what they want (and presumably feel they need). Human services' delivery, however, rarely takes place on a competitive basis and when it does the needs of those who cannot afford certain services are not effectively communicated to service providers.

We have already seen that in new town development

user participation in devising certain human services can only be simulated at the outset. Moreover, it was pointed out that certain innovative approaches to service delivery sometimes can be installed only before settlement begins because of the attitudes of prospective clients who might reject some of the less familiar innovations which appeal to planners and technical experts.

The process of involving users in the design of service delivery systems must be thought through carefully. It is important to avoid the extreme of asking citizens to rubber stamp a completely thought through plan to which the development team is already committed. None of us appreciates—and many of us deeply resent—being used as window dressing or being covertly manipulated into accepting what others think we need for our own good. It is equally essential that lay people not be treated as if they were equipped automatically to participate as planners or experts in the task of devising human services. The optimal approach falls between the two extremes; it neither solves problems for citizens nor expects them to come up with technical solutions beyond their competence.

There is no single pattern or sequence of involvement that is suitable for all cases of user participation in planning. There are, nonetheless, certain steps which are desirable. Among them are the following:

(a) The area of concern or the focus for planning is carefully defined by the convenors; users are asked to consider whether the scope of the task as defined is congruent with their expectations and definitions of what is needed. If it is, fine; if it is not, there is need for discussion of differences and resolution of them before further work is done.

(b) Resources and limitations are set forth from the convenors' perspective; users are asked to contribute their own ideas on what financial and other resources might be needed and on what barriers to planning or problem-solving exist.

(c) Users are asked to explore their own experiences and understandings of the delivery system; in what ways have their needs been met, in what ways have they experienced disappointment and frustration?

(d) Planners, experts, and users alike undertake to state what they hope can be achieved by an effective delivery system. What would constitute an effective health maintenance system, for example? Is it limited to early treatment? Does it include special attention to the prevention of accidents and injuries in young children? Should it provide easy access to parent counseling and support when worried mothers and fathers feel the need for advice? Is there a place for parent effectiveness training?

(e) Alternatives and choice points are carefully spelled out by the planning experts insofar as possible. Users are asked to contribute to a discussion of both gains and drawbacks involved in each and, where possible, arrive together with the planners at a solution that appears to match most closely the possibilities already set forth as desirable.

Once residents have begun to arrive and service delivery is underway, there is value in involving users in monitoring services and evaluating the extent to which they are responsive to actual needs. It is unlikely that, even though carefully planned, services will meet residents' needs in all respects. Problems of two kinds may be expected: (1) services turn out not to be fully responsive to users' needs; and (2) needed services exist but are not fully used because residents either do not know about them or do not perceive them to be relevant.

It is important, as the NewCom team emphasized, to vest monitoring and evaluative responsibility in groups that are not composed of agency staff members or their governing boards alone. If service delivery objectives are carefully specified in advance and if data are available regarding awareness of services and their utilization by prospective users, it should be possible for citizen panels to determine whether gaps exist and modifications are required.

Choices Among Available Services. It was noted earlier that few opportunities exist for providers and users of services in public facilities to choose one another. A classic example is the public school system. With few exceptions, neither pupils nor educators have anything to say about selecting each other. There are, of course, ways in which knowledgeable and resourceful individuals circumvent such a system. School personnel exercise the prerogative of "lateral transfer"to remove a child from a situation in which the teacher-pupil relationship leaves something to be desired. Affluent parents select school districts and neighborhoods which provide the educational approach that appears most desirable for them. But the great bulk of teachers and pupils (and their families) alike are—and often feel—stuck with one another.

An obvious approach would be to enable more service deliverers and prospective users to make some choices from among available alternatives. Experiments along these lines are already underway in some inner city schools. In at least one new town development—the Welfare Island project being designed by the New York State Urban Development Corporation—thought is being given to developing relatively small educational centers dispersed through the new city area, each with a relatively autonomous staff committed to a clearly stated and somewhat unique educational philosophy and approach. Within the limits of available space and transportation, pupils and their families would be invited to choose the educational center most suited to their felt needs and educational convictions.

Accessibility of Services to All Those Needing Them. Anyone familiar with human service delivery systems knows the patchwork nature of what is available—whether in health, education, recreation, child care, or any other area. There is little need to dwell on either the physical problems involved (e.g., in the optimal location of facilities) or the financial limitations which restrict high quality services all too often to those able to pay for them.

It is important to recognize that—given current national policies in the several delivery areas—new towns are not in a position to do more than ameliorate some of the more obvious inequities. Various approaches—such as prepaid medical, legal, and other plans—have already been discussed. For middle-income groups it is possible to incorporate the cost of essential services in the annual assessments which support either special mechanisms such as Columbia's Parks and Recreation Association or the services of municipal or county government. A limited range of lower income residents may be supported by means of subsidization. Special pilot programs may be funded by Federal or foundation funds. Social and rehabilitation programs of the Federal government or at the state level may provide for the needs of the very poor or those with special problems.

Ideas are not lacking for comprehensive, multiservice programs located within easy reach of the consumer. The barriers are in the pocketbook, not the mind of man. Until social policy shifts occur in the United States, new town planners—however competent and well-intentioned — can only install systems that fall short of making services available to all those needing them.

Orientation of Services to Human Growth and Problem Prevention. As was pointed out earlier, direct services for those with problems or handicaps often take precedence over preventive services designed to promote physical and emotional well-being. Orientation of services to human growth and problem prevention on a community-wide basis probably cannot be achieved if they are conceived of as extensions or outreaches from service delivery facilities designed for immediate clientele.

The design of growth-oriented services must follow from the careful delineation of objectives. The goals, as Molinaro (1971) emphasized, need to be simply stated and concrete; the consequences of their attainment must be clearly spelled out in advance. Consider, for example, a program designed to "strengthen family life" in the new city. It is generally assumed that the divorce rate for marriages within the past 10 years has risen from about one in four to a ratio that is close to one in two. It can be expected, therefore, that there will be many single-parent families in new communities. What should the goals be in reference to such families? One goal might be that no mother in such a family be cut off from recreational activities, social gatherings, and companionship of both other women and men. To achieve such a goal a number of resources must be provided. Among them are: ready access to both day-care and baby-sitting services, singles bars or other gathering places designed to provide male-female companionship, opportunities for voluntary involvement in civic activities for those who do not require paid employment, consciousness-raising groups for women wishing to explore their identity, ready availability of personal counseling focusing on life planning for those adjusting to single-parent status, and a deemphasis of school or other programs in which the norm is the involvement of parental pairs in social or recreational activities with the children.

As things stand today, the provision of the above resources or opportunities are the concern of no single human resources agency. To provide them would require the active concerned involvement of a great number of institutions, including mental health, religious organizations, day-care services, those responsible for planning commercial as well as civically-sponsored entertainment centers, facilitators of voluntary organizations, as well as representatives of the women themselves.

Perhaps some day we will take for granted the existence in every community of a human resources agency which has the responsibility for identifying the special needs of those whose normal development is endangered and for mobilizing the inputs needed to help them cope successfully with the hazards with which they are faced. In the meanwhile, it is to be hoped that health and mental health agencies in new communities will be encouraged to orient major components of their services to human growth and problem prevention.

Delineation of Linkages Among Service Delivery Systems. It has already been emphasized that no single institution's services is equivalent to the total array of resources required for a comprehensive delivery of services in any single area such as health or education. The health delivery system is not equivalent to the community's hospital or clinic; the educational system is not equivalent to the public schools. It is also true that the sum total of all health institutions is less than the total health delivery system of a community. Health is also the concern of other agencies, among them the public schools, day-care centers, fire fighting and prevention, police and other public safety organizations, and business and industry.

A comprehensive approach to health promotion, maintenance, treatment, and rehabilitation is possible only to the extent that traditional boundaries between service delivery institutions are bridged.

Linkages can be accomplished in various ways. One of the most successful mechanisms involves the pooling of personnel from several agencies in a multipurpose delivery center located within a target population area. Another approach makes use of detached workers from one agency located within another (e.g., a health department child health team based within the public schools). Consultants from one agency can be assigned to work with client organizations, a model widely employed by mental health centers in their work with schools, churches, police departments, and other caretaking groups.

An essential component for interagency linkage—and one that has rarely been employed — is a means for keeping track of the flow of clients among the various human service organizations. It has long been apparent that certain individuals and families occupy a disproportionate amount of time and attention from help-giving organizations. It has been equally apparent that such high-need individuals are parcelled out among several agencies according to presenting complaints. Rarely does any single agency maintain coordinative contact in such cases. Keeping track can and should be done at two levels: first, by having a single helping source remain in contact with the family to help coordinate among the several agencies; second, by installing computer-based record keeping systems that can help agencies monitor the referral of clients among them.

Finally, mechanisms should be developed that will enable two or more agencies and citizen representatives to focus attention on problems which require the concentrated and coordinated attention of multiple groups.

Coordinative councils, though sometimes valuable as means of pooling information and improving communication between agencies, are rarely sufficient. What is needed are working task forces composed of specialists from all relevant areas. Each task force must be given a clear mandate and the financial resources needed to do the job. And it must be accountable to some supraordinate administrative body that will see to it that task forces are formed when needed and that they are in a position to achieve their objectives. Again it would appear that the logic of effective delivery of services points to the formation of a coordinative human resources agency in order to ensure effective linkages when they are most needed.

Encouragement of Effective Self-Help Approaches. Professionalization of human services leads inevitably to situations where only the most highly qualified practitioners are certified or licensed to provide certain kinds of technical assistance. The medical field is a prime example of one in which nonphysicians have not in most settings been able to perform badly needed functions. To protect the public against unqualified practitioners the medical profession was, until quite recently, well on its way to creating a monopolistic situation in which only physicians, in short supply almost everywhere and nonexistent in some places, could make diagnoses and administer drugs.

As professionalization occurs there is a corresponding tendency for the general public to become increasingly dependent on highly trained experts even for services that could be provided by others, such as less trained paraprofessionals or even interested concerned neighbors. The result is that more and more of a service delivery area is left up to the highly trained practitioners, including aspects which often can be more promptly and adequately performed by others. An example in many communities is the ambulance and emergency rescue service. Rarely performed by qualified medical personnel, the pick-up of accident, heart attack, and other victims has often been left in the hands of untrained driver-helper teams. In recent years, however, medical groups have cooperated with citizens in forming well-schooled volunteer rescue squads, usually working in coordination with police and fire services, which have been responsible for saving many lives.

The self-help concept can be extended to many areas of caregiving. The Friendship Exchange in Columbia, mentioned earlier, was an example of a neighbor-helping-neighbor arrangement that made emergency resources available to any resident on a round-the-clock basis at a time when few agencies or services of any kind were available.

There need be no essential conflict between the encouragement of self-help approaches and the provision of highly skilled technical and professional resources in a new community. It would be desirable for all self-help efforts to be supplemented by qualified professionals especially if the latter can master the art of facilitating the work of others.

Provision of Services Within the Immediate Locale of Users. As already suggested, it would be desirable to provide front-line services within the immediate locale of potential users whenever possible. To do so, however, will mean reversing a trend in such major human services areas as education and health which in recent years has led to ever larger consolidations of facilities and technical personnel in institutions that are often far removed from the homes of clients.

There are understandable reasons for such consolidation. By pooling financial resources communities are able to provide better equipped and staffed facilities.

Training centers can be associated with the largest institutions, thereby ensuring high-caliber supervision and the stimulation of an academically-related setting. Few professionals have been interested in exiling themselves to financially and professionally less rewarding isolated locations in small communities or out-of-the-way neighborhoods in large cities.

It is now technically possible, by means of computerized diagnostic procedures and closed circuit TV, to establish vital linkages between front-line delivery centers and the more centralized better equipped institutions. Theoretically, at least, every neighborhood elementary school in a new town could be staffed by nurses and paramedical personnel to serve as the front-line health maintaining, early case finding, and minor treatment center for all residents of that neighborhood. Extending the concept somewhat, it would be possible for a front-line center to serve as the locale for parental guidance programs and for provision of information about all helping services in the region. Nonprofessional community helpers could be trained as ones to whom neighbors might turn for immediate help or support, for referral elsewhere, and for continuing assistance and encouragement until the need for help has ended. With easy access to highly qualified professionals by means of closed circuit TV and other techniques, such local helpers are in the best position to mobilize quickly the resources needed to help restore an individual or a family to a state of well-being.

Once again it should be emphasized that no new community can be expected in the immediate future to fulfill all seven criteria in its development of human service delivery systems. Nevertheless, such criteria can help guide the process of institutional development and encourage the examination of alternatives that might otherwise be overlooked. Hopefully each new community will be in a position to experiment with one or more aspects of the problem. On the basis of such experiments it should be possible to develop more comprehensive models that can be tested in successive waves of new community development.

THE NEED FOR MODELS

Soon after establishing the NTL laboratory in Columbia I became aware that models for social and institutional development in new communities were lacking. Behavioral scientists have been able in the past to amass a body of research and experience which has led to useful models for developing well-functioning groups and for facilitating change within existing business and other organizations, that is, for what has been termed group and organizational development. At one point I hoped to formulate, with the help of planners and designers who had engaged in the creation of new institutions, a provisional model for a new area of inquiry and practice known as *Institutional Development*. In fact, a series of seminar meetings were held at which a number of the ideas contained in this study were formulated. Nonetheless, it is no doubt clear from this publication that a full social and institutional model has yet to be devised. The period of greatest creativity in the development of social institutions for new towns lies ahead. So far people in the field are for the most part flying by the seat of their pants. However, each group's experience with each new town has the potential for adding to the body of both theory and practice. The challenge is clearly for students of human behavior to become increasingly engaged in the process. Out of the full collaboration of social scientists with physical and economic planners will, I am hopeful, emerge designs for large-scale human communities that will indeed foster a high quality of life.

REFERENCES

Barker, R. *Ecological psychology.* Stanford, Calif: Stanford University Press, 1968.

Barker, R. & Gump, P. *Big school, small school.* Stanford, Calif: Stanford University Press, 1964.

Berkeley, E. P. The new process in Hartford's North End. *City,* Summer 1971, 36–37.

Blake, P. Mickey Mouse for mayor. *New York,* February 7, 1972.

Buder, S. Ebenezer Howard: The genesis of a town planning movement. *Journal of the American Institute of Planners,* 1969, *35,* 390–397.

Department of Housing and Urban Development. Large developments and new communities completed or under construction in U.S. since 1947. *Urban Land,* Jan. 1970.

Department of Housing and Urban Development. *Draft Regulations for Urban Growth and New Community Development Act of 1970.* Federal Register, 36 F.R. 14205-14, July 31, 1971.

Dewey, R. E. *Report of the Howard County Human Services Community Action Seminar.* January 15, 1972; *Howard County Human Services Project Report Part II,* June 30, 1972. Columbia, Md.: Howard County Association of Community Services and Howard Community College.

Downs, A. Private investment and the public weal, *Saturday Review,* May 15, 1971.

Eichler, F. P. The larger concerns of new community building. In S. Weiss, E. Kaiser, and R. Burly, III, (Eds.), *New community development,* Vol. 2. Chapel Hill, No. Carolina: Center for Urban and Regional Studies, 1971.

Gans, H. J. Planning for the everyday life and problems of suburban and new town residents. *People and plans: Essays on urban problems and solutions.* New York: Basic Books, 1968.

Godschalk, D. R. Comparative new community design. *Journal of the American Institute of Planners,* 1967, *33,* 6, 371–386.

Group Legal Services News, 1972, *1,* 1, p. 4.

Hoppenfeld, M. A sketch of the planning-building process for Columbia, Maryland. *Journal of the American Institute of Planners,* November, 1967, 398–409.

Howard, E. *Garden cities of tomorrow.* Cambridge, Mass.: MIT Press Paperback Edition, 1965.

Kinkade, K. *A Walden Two Experiment.* New York: William Morrow & Co., Inc., 1973.

Lawson, S. New towns in old cities. *City,* May-June, 1971.

Lemkau, P. The planning project for Columbia. In M. Schore and F. Mannino (Eds.), *Mental health and the community.* New York: Behavioral Publications, 1969.

Levin, A. Financing social work services through prepaid social insurance. In W. Richan (Ed.), *Human services and social work responsibility.* New York: National Association of Social Work, 1969.

Lieberman, M. New communities: New business on the urban frontier. *Saturday Review,* May 15, 1971.

Lieberman, M. Education in new cities. *Phi Delta Kappan,* March, 1972.

Likert, R. *New patterns of management.* New York: McGraw-Hill, 1961.

Logue, E. Piecing the political pie. *Saturday Review,* May 15, 1971.

Ministry of Housing and Local Government. *The first hundred families.* London: Her Majesty's Stationery Office, 1965.

Ministry of Housing and Local Government: *The needs of new communities.* London: Her Majesty's Stationery Office, 1967.

Molinaro, L. Truths and consequences for older cities. *Saturday Review,* May 15, 1971.

Murrell, S. *Community psychology and social systems.* New York: Behavioral Publications, 1973.

Peachey, P. *New town, old habits: Citizen participation at Fort Lincoln.* Washington, D. C.: Series of Community Governance No. 1, Washington Center for Metropolitan Studies, 1970.

Rosenthal, J. A tale of one city. *New York Times Magazine,* December 26, 1971.

Rouse, J. Cities that work for man — victory ahead. Address to symposium on The City of the Future, U. of Puerto Rico, San Juan, P. R., October 18, 1967.

Skinner, B. F. *Walden Two.* New York: The Macmillan Co., 1948.

Spillhaus, A. The experimental city. *Daedalus,* Fall, 1967.

Towle, W. New city, new hospital. *Hospitals, Journal of the American Hospital Association,* 1972, *46.*

Underhill, J. European new towns: One answer to urban problems? *HUD Challenge,* Mar.-Apr., 1970, 19–23.

Urban Studies Center. *NEWCOM, Volume II, the psychosocial environment* (D. Nunn, Ed.). Louisville, Kentucky: Urban Studies Center, U. of Louisville, 1971.

Warmington, C. A description of a prepaid adversity insurance concept. Working paper, American City Corporation, Columbia, Md., March, 1972.

White, L. The social factors involved in the planning and development. Background paper No. 8 prepared for United Nations Symposium on the Planning and Development of New Towns, Moscow, August 24-September 7, 1964.

Willmott, P. Social research and new communities. *Journal of the American Institute of Planners,* 1967, *33,* 6. 387–397.

Ylvisaker, P. Socio-political innovations and new communities. Paper presented at conference on Innovation and New Communities, Princeton University, September 28, 1970.

Additional Readings

Nunn, D. (Ed.) *The new town movement: Selected readings.* Louisville, Kentucky: Urban Studies Center, U. of Louisville, June, 1971.

Weiss, S., Kaiser, E. J., & Burby, F. J., III (Eds.) *New community development: Planning process, implementation and emerging social concerns,* Vols. I and II. Chapel Hill, No. Carolina: Center for Urban and Regional Studies, U. of No. Carolina, 1971.

Davis, G. K. *City building: Experience trends and new directions.* Columbia, Md.: American City Corporation, 1971.

Twentieth Century Fund Task Force on Governance of New Towns. *New towns: Laboratories for democracy.* New York: Twentieth Century Fund, 1971.

INDEX

"Fiscal integrity," of system, 49
Fiscal policies/requirements
  and balance in manpower
      utilization, 33
  and options for program linkages,
      24
Follow-up services
  poor, in categorical systems, 64
  in new town development, 265
  See also Continuity of care
Fort Lincoln new town,
      Washington, D.C., 259, 293
  citizens' planning council, 293
Foster, J. T., 229, 234
Foster care homes, 98
  as specialized service programs,
      64
Foster City, as peripheral new town,
      258
Fragmentation of services
  and community linkage
      requirements, 87
  and consumer movement toward
      integration, 139–140
  and idealized model, 117, 132
  reduced by neighborhood
      multiservice centers, 21
  and special interest groups,
      31–32
  of specialist system, 59, 64, 65
Francis, J. O'S., 227
Franklin Mental Health Center,
      Boston, Mass.
  Family Life Center, Model Cities
      program in, 80
    and neighborhood service
        center, 91
Free society, and value initiatives, 6
Freeman, H. E., 232
Free-standing new town, 259–260
Friedman, B., 202, 234
"Functional job analysis," of Utah's
      agencies, 32
  and optimal manpower
      utilization, 33, 35
Funding (of human services)
  Federal, conflicting patterns of,
      138
  and general hospital model, 107
  and influence of community on
      programs, 53
  for new cities, 263
  and quality of services, 350–351
  shifting sources of, and
      constraints on service
      delivery, 207–208
  and supply, 204, 205
Funds
  and bureaucratic control of

service delivery, 137
common source of, and
    decision-making, 85
for community development, in
    new towns, 319
endowed, and restrictions on
    service delivery, 208
for intervention in services
    market, 188
public, and human services, 1960
    to 1972, 170
rationale for spending of, 7
source of, and administrative and
    policy decisions, 51
transfer of, in federated system,
    81
Future, probable realities of,
    133–140

Gananda, New York (new town)
    Facilities Corporation, 339
Gans, Herbert, 299, 315, 371
Garden cities, of Ebenezer Howard,
    266
Garfield, S. R., 109–110, 141
Geiger, J., 228
General hospital, as linkage model,
    106–108
General practitioner
  decline of, 118
  patient relationship, importance
      of, 118
Generalist role, of staff person, and
    responsibility for client, 33
Generalist(s)
  Associate in Arts degree for, 58
  basis of assignment to client, 126
  benefits of integrative-
      supportive role, 130
  functions of, in idealized systems
      model, 119
  need for, 124–127
  future of, 133
  isolation from system, 65
  range of interests of, relevance to
      client's needs, 56
  receiving training from specialists,
      121
  referral to, 125
  vs. specialists, in manpower
      utilization, 31, 32
    problem of relating, 55
    roles in idealized systems
        model, 119–120
    tasks in comprehensive system,
        34
    upgrading to skills of, 122
Generalist/specialist, differentiated
    by role, 127